The Societal Relevance of Management Accounting

T0316051

This book explores the relevance of management accounting research and practice for a range of broader, societal phenomena related to corporate governance and regulation, the creation and maintenance of markets and their concomitant social and political implications. It also explores the theoretical and methodological implications of pursuing a research agenda exploring such phenomena in greater detail.

Containing a number of theoretical, methodological and empirical contributions by leading management accounting scholars, *The Societal Relevance of Management Accounting* seeks to advance novel research approaches that go beyond the traditional intra-organisational focus that has long dominated management accounting research. As such, it seeks to enhance the relevance of management accounting research for a broader range of stakeholders and interest groups in and around individual organisations.

This book was originally published as a special issue of *Accounting and Business Research*.

Sven Modell is Professor of Management Accounting at Manchester Business School, University of Manchester, UK. His research interests pivot on a broad range of management accounting topics, especially related to performance management, costing and resource allocation practices. He is an Associate Editor of *Accounting and Business Research* and has published widely in a number of leading accounting journals.

The Societal Relevance of Management Accounting

Edited by
Sven Modell

Routledge
Taylor & Francis Group

LONDON AND NEW YORK

First published 2016 by Routledge

2 Park Square, Milton Park, Abingdon, Oxon OX14 4RN
711 Third Avenue, New York, NY 10017, USA

Routledge is an imprint of the Taylor & Francis Group, an informa business

First issued in paperback 2017

British Library Cataloguing in Publication Data
A catalogue record for this book is available from the British Library

ISBN13: 978-1-138-93000-1 (hbk)
ISBN13: 978-1-138-08939-6 (pbk)

Typeset in Times
by RefineCatch Limited, Bungay, Suffolk

Publisher's Note
The publisher accepts responsibility for any inconsistencies that may have arisen during the conversion of this book from journal articles to book chapters, namely the possible inclusion of journal terminology.

Disclaimer
Every effort has been made to contact copyright holders for their permission to reprint material in this book. The publishers would be grateful to hear from any copyright holder who is not here acknowledged and will undertake to rectify any errors or omissions in future editions of this book.

Contents

Citation Information

The chapters in this book were originally published in *Accounting and Business Research*, volume 44, issue 2 (April 2014). When citing this material, please use the original page numbering for each article, as follows:

Chapter 1
The societal relevance of management accounting: An introduction to the special issue
Sven Modell
Accounting and Business Research, volume 44, issue 2 (April 2014) pp. 83–103

Chapter 2
In our ivory towers? The research-practice gap in management accounting
Basil Tucker and Lee Parker
Accounting and Business Research, volume 44, issue 2 (April 2014) pp. 104–143

Chapter 3
The societal relevance of management accounting innovations: economic value added and institutional work in the fields of Chinese and Thai state-owned enterprises
Pimsiri Chiwamit, Sven Modell and Chun Lei Yang
Accounting and Business Research, volume 44, issue 2 (April 2014) pp. 144–180

Chapter 4
The 'performativity thesis' and its critics: Towards a relational ontology of management accounting
Ed Vosselman
Accounting and Business Research, volume 44, issue 2 (April 2014) pp. 181–203

Chapter 5
Relevant interventionist research: balancing three intellectual virtues
Kari Lukka and Petri Suomala
Accounting and Business Research, volume 44, issue 2 (April 2014) pp. 204–220

For any permission-related enquiries please visit:
http://www.tandfonline.com/page/help/permissions

Notes on Contributors

Pimsiri Chiwamit is a Lecturer in Commerce and Accountancy at the Chulalongkorn Business School, Bangkok, Thailand.

Kari Lukka is the Head of the Department of Accounting and Finance, Turku School of Economics, Finland. His research interests and his international publication record cover a wide range of management accounting topics as well as accounting theory and methodology.

Sven Modell is Professor of Management Accounting at Manchester Business School, University of Manchester, UK. His research interests pivot on a broad range of management accounting topics, especially related to performance management, costing and resource allocation practices. He is an Associate Editor of *Accounting and Business Research* and has published widely in a number of leading accounting journals.

Lee Parker is Professor of Accounting at RMIT University, Melbourne, Australia. His research appears in over 200 articles and books on management and accounting internationally. His interests include strategic management and control, corporate governance, accounting history and social and environmental accountability.

Petri Suomala is Professor in the Department of Industrial Management at Tampere University of Technology, Finland. His areas of interest include profitability management and management accounting within various corporate functions and activities (R&D, production, and marketing).

Basil Tucker is a Senior Lecturer in the University of South Australia Business School, Adelaide, Australia. His research interests include the relationship between management control systems and strategy; management control; the management techniques developed by Ricardo Semler; social network theory; and structural equation modelling.

Ed Vosselman is Professor of Accountingat Radboud University, Nijmegen, The Netherlands, and Professor of Management Control in the Public Sector at the Vrije Universiteit Amsterdam, The Netherlands. His current research interests are in the field of control in intra- and interfirm relationships, as well as in performance management in both the private and the public sector.

Chun Lei Yang is a Lecturer in Accounting at Manchester Business School, University of Manchester, UK. Her current research interests include management accounting and organisational change, complexity and contradictions in the process of change, public sector financial reform, and performance measurement.

The societal relevance of management accounting: An introduction

SVEN MODELL[a,b]

[a]*Manchester Business School, University of Manchester, Manchester, England;*
[b]*Norwegian School of Economics (NHH), Bergen, Norway*

This essay introduces the special issue of *Accounting and Business Research* exploring the societal relevance of management accounting and locates the individual contributions within this research agenda. In contrast to prevailing, managerialist conceptions of relevance, the discussion is guided by an over-riding ambition to turn management accounting research "inside out" to examine the effects of management accounting practices on a broader range of constituencies and interests in society and the formation of such practices beyond individual organisations. I start by charting the development of extant and emerging debates on the relevance of management accounting research and practice and then outline some pertinent research themes worthy of further exploration. In doing so, I pay particular attention to emerging research illustrating how management accounting becomes implicated in the external regulation and governance of organisations, the shaping of markets and the wider, societal consequences of such processes. I also discuss some theoretical and methodological implications of exploring such topics.

Keywords: governance; management accounting; markets; regulation; relevance; research-practice gap; society

1. Introduction

The relevance of management accounting research and practice has received ample attention over the past three decades and continues to generate considerable debate in the academic research literature. This special issue of *Accounting and Business Research* seeks to contribute to this debate by taking it in a slightly different direction. Earlier and emerging debates about the relevance of management accounting have tended to cast the topic in relatively narrow terms centred on its usefulness for managerial decision-making and control in specific organisational locales. By contrast, the contributions to this issue widen this perspective by illustrating how management accounting can also be implicated in processes that go beyond individual organisations and managerialist concerns with enhancing their performance. Individually and collectively, they draw attention to how we may conceive of the notion of relevance from a somewhat broader, societal perspective and how this may prompt some rethinking of our research agenda as management accounting scholars. To paraphrase van der Stede (2011), the nurturing of such an agenda implies a need to adopt an "inside out" perspective on management accounting. Rather than confining research to intra-organisational practices and processes, it requires us to explore how management accounting affects and becomes more or less useful to a broader range of interests and constituencies in society. Also, it compels us to examine how management accounting practices take shape beyond individual organisations as an integral part of societal processes where multiple actors with more or less conflicting interests vie for power and influence. Shedding further light on such issues may widen the view of the potential audiences to which management accounting is seen as relevant. It may also open up new or under-explored research opportunities and ways of theorising management accounting.

This introductory essay outlines what such an extended research agenda may entail by way of specific research themes as well as theoretical and methodological implications. It also locates the individual contributions to the special issue in relation to these topics. I start by briefly revisiting the notion of relevance and how debates around this issue have evolved in the management accounting literature. I then identify a number of emerging research themes which would seem worthy of further exploration to enhance the societal relevance of management accounting research. This is followed by a discussion of how the pursuit of such research themes may influence our use of some theories currently deployed to explore the societal relevance of management accounting and what methodological implications this may have. I close the essay with some brief concluding remarks summarising how we may take this research agenda forward.

2. The notion of relevance revisited

More than any other individual text the contemporary debate about the relevance of management accounting is probably most intimately associated with Johnson and Kaplan's (1987) treatise *Relevance Lost: The Rise and Fall of Management Accounting.*[1] Drawing attention to the alleged obsolescence of especially product costing and performance measurement practices, Johnson and Kaplan outlined a programme for research and innovation with tremendous impact on the discipline of management accounting over the following decades. Their key concerns pivoted on the need to enhance the managerial decision-making relevance of accounting in an increasingly globalised and deregulated market environment infused with technological breakthroughs causing extant management accounting practices to provide misleading information. To overcome such problems, they prescribed a re-engagement with innovative practices aimed at improving the informativeness of costing as well as addressing more perennial issues, such as the tendency of financial indicators to reinforce a backward-looking and myopic view of organisational performance. Addressing such issues was seen as imperative for restoring the commercial viability and long-term competitiveness of especially US business organisations in the wake of growing, international competition.

Johnson and Kaplan (1987) primarily attributed the obsolescence of management accounting practices to the pervasive influence of financial accounting conventions and the embeddedness of such practices in organisational structures and information systems evolving over the course of the twentieth century. However, some of the blame was also laid at the door of the academic research community. Contrasting research on cost accounting with the progress made in understanding the wider phenomenon of management control since the 1950s, they chastised accounting scholars for continuing to provide overly simplified and abstract portrayals of costing systems far removed from actual costing practices. Such criticisms sparked a flurry of innovation and research seeking to enhance the usefulness, or relevance, of management accounting practices for managerial decision-making and control over the following decade. The foremost manifestation of this is the emergence of novel costing and performance measurement techniques, such as Activity-Based Costing and the Balanced Scorecard. The diffusion of such innovations across private as well as public sector organisations has also been an important source of rejuvenation for management accounting research. This is notably manifest in the exponential growth of empirical studies exploring the roles of management accounting innovations in the context of strategic management and operational decision-making and control (Ittner and Larcker 2001, Zawawi and Hoque 2010).

Nevertheless, concerns with a prevailing gap between academic research and evolving management accounting practices have continued to surface (Hopper *et al.* 2001, Mitchell 2002, Hopwood 2008) and have recently sparked a new wave of reflection on the nature of this problem and how it may be overcome. This is evident in special issues and sections of various accounting journals debating the relevance of research for practice (Baldvinsdottir *et al.* 2010, ter Bogt and van Helden 2012) and separate commentaries by prominent accounting scholars (Malmi and Granlund 2009, van Helden and Northcott 2010, Kaplan 2011, Merchant 2012). Malmi and Granlund (2009) lamented how the quest for academic standing and the borrowing of theories from other social sciences have detracted from the development of unique, discipline-specific theories of more direct relevance to management accounting practice. Similarly, van Helden and Northcott (2010) documented how management accounting research in the public sector has moved towards increasing theoretical sophistication whilst remaining relatively mute about how research findings may be translated into more specific guidelines for practice. Finally, both Kaplan (2011) and Merchant (2012) have recently argued that such tendencies to privilege theoretical refinement over practical usefulness are reinforced by the research training, publication standards and the broader incentive and governance structures permeating accounting academia.

A consistent theme throughout this long-standing debate about the relevance of management accounting research and practice is the rather narrow, managerialist focus dominating the discourse. To the extent that the presumed or intended users, or practitioners, of management accounting have made explicit that they have mainly been confined to managers at different organisational echelons or other employees using accounting information to improve business processes and organisational performance. This testifies to a functionalist and rather instrumental notion of relevance pivoting on the continuous fine-tuning of management accounting to help managers meet pre-specified organisational goals (cf. Nicolai and Seidl 2010, van der Meer-Kooistra and Vosselman 2012). Whilst this is perhaps not surprising given the primarily intra-organisational and managerial focus traditionally dominating our conception of management accounting, some deviant voices have recently emerged and called for a somewhat broader view of who the "relevant" practitioners might be. Quattrone (2009) critiqued Malmi and Granlund (2009) for remaining vague about which specific practitioner audiences they have in mind whilst subscribing to a relatively narrow and instrumental definition of management accounting as a primarily managerial practice concerned with enhancing organisational performance and accountability. This, he argued, conveys an overly homogeneous view of who the users of management accounting are and detracts from concerns with the often unpredictable consequences of the use of accounting information for a broader range of interests in and around organisations. As an alternative to such a conception of relevance, he called for a widening of the discourse to acknowledge how management accounting may concern a wider set of constituencies in organisations and society and how this varies with the social contexts in which it operates. Similar sentiments underpin van der Stede's (2011) call for further research into how management accounting is turned "inside out" as a broader range of societal actors (e.g. politicians and regulators) take an increasing interest in it and strive to influence its development. Rather than constituting the unique preserve of managers of individual organisations, the design and use of management accounting practices thus need to be re-conceptualised as implicated in much wider societal processes and phenomena.

At one level, this recent "rediscovery of the societal" in debates about the relevance of management accounting would seem somewhat peculiar or even paradoxical. Over 30 years ago, Burchell *et al.* (1980) called for a widening of the accounting research agenda to explore the broader roles of accounting in organisations as well as in society. Since then, management accounting research adopting an interpretive or critical perspective has come of age and extended the research frontier considerably beyond the narrow managerialist focus dominating debates about its relevance for practice (Baxter and Chua 2003, Cooper and Hopper 2007, Parker 2012). Much of this research pays explicit attention to how management accounting practices influence the interests of a broader range of constituencies and are effectively implicated in entrenching the power and influence of some actors at the expense of others. However, it has largely failed to engage in any deeper or sustained dialogue with research seeking to enhance the relevance of management accounting from a more managerialist perspective. Even though some sanguine projections for rapprochement between these bodies of research have emerged (Roslender 1996) there has been little reciprocal sharing of knowledge. Whilst historical accounts of the development of management accounting practices such as those provided by Johnson and Kaplan (1987) have often been taken as a starting point, they have rarely functioned as more than objects of critique in attempts to advance alternative, sociologically informed explanations (Ezzamel *et al.* 1990, Hopper and Armstrong 1991, Miller 1991, Ahmed and Scapens 2000). Over time, this has fostered a fragmented communication structure in accounting academia, where interpretive and critical research draws considerable inspiration from the functionalist and managerialist literature on management accounting but offers little back by way of insights thoroughly incorporated into the latter (Lukka and Granlund 2002, Englund and Gerdin 2008, Modell 2012a). One explanation of this may be that much interpretive and critical research has been more pre-occupied with developing increasingly sophisticated theoretical explanations of the social and political processes surrounding management accounting than delving into the technical practicalities still constituting an important part of the everyday lives of accounting practitioners (Ahrens and Chapman 2007, Seal 2012).

In so far as debates about the relevance of management accounting are concerned, research genres underpinned by different paradigmatic vantage points thus seem to have "talked past" each other. As indicated by Tucker and Parker (2014), however, the positions taken by management accounting scholars on this issue are not necessarily related to their paradigmatic affiliations. In their global survey of senior management accounting academics, they found no statistically significant differences between respondents of either a predominantly functionalist/positivist or interpretive/critical persuasion as to whether they perceive a gap between research and practice and see such a gap as problematic. Rather, accounting scholars across the paradigmatic spectrum seem to harbour a very diverse set of views about what it means to render research relevant for practice and whether this should indeed be a key concern of academics. Whilst a clear majority of the respondents see a considerable and widening gap between research and practice and consider this problematic, a significant minority group takes a somewhat different view that often entails objections to a conception of relevance in narrow, managerialist terms. This leads the authors to deepen the analysis of what it means to pursue practically relevant research. In doing so, they develop an empirically grounded typology distinguishing between basic and applied research and broader and narrower conceptions of the users of management accounting research. Echoing arguments set out in other, recent papers about the relevance of research to practice (Nicolai and Seidl 2010, van der Meer-Kooistra and Vosselman 2012), they extend the conception of this issue beyond the conventional, instrumental view as mainly a matter of enhancing managerial decision-making relevance and improving organisational control practices. Whilst this conventional view of relevance is still firmly endorsed by especially the majority group, Tucker and Parker find that applied management accounting research can also have a "policy-driving" role in informing debates about issues of broader, societal significance, such as the development of regulatory frameworks and their effects on a wider range of constituencies. Moreover, they reject the argument that basic research is of little relevance for practice. Instead, they find support for the view that a broadening of the theorisation of management accounting practices to account for their impact on a wider range of users may enhance the societal relevance of research.

Tucker and Parker's survey is a particularly valuable contribution to the debate about the relevance of management accounting research in that it provides a systematic empirical documentation of an issue that has previously been subject to commentaries based on mainly personal experiences of individual accounting scholars and relatively anecdotal evidence. It also opens up the debate about what the broader relevance of management accounting research might be and how it may serve a wider range of societal constituencies and interests than the ones typically seen as the predominant users, or practitioners, of management accounting. However, it begs the question of which specific issues or research themes may be worth pursuing to this end. I now turn to examine this issue in some detail.

3. Emerging research themes

In approaching the issue of how management accounting research may be of greater societal relevance, it is helpful to locate management accounting practices in broader change and reform projects aimed at transforming various socio-economic fields, such as specific industries, sectors or, indeed, society in general. A useful starting point to this end is to ask what broader, societal *programmes* management accounting is implicated in (Miller 1991). Such programmes denote the more general objectives that specific accounting practices get tied up with as they traverse different spheres of society. Examining the development of capital budgeting in the UK in the 1960s, Miller (1991) drew attention to how techniques for this purpose (e.g. discounted cash flow analysis) came to epitomise broader, societal concerns with how to stimulate economic growth through sound investment behaviours. This, he argued, extends our understanding of how management accounting practices take shape beyond individual organisations and come to represent more than merely technical, or instrumental, concerns with enhancing their performance. Rather, his analysis shows how evolving capital budgeting techniques became implicated in intricate political processes where a range of actors bestowed diverse meanings on them as a vehicle of meeting broader, societal objectives and what they did to entrench such objectives in capital budgeting practices. It is germane to extend this line of enquiry to ask what societal programmes management accounting is implicated in *today*. In what follows, I identify two broad programmes that have recently come to the fore and are beginning to attract the attention of management accounting scholars. Whilst this discussion is by no means exhaustive, it gives an indication of how we may expand management accounting research to explore societal issues of high contemporary relevance.

3.1. *The role of management accounting in external regulation and governance*

An emerging theme already hinted at is the implication of management accounting in the external regulation of organisations and the formation of rules and standards for this purpose. This is not necessarily a "new" phenomenon per se. For instance, historical research into the evolution of costing practices reveals how this has long been imbued with broader societal concerns with ensuring competitive neutrality and fairness and mitigating predatory pricing to safeguard wider socio-economic interests. Some accounting researchers demonstrate how such concerns prompted the State, trade associations and various professional bodies to play an active role in the shaping of legal rules with a long-standing influence on cost management practices (Ahmed and Scapens 2000, 2003, Edwards *et al.* 2003). Other scholars have drawn attention to how such practices were regulated through more voluntary processes of standardisation exercising a considerable influence on specific industries or societal sectors (Jönsson 1991). This suggests a need to extend inquiries into the notion of relevance by exploring whose interests are being served by the evolution of particular management accounting practices and what different actors do to entrench such interests through the regulatory process. However, such lines of inquiry have not loomed large in contemporary debates about the relevance of management accounting. Johnson and Kaplan (1987) paid little attention to how management accounting influences regulatory processes as a result of their emphasis on economic and technological imperatives as the key drivers of its historical evolution (Ahmed and Scapens 2000). Indeed, one may go as far as arguing that they effectively reified a view of management accounting as ideally operating in some relatively unregulated space by emphasising the need to sever its ties to the regulatory conventions governing financial accounting. Their prescriptions for enhancing the relevance of management accounting as mainly a matter of tailoring it to increasingly deregulated and globalised market environments may also have detracted from scholarly interest in exploring its implication in regulatory processes. This is notably manifest in the limited concerns with external regulation in empirical research heeding Johnson and Kaplan's call for exploring and enhancing the relevance of management accounting (Zawawi and Hoque 2010, Modell 2012a).

Nevertheless, the conception of management accounting as an increasingly deregulated sphere of practice has been challenged by empirical inquiries revealing how financial accounting conventions and other forms of external regulation continue to exercise a more or less direct influence on contemporary management accounting practices (Hopper *et al.* 1992, Joseph *et al.* 1996, Byrne and Pierce 2007, Lantto in press). There is also evidence of how management accounting innovations emerging in the wake of the debate about the relevance of management accounting are directly implicated in the shaping of regulatory standards. One notable example is Hopper and Major's (2007) study of the role of Activity-Based Costing in the regulation of the telecommunications industry in the European Union. Their analysis reveals how international consulting firms, such as Arthur Andersen, mobilised Activity-Based Costing as a recommended costing technique and how this had a decisive impact on political decisions to adopt it as a basis for cost-based price regulation. This illustrates how a management accounting innovation partly originating in concerns with reversing the influence of financial accounting regulation on organisational costing practices finds a new role in the shaping of extra-organisational, regulatory standards. It is thus a fine example of how such innovations are turned "inside out" (cf. van der Stede 2011) and come to fill important societal roles beyond individual organisations. Similar tendencies are discernible with respect to other prominent innovations such as the Balanced Scorecard. In addition to constituting a mechanism of strategic goal alignment in individual organisations, there is growing evidence of its use as a template for reforms and political regulation of especially public services in various countries (McAdam and Walker 2003, Northcott and France 2005, Chang 2009, Modell 2012b). The appeal of the Balanced Scorecard to this end would seem to be that it enables a formalisation of regulation as structured around a set of financial and non-financial performance aspects representing a broad range of societal interests, although some studies suggest that such ideals are only honoured in the breach (Chang 2009, Modell 2012b).

The discussion above is indicative of how management accounting is implicated in emerging, societal programmes of regulation with important implications for a multitude of actors with diverse interests. The significance of this observation becomes clear when considering how regulation is not only increasing, but also changing, in contemporary society. Rather than naively accepting the oft-cited neo-liberal view that society has undergone an era of rapid deregulation, scholars across diverse disciplines have shown how the face of regulation of both the private and public sectors has changed over the past decades (Ayres and Braithwaite 1992, Hall *et al.* 1999, Hood *et al.* 1999, 2000, Mörth 2004, Broadbent *et al.* 2010). These changes are partly epitomised by such notions as "responsive regulation" (Ayres and Braithwaite 1992) and "soft law" (Mörth 2004), signifying a more collaborative approach to regulation that is no longer necessarily dominated by the State. Rather, regulation increasingly takes shape through some intricate interplay between various expert bodies and interest groups, often working in close collaboration with the State, and entails a significant element of self-regulation. To accounting scholars, the most well-known account of how such regulatory regimes manifest themselves is perhaps Power's (1997) analysis of the development of auditing as an increasingly pervasive phenomenon that not only affects financial reporting but also penetrates a range of societal phenomena, including the internal control practices of organisations. According to Power (1997), this signifies a new mode of governance where auditing, and indeed accounting more generally, is intricately tied up with social and political processes where multiple actors, including the State, seek to influence emerging regulatory priorities. However, relatively little is still known about how management accounting practices are turned "inside out" to become part of such emerging programmes of governance and regulation.

An empirical illustration of how management accounting becomes implicated in such programmes and assumes broader, societal relevance can be found in Chiwamit *et al.*'s (2014) comparative analysis of how Economic Value Added (EVA^{TM}) evolved as a governance mechanism for Chinese and Thai state-owned enterprises (SOEs). Rather than assuming that EVA^{TM} primarily serves capital markets' interests in some deregulated global economy, they show how it was effectively co-opted by powerful actors with strongly vested interests in pursuing particular paths of economic and political reform. As such, EVA^{TM} became intricately intertwined with broader, societal processes of devising novel forms of regulation and governance practices. Chiwamit *et al.* analyse this development by broadening the conception of relevance to ask which societal interests were being served by EVA^{TM} as it contributed to the institutionalisation of such governance practices. Their analysis shows how similarities and differences in this regard across Chinese and Thai SOEs were conditioned by the need to coordinate more or less conflicting constituency interests. To achieve such coordination, key actors, such as regulatory agencies, had to engage in complex negotiations with individual SOEs and make significant adjustments to their demands to render EVA^{TM} useful. Rather than being imposed on individual SOEs in a unilateral, "top-down" process of governance reforms, EVA^{TM} only grew more firmly institutionalised through protracted political processes where important concessions to diverse societal interests, pivoting on concerns with equity and social welfare, were made. This underlines the usefulness of adopting an "inside out" perspective on management accounting innovations to understand how they constitute a medium, rather than merely an outcome, of governance reforms and accounting regulation. Chiwamit *et al.* call for further research of this kind and draw particular attention to how this may help bridge the prevailing gap between management accounting research and cognate areas of scholarship, such as research on financial accounting regulation and corporate governance.

Two additional, emerging strands of research would seem to have considerable potential to extend this focus on how management accounting practices get tied up with and indeed influence external regulation and governance. The first is the burgeoning body of management accounting research engaging with the broader literature on social and environmental accounting (SEA). Bebbington and Thomson (2013) explicitly recognised how such research has the potential to nurture an "inside out" perspective on management accounting and address issues of considerable societal relevance. Yet, in reviewing emerging research in the area, they lamented how much of it continues to primarily reflect managerial concerns with organisational performance, epitomised by such notions as eco-efficiency and corporate social responsibility reporting, and largely fails to engage with wider, societal issues on the sustainability agenda such as social justice and the effectiveness of social and environmental regulation. This does not mean that the interactions between management accounting and the external regulation and governance of social and environmental issues have gone unnoticed. For instance, there are some interesting attempts to unpack the complex interplay between management accounting practices and external reporting (Bouten and Hoozee 2013, Contrafatto and Burns 2013). However, the emphasis of these studies is still very much on the intra-organisational processes shaping this interplay rather than its wider effects on society. An attempt to extend this perspective can be found in Moore's (2013) multi-level analysis of how SEA practices became embedded in an individual organisation but also got entangled in wider regulatory processes and, indeed, influenced the development of sustainability strategies of relevance for similar organisations. This testifies to how such practices may be turned "inside out" and affect, rather than merely being affected by, the governance of social and environmental issues. Yet Moore's analysis of the effects of management accounting on such broader, societal phenomena was relatively limited in scope. There would thus seem to be con-siderable opportunities to extend extant empirical research into the interactions between manage-ment accounting and the external regulation of SEA. One way of doing so would be to explore the interplay between evolving management accounting practices and the voluntary and mandatory environmental audits now flourishing in several countries (cf. Power 1997).

The other emerging strand of research with potential to shed further light on the societal rel-evance of management accounting is the growing literature on its relationship to risk management practices. Calls for further research into this relationship have emerged in the wake of the recent financial and economic crisis (Hopwood 2009, van der Stede 2011) and at least two special issues on the topic have already appeared (Bhimani 2009, Soin and Collier 2013). A particularly prom-ising line of inquiry was set forth by Bhimani (2009), who forged a connection between manage-ment accounting, risk management and emerging corporate governance regulations and practices. Exploring the interconnections between the three would seem worthwhile given the trust that society places in both corporate governance and risk management as means of ensuring that organisations effectively serve diverse, extra-organisational constituencies. It would also seem apposite in light of Power's (2007) observation that the regulation of risk management increas-ingly constitutes a phenomenon that not only exerts external pressures for compliance, but also requires organisations to disclose its potential effects and effectiveness. This opens up possibili-ties of exploring the reciprocal interplay between such regulations and management accounting practices and enhancing our understanding of how this affects the internal management of risks as well as the wider, societal consequences of such management practices. Empirical inqui-ries of this kind may also be enriched by insights from emerging corporate governance research steering away from the economics-based perspective dominating such research to probe into the social and political processes associated with the shaping of governance rules and practices (Ahrens and Khalifa 2013, McNulty et al. 2013, Westphal and Zajac 2013).

3.2. *The role of management accounting in the shaping of markets*

The second over-riding theme with considerable potential to enhance the societal relevance of management accounting research is how management accounting practices are implicated in the shaping of markets. Whilst Johnson and Kaplan (1987) placed considerable emphasis on the need to tailor management accounting practices to increasingly globalised and presumably deregulated product markets, we still know surprisingly little about how management accounting contributes to the construction and maintenance of such markets. As noted by Vollmer *et al.* (2009), this is primarily due to the predominantly intra-organisational focus of management accounting research. This lacuna is significant given the expansion of markets as an arena for the organisation of growing swathes of socio-economic life over the past decades. The programmatic nature of this development is notably epitomised by the fact that the diffusion of market forces has often been closely affiliated with broader, neo-liberal reform projects sweeping across the private as well as public sectors over large parts of the world. The social and political processes of bringing market forces into play have received ample attention especially in research evolving within the broad paradigm of the sociology of markets (Fligstein and Dauter 2007, Fourcade 2007). However, despite the long-standing recognition that accounting can have powerful constitutive effects on such socio-economic phenomena (Burchell *et al.* 1980, Hopwood and Miller 1994), research exploring how management accounting is turned "inside out" to shape programmes of marketisation is still relatively scarce. Whilst there is no shortage of studies exploring how market-led reforms influence the development of management accounting practices in individual organisations, especially in the context of the transformation of public services (van Helden 2005, Broadbent and Guthrie 2008), much less is known about how such practices contribute to establish, stabilise and possibly disrupt markets and shape their broader effects on society.

A few notable exceptions to this pattern and potentially promising lines of inquiry are discernible in the management accounting literature. One major strand of research has been concerned with how novel costing and performance measurement practices contribute to transform conceptions of the beneficiaries of public or newly privatised services by re-casting them as "customers" with distinct preferences or needs and how this affects the allocation and delivery of such services (Ogden 1997, Preston *et al.* 1997, Lawrence and Sharma 2002, Samuel *et al.* 2005, Modell and Wiesel 2008, Wiesel *et al.* 2011). This research has drawn on a variety of theoretical perspectives[2] and shows how the re-casting of beneficiaries as customers is an integral, if not necessary, part of the marketisation of public services and how management accounting mediates such transformations. One particularly provocative insight with far-reaching societal implications is how the use of costing practices devised to price the services delivered to specific groups of beneficiaries can mask and enable politically charged rationing processes (Preston *et al.* 1997, Samuel *et al.* 2005). Such rationing processes not only influence the distribution of social welfare across various strata of society, but may also have wider, macro-economic implications as they come to impinge on public spending decisions. As noted by Wiesel *et al.* (2011), however, effective rationing is neither an inevitable nor universal outcome of the re-casting of beneficiaries of public services as customers. Rather, their analysis shows how a relatively ambitious attempt to divide service users into different customer segments as a basis for resource allocation failed due to the intricate political dynamics unfolding in specific decision-making episodes. This suggests a need for more detailed inquiries into how management accounting becomes implicated in and, indeed, shapes the politics of resource allocation in markets for public services.

A useful analytical approach to advance a more detailed understanding of how management accounting contributes to the process of marketisation can be found in the work on performativity emerging within the sociology of markets over the past decade. Originating in Callon's (1998) critique of mainstream economics as well as the conception of markets as socially embedded entities, the performative perspective has informed a burgeoning literature concerned with how various calculative practices,[3] often derived from formal economic theories, contribute to the shaping of markets (MacKenzie *et al.* 2007, Caliskan and Callon 2009, 2010). The key premise of this perspective is that such practices not only reflect socially embedded market transactions, but also play a direct role in formatting and, indeed, performing such transactions. Through such performative processes the predictions and prescriptions of economic theories and models may become nearly self-fulfilling and foster behaviours resembling those of self-interested economic agents in a market economy. A critical, yet sympathetic review of management accounting research following this school of thought is offered by Vosselman (2014). Similar to Callon's (1998) original work, much of this research is firmly grounded in the actor-network theory (ANT) (see below) and examines how accounting calculations are entangled in complex power struggles and obtain their performative capacity from their ability to mobilise diverse social actors around particular matters of concern. Whilst most of it has focused on accounting phenomena that are not directly associated with market transactions, Vosselman argues that the societal relevance of such research may be enhanced by examining how management accounting becomes implicated in actor-networks extending beyond the boundaries of individual organisations. This may entail deeper inquiries into the wider societal consequences of the role of accounting calculations in performing market transactions, such as their effects on the stratification of social actors into more or less favoured and marginalised segments of markets and society. Whilst such broader, societal concerns are increasingly occupying scholars advancing the sociology of markets (Beamish 2007, Fourcade and Healy 2013), they have yet to permeate management accounting research mobilising a performative perspective.

A significant amount of work thus remains to be done to enhance our understanding of how management accounting practices are implicated in the shaping of markets and the wider, societal consequences of such processes. Whether researchers follow the general intuition that accounting plays a constitutive role or focus on the more specific, performative effects of accounting calculations, more careful attention to the effects of such practices on the evolution of markets is required to nurture an "inside out" perspective on management accounting. It would also seem worthwhile to extend such research beyond the public sector, where the implication of management accounting in programmes of marketisation has perhaps been most palpable, to explore its wider, societal relevance in settings presumably characterised by less constrained pursuit of profits and shareholder value.

4.   Theoretical implications

Several theoretical implications follow from the above discussion of how to advance the societal relevance of management accounting research. In what follows, I concentrate the discussion to the theoretical perspectives guiding the contributions to this special issue. Particular attention is paid to the institutional theory and ANT, which have both exercised a powerful influence on interpretive management accounting research over the past decades and which offer a distinct alternative to the functionalist perspective guiding much of the debate on the relevance of management accounting. I also discuss some implications for critical accounting research related to my review of these theoretical perspectives. Rather than offering a comprehensive review, however, I focus on how research following these perspectives might need to be extended to further the quest for the societal relevance of management accounting and inform unfolding scholarly debates on the topic.

4.1.   *Institutional theory*

Institutional theory initially emerged as a reaction against functionalist theories of organisations (Meyer and Rowan 1977, DiMaggio and Powell 1983) and has had a long-standing influence on management accounting research seeking to understand the role of social and political processes in and around organisations (Dillard *et al.* 2004, Moll *et al.* 2006, Modell 2009). Rather than assuming that organisational design choices are driven by purely efficiency-centred concerns with organisational performance, it emphasises the social embeddedness of action and draws attention to the social values, norms and rules endorsed by various constituencies and dominating organisational life. Organisational constituencies are seen as situated in larger networks of social relations, or institutional fields, held together by common beliefs systems and conditioning the action repertoires of individual organisations. Institutional theory has increasingly come to focus on how fields emerge and are transformed over time by paying closer attention to the intricate political processes involved in the (re-)shaping of such beliefs systems (Wooten and Hoffman 2008). In doing so, it has highlighted the power struggles between diverse constituencies with more or less conflicting interests and how such struggles lead specific interests to become more or less dominant within institutional fields. Institutional research following this lead would seem to have considerable potential to contribute to our understanding of the societal relevance of management accounting.

However, at least two significant strands of development within institutional research on management accounting have detracted from its broader, societal relevance. The first is the predominantly intra-organisational focus permeating much of this research. Considerable emphasis has been placed on how management accounting rules and routines evolve in individual organisations, whilst comparatively little attention has been paid to broader developments in institutional fields and the recursive institutional dynamics unfolding across the two levels (Dillard *et al.* 2004, Modell 2009). This has had the unfortunate effect of researchers treating the external, institutional environment as a "given", or largely exogenous entity influencing organisational practices and failing to recognise the broader, societal consequences of the institutionalisation of management accounting. The primary emphasis has been on the institutional effects *on*, rather than *of*, management accounting practices (Modell 2009). In other words, research in the area has tended to nurture an "outside in", rather than an "inside out" perspective on the role of management accounting. Notable exceptions to this pattern can be found in the multi-level studies of the process of institutionalisation by Hopper and Major (2007) and Moore (2013) reviewed in the foregoing. Recent advances in institutional theory, pivoting on the notion of institutional work unfolding across different field levels, also inform Chiwamit *et al.*'s (2014) analysis of the development of EVA^{TM} as a governance mechanism for Chinese and Thai SOEs. However, much more empirical research into such multi-level dynamics is required to enhance our insights into the broader, societal consequences of the institutionalisation of management accounting.

The second development in institutional research on management accounting detracting from its societal relevance is its tendency to bracket the more critical insights and implications potentially emerging from institutional analyses (Modell 2012b). Institutional theory has increasingly been criticised for posing as an essentially value neutral perspective whilst harbouring some "elite bias" as a result of mainly focusing on the actors and interests that dominate institutional fields or processes of institutional change (Cooper *et al.* 2008, Zald and Lounsbury 2010), societal constituencies and interests being marginalised as a result of the institutionalisation of particular accounting practices have received scant attention. Moreover, the moral and ethical implications of such marginalisation rarely feature as key theoretical or practical concerns in institutional analyses. This has led some observers to argue that much institutional research on management accounting has effectively reified a rather managerialist view of change (Modell 2012b). Even though this body of research has paid considerable attention to the inertia and resistance that often accompany attempts to institutionalise novel management accounting practices, empirical analyses rarely go beyond the organisational and managerial implications of such phenomena.

The broader, societal consequences of the institutionalisation of management accounting are typically absent from discussions of how to extend such research.

Attempts to enhance the societal relevance of institutional research on management accounting would thus need to entail greater emphasis on multi-level analyses within institutional fields as well as a commitment to imbue such research with more critical intent. This may necessitate some combination of institutional theory with insights gleaned from critical accounting research. But pursuing such theoretical combinations raises a number of ontological and epistemological issues that have not yet been satisfactorily addressed (see, e.g. Cooper *et al.* 2008). One of the main obstacles to such research would seem to lie in the value system and epistemology in which institutional research is embedded. Whilst posing as value neutral, some critics have argued that institutional theory embodies a fundamentally conservative approach to knowledge formation centred on a normal science conception of scientific progress (Cooper *et al.* 2008). In the short term, such conceptions tend to be highly resilient and insensitive to challenges calling for radical change in the theoretical and methodological priors guiding researchers' view of the world. However, this does not mean that institutional research on management accounting cannot make less dramatic, incremental progress to incorporate more critical insights and thus advance its societal relevance.

4.2. *Actor-network theory*

The second, major strand of theoretical thought represented in the contributions to this special issue is ANT. Growing out of the seminal works of Latour (1987) and, to a lesser extent, Callon (1986, 1998), ANT-inspired accounting research now constitutes a voluminous literature and has inspired investigations of a broad range of accounting phenomena (Hansen 2011, Justesen and Mouritsen 2011). The key tenet of ANT is that social action is constituted by constantly evolving networks of human and non-human actors (or actants) clustered around specific issues, or matters of concern, and shaping societal development. In doing so, diverse actors "translate" various interests, ideologies and agendas into evolving practices. Such translation processes are inherently political phenomena imbued with power struggles over the meanings of evolving practices and the direction of social action. According to Justesen and Mouritsen (2011), empirical analyses of how management accounting is implicated in such translation processes have sought to transcend the division of sociologically informed accounting research into studies that either explain its development with reference to macro-level structures or socio-cognitive processes operating at a more personal level. A notable feature of ANT is its ambition to dissolve such notions of "macro" and "micro" and rather direct our attention to how actor-networks evolve across various societal levels over time. Following this tenor, several ANT-inspired studies have paid explicit attention to how management accounting practices transcend formal organisational boundaries and come to have broader societal impact. Indeed, ANT formed a stepping stone for Miller's (1991) historical analysis of the societal programme formed around capital budgeting in the UK. Other examples include the studies by Lawrence *et al.* (1994), Chua (1995) and Llewellyn and Northcott (2005) of how costing techniques associated with public health care reforms not only shape intra-organisational networks and accounting practices but also serve to commodify and standardise health services and thus impinge on broader, societal interests.

Another significant feature of ANT-inspired accounting research is that it brings calculations centre stage without submitting to a functionalist view of accounting as some under-socialised technicality (Justesen and Mouritsen 2011). Rather, accounting calculations are seen as intricately intertwined with evolving actor-networks whilst having a capacity to act and shape socio-economic behaviour in their own right. Such performative effects of accounting calculations are perhaps most notable in studies following Callon's (1998) elaboration on ANT (Vosselman

2014). As noted in the foregoing, research following this lead may enhance our understanding of how management accounting is implicated in the shaping of markets and the broader, societal consequences of such marketisation efforts. Mobilising ANT to this effect may enable researchers to overcome the aforementioned tendency of much sociologically informed accounting research to distance the analysis of social and political processes from the practical minutiae of accounting calculations (cf. Ahrens and Chapman 2007, Seal 2012).

Notwithstanding these merits, however, ANT-inspired management accounting research would seem to require some further development to nurture more innate concerns with issues of broader, societal relevance. Similar to institutional theory, ANT has not escaped criticisms for embodying a rather conservative epistemology and harbouring limited concerns with the plight and possibilities of emancipation of marginalised constituencies (Whittle and Spicer 2008). This criticism is discussed at some length by Vosselman (2014), who argues that it is partly based on a misplaced conception of ANT as representing some relatively value-free and apolitical approach to the examination of accounting. As a remedy to such conceptions he advances a relational ontology, which recognises that the real is inherently political and that the formation of any social relations that constitute actor-networks is imbued with negotiations of power and influence. Similar to much critical accounting research, the adoption of such ontological premises should lead us to recognise that things could always be otherwise. ANT arguably has an inherent advantage in this respect in that it compels researchers to continuously search for the unanticipated yet significant elements of actor-networks emerging in specific instances of time and space (Justesen and Mouritsen 2011). This could entail elucidation of previously unknown or unrecognised opportunities for emancipation. However, Vosselman also emphasises the need to explore the more "un-localisable", or durable, forces impinging on actor-networks and often constraining such opportunities. Such "un-localisable" forces may include political ideologies and reform projects with potentially oppressive effects being enrolled in specific actor-networks and imbued with performativity, although they also have an existence that is independent of the time- and space-specific configurations of actor-networks. By exploring the role of management accounting in such processes of enrolment, researchers may gain deeper insights into its broader, societal implications and be sensitised to the need to intervene in practice if vital constituency interests are at risk of being jeopardised. This might, in turn, give ANT-inspired management accounting research a more explicit, critical edge.

4.3. Critical accounting research

Whilst the discussion in the foregoing has emphasised how researchers using well-established social theories may enhance the societal relevance of management accounting research by taking a "critical turn", it is vital not to downplay the strides made to this end by critical accounting scholars. In contrast to institutional theory and ANT, management accounting research applying various critical theories has long had an explicit ambition to highlight and, at least occasionally, intervene in organisational and societal processes causing particular constituencies and interests to become marginalised (Neu et al. 2001, Cooper and Hopper 2007). However, in doing so, critical accounting scholars have often sought to deliberately distance their research agenda from more managerialist debates on the relevance of management accounting (Roslender 1996). They have also voiced repeated concerns about research being captured by management or other dominant actors with interests detracting from broader, societal issues, unless such a distance is maintained (Baker 2010). This is likely to have reinforced the fragmented communication structure in management accounting academia discussed in the foregoing. I do not envisage this situation to change in the foreseeable future. Nor do I necessarily see it as particularly urgent or even desirable to seek to address this as yet another "gap" that needs to be bridged in order to enhance the overall relevance or usefulness of management accounting research. As Tucker and Parker's (2014) survey reminds us, management accounting scholars conceive of relevance in very different ways and it would be fallacious to privilege one view over the other. The raison d'etre of the critical accounting project is to challenge taken-for-granted assumptions about whose interests matter and are being served by particular accounting practices. It seeks to do so by imagining how things could be different whilst mapping out the often unintended consequences of the use of accounting. Hence, its definition of relevance has tended to differ vastly from the more conventional conception of it as a matter of enhancing managerial decision usefulness and control and is much more concerned with bringing out the voices of multiple constituencies in organisations and society (van der Meer-Kooistra and Vosselman 2012).

Nevertheless, there are some merits in at least pondering how critical management accounting scholars might re-engage with debates about relevance in other strands of accounting scholarship. Although there is occasionally a tendency amongst critical accounting scholars to ascribe a certain naivety to researchers working within other paradigms (Tinker 2005, Roslender 2013), there is also some recognition of the difficulties in clearly demarcating the critical paradigm from other strands of especially sociologically informed accounting research (Roslender and Dillard 2003). As noted by Mouritsen *et al.* (2002), it is also fallacious to conceive of critique and naivety in overly dichotomous terms. Whilst some form of critical, or reflexive, bearing is expected from any knowledge claim that aspires to scholarly status, the kinds of critiques that are likely to be legitimate and effective in various societal contexts are a highly contingent phenomenon that varies with a multitude of social, cultural and political factors embedded in such contexts. Hence making an overly strict, universal distinction between what counts as "critical" and "non-critical" scholarship is unlikely to be a very productive starting point for enhancing the societal relevance management accounting research. Relaxing this distinction may also lower the barriers to communication between researchers with a critical orientation and accounting scholars with more functionalist leanings and thus further the long-awaited rapprochement between the two (cf. Roslender 1996). However, for such rapprochement to be fruitful also requires some receptiveness from scholars with a functionalist outlook, which cannot always be taken as a given (cf. Parker 2012). Such receptiveness needs to go beyond general recognition to more fully appreciate how a critical understanding of conflicting interests and power struggles compels us to rethink and possibly revise functionalist postulates concerning how management accounting obtains its relevance.

5. Methodological implications

The pursuit of an extended research agenda to explore the societal relevance of management accounting also has important methodological implications. As the preceding discussion has made plain, a narrow, functionalist perspective exclusively concerned with how accounting is deployed in the internal management of organisations is unlikely to take this research agenda forward. At the same time, it would be fallacious to distance the quest for the societal relevance of management accounting from the calculative practices constituting its very core. Such practices still form an important part of the everyday lives of accounting practitioners in individual organisations. However, to explore their wider, societal relevance it is vital to extend empirical research to examine the formation and consequences of such practices beyond the boundaries of individual organisations.

At one level, such a widening of the scope of management accounting research from individual organisations may be interpreted as a call for connecting empirical inquiries to broader, macro-level phenomena in a manner that goes against the grain of methodological approaches currently gaining momentum in accounting academia. The discussion throughout this essay has emphasised the primacy of exploring issues with distinct macro-level connotations, such as the societal power struggles and processes of institutionalisation implicated in the formation of external regulation, corporate governance practices and markets. By contrast, it has lately been in vogue to call for more detailed, micro-level studies of management accounting practices as they evolve in particular organisational locales and get implicated in highly specific episodes of organisational decision-making and control. This is notably manifest in the recent "practice turn" in management accounting research, which grew out of a pronounced disenchantment with detached and abstract accounts of how management accounting obtains its relevance (Ahrens and Chapman 2007, Chua 2007, Jørgensen and Messner 2010). It is also obvious in research inspired by ANT with its ambition to dissolve notions of "macro" and "micro" whilst directing the analytical search light to the minutiae of ongoing interactions between human and non-human actors (Justesen and Mouritsen 2011). However, it is perhaps erroneous to pitch such perspectives against methodological approaches furthering the quest for the societal relevance of management accounting. To be clear, I see a considerable need for more detailed analyses of the micro dynamics shaping the macro-level phenomena in which management accounting is implicated and the complex processes through which it comes to affect and be affected by diverse, societal interests. It is only by doing so that we will gain a deeper understanding of the inherently political processes causing particular interests to become increasingly dominant or marginalised and be able to imagine how things could be different.

Through further inquiries of this kind, I envisage some rapprochement between management accounting research and emerging attempts to enhance the societal relevance of research on external reporting standards (Cooper and Morgan 2013), regulation of corporate governance practices (McNulty *et al.* 2013) and the shaping of markets (Caliskan and Callon 2009, 2010). As noted in the foregoing, however, there is also a need to extend analyses of the societal relevance of management accounting to individual organisations and conduct empirical research that straddles multiple levels of analysis. Research of this kind may include examinations of the dynamic and reciprocal interplay between management accounting and the external reporting, corporate governance practices and market relations of individual organisations. Some insights into this interplay may be gleaned from archival data of either proprietary origin or more readily available in the public domain. But such data sources may also need to be substituted or complemented with other methods of data collection such as interviews or observations. This requires us to extend direct engagements with managers and employees within organisations, which currently inform most field research in management accounting, to extra-organisational constituencies, such as customers and societal interest groups, and possibly relevant actors at higher levels of society, such as regulators and politicians, who may be less easily accessible. Conducting such multi-level research may seem like a daunting task and is no doubt likely to add to the time required to complete research projects. It also brings the additional challenge of exploring relationships which may be politically charged, especially if the societal implications of management accounting are potentially detrimental to organisational legitimacy or the interests of particular actors or constituencies. On the other hand, extended time for empirical inquiries may be necessary to more fully observe intended and unintended, societal consequences and unpack the complex processes in which they are embedded. Extending research to a broader range of constituencies may also enhance the possibilities of researchers to critically reflect on such consequences from multiple perspectives and may thus mitigate tendencies for research to be captured by any one actor with an interest in furthering a particular agenda.

Advancing the quest for the societal relevance of management accounting also prompts us to rethink extant methodological approaches which have spearheaded earlier attempts to enhance the relevance of research to practice. This issue is addressed by Lukka and Suomala (2014) with specific reference to interventionist research in management accounting. Whilst interventionist research has long been recognised as a valuable, yet under-utilised, way of connecting management accounting research to evolving practices, Lukka and Suomala argue that much of it has suffered from an unduly narrow emphasis on advancing technical solutions of immediate, practical relevance to managers and accountants in individual organisations. Whilst such research typically offers detailed insights into the technicalities of accounting as a calculative practice, they raise concerns that it often appears void of deeper, critical deliberations on whose interests and values are being served by management accounting and how it gets tied up with power in organisations and society. Drawing on Flyvbjerg (2001), they argue that the nurturing of more pronounced sensitivity to such broader, social and political aspects constitutes the hallmark of any social science inquiry striving to make an impact in society. Increasing the societal relevance of interventionist research in management accounting implies paying more conscious and explicit attention to such aspects and ensuring that multiple interests are given a voice. One research strategy to achieve this end might be to combine interventionist research with a multi-level approach to data collection and analysis. As noted above, extended, multi-level analyses involving a broader range of constituencies may enhance the propensity for critical reflections on the values, interests and power relations served by management accounting.

Lukka and Suomala also remind us of the indispensable role of theory in interventionist research or, for that matter, any research with the ambition to enhance the societal relevance of management accounting. In contrast to Flyvbjerg's (2001) somewhat caricatured portrayal of theorising in the social sciences as ineluctably trapped within a positivist, natural science-dominated paradigm, they argue that greater attention to context-sensitive theory building is likely to improve the standing of interventionist research. Whilst they see a frequent lack of clearly articulated theoretical contributions as a likely reason for the paucity of interventionist research studies in highly ranked accounting journals, they do not merely argue for its necessity as a way of boosting the academic status of such research. Similar to Tucker and Parker (2014), they also endorse the view that theorising aimed at giving voice to a broader range of interests may enhance the societal relevance of interventionist research. They thus end up advocating a position that entails some balancing between the practical, theoretical and societal relevance of such research whilst emphasising the need to continuously nurture an element of each. Consistent with a contingent conception of what counts as more or less legitimate forms of critique, such balancing acts would also need to include some deliberations on the specific social, cultural and political context in which researchers are embedded such that various kinds of critical interventions are not rendered ineffective.

6. Concluding remarks

This introductory essay has sketched the contours of what an extended research agenda exploring the societal relevance of management accounting might entail. Guided by an over-riding ambition to turn management accounting research "inside out", it has highlighted a number of emerging research themes and opportunities for developing such research as well as some theoretical and methodological implications of doing so. A considerable amount of work remains to be done to take this research agenda forward. In particular, I have highlighted research opportunities related to how management accounting is implicated in the development of external regulation and governance of organisations and the shaping of markets. In doing so, I have called for some rapprochement between research exploring the societal relevance of management accounting and cognate areas of scholarship, such as research on auditing, financial accounting, corporate governance, regulation and the constitution and performance of markets. I have also emphasised the need to develop research in such a way that it gives voice to a broader range of constituency interests in society. To this end, we may need to extend some of the theories exercising an increasingly dominant influence on interpretive management accounting research, such as institutional theory and ANT, so that researchers employing them nurture a stronger sense of engagement with broader, societal issues of marginalisation and emancipation. Whilst this has long been a key concern of critical accounting scholars, I have argued against an overly strict distinction between what counts as more or less "critical" research and in favour of a contingent conception of what kinds of critiques and interventions may be effective in various societal contexts. This has important methodological implications, especially for research that seeks to intervene directly in organisational and societal practices in the quest for relevance. The relative effectiveness of various kinds of interventions is likely to depend on the social, cultural and political context in which researchers are embedded. Any interventions aimed at exploring and enhancing the societal relevance of management accounting need to be undertaken with such specific contingencies in mind.

Acknowledgements

The original ideas behind this paper were presented in a panel session at the *6th Workshop on Management Accounting as Social and Organizational Practice* (MASOP), Copenhagen, 2013. I thank the workshop organisers and participants for the opportunity to discuss these ideas at an early stage. Helpful comments by Vivien Beattie and the contributors to this special issue on the "Societal Relevance of Management Accounting" are also acknowledged.

Notes

1. As of 5 December 2013, the 1991 paperback edition of Johnson and Kaplan (1987) had generated 3582 Google Scholar citations.
2. Theoretical approaches used to study this phenomenon include *inter alia* garbage can theory (Wiesel *et al.* 2011), institutional theory (Modell and Wiesel 2008), sociology of professions (Samuel *et al.* 2005) and various critical theories (Preston *et al.* 1997, Lawrence and Sharma 2002).
3. The notion of calculative practices has tended to be rather loosely defined in the accounting literature. Following Vollmer *et al.* (2009), it is here conceived of as a set of social practices clustered around some calculative techniques such as costing or performance measurement.

References

Ahmed, M.N. and Scapens, R.W., 2000. Cost allocation in Britain: an institutional analysis. *European Accounting Review*, 9 (1), 159–204.

Ahmed, M.N. and Scapens, R.W., 2003. The evolution of cost-based pricing rules in Britain: an institutionalist perspective. *Review of Political Economy*, 15 (2), 173–191.

Ahrens, T. and Chapman, C.S., 2007. Management accounting as practice. *Accounting, Organizations and Society*, 32 (1), 1–27.

Ahrens, T. and Khalifa, R., 2013. Researching the lived experience of corporate governance. *Qualitative Research in Accounting and Management*, 10 (1), 4–30.

Ayres, L. and Braithwaite, J., 1992. *Responsive Regulation: Transcending the Deregulation Debate*. Oxford: Oxford University Press.

Baker, M., 2010. Re-conceiving managerial capture. *Accounting, Auditing and Accountability Journal*, 23 (7), 847–867.

Baldvinsdottir, G., Mitchell, F., and Norreklit, H., 2010. Issues in the relationship between theory and practice in management accounting. *Management Accounting Research*, 20 (2), 79–82.

Baxter, J. and Chua, W.F., 2003. Alternative management accounting research – whence and whither. *Accounting, Organizations and Society*, 28 (1), 97–126.

Beamish, T.D., 2007. Economic sociology in the next decade and beyond. *American Behavioral Scientist*, 50 (8), 993–1014.

Bebbington, J. and Thomson, I., 2013. Sustainable development, management and accounting: boundary crossing. *Management Accounting Research*, 24 (4), 277–283.

Bhimani, A., 2009. Risk management, corporate governance and management accounting: emerging inter-dependencies. *Management Accounting Research*, 20 (1), 2–5.

ter Bogt, H. and van Helden, J., 2012. Guest editorial: the practical relevance of management accounting research and the role of qualitative methods therein. *Qualitative Research on Accounting and Management*, 9 (3), 201–204.

Bouten, L. and Hoozee, S., 2013. On the interplay between environmental reporting and management accounting change. *Management Accounting Research*, 24 (4), 333–348.

Broadbent, J. and Guthrie, J., 2008. Public sector to public services: 20 years of "contextual" accounting research. *Accounting, Auditing and Accountability Journal*, 21 (2), 129–169.

Broadbent, J., Gallop, C., and Laughlin, R., 2010. Analysing societal regulatory control systems with specific reference to higher education in England. *Accounting, Auditing and Accountability Journal*, 23 (4), 506–531.

Burchell, S., Clubb, C., Hopwood, A., Hughes, J., and Nahapiet, J., 1980. The roles of accounting in organizations and society. *Accounting, Organizations and Society*, 5 (1), 5–27.

Byrne, S. and Pierce, B., 2007. Towards a more comprehensive understanding of the roles of management accountants. *European Accounting Review*, 16 (3), 469–498.

Caliskan, K. and Callon, M., 2009. Economization, part 1: shifting attention from the economy towards processes of economization. *Economy and Society*, 38 (3), 369–398.

Caliskan, K. and Callon, M., 2010. Economization, part 2: a research programme for the study of markets. *Economy and Society*, 39 (1), 1–32.

Callon, M., 1986. Some elements of a sociology of translation: domestication of the scallops and the fishermen of St Brieuc's Bay. In: J. Law, ed. *Power, Action and Belief. A New Sociology of Knowledge*. London: Routledge Kegan & Paul, 196–229.

Callon, M. ed., 1998. *The Laws of the Market*. Oxford: Blackwell/The Sociological Review.

Chang, L.-C., 2009. The impact of political interests upon the formulation of performance measurements: the NHS star rating system. *Financial Accountability and Management*, 25 (2), 145–165.

Chiwamit, P., Modell, S., and Yang, C., 2014. The societal relevance of management accounting innovations: Economic Value Added and institutional work in the fields of Chinese and Thai state-owned enterprises. *Accounting and Business Research*, 44 (2), 144–180.

Chua, W.F., 1995. Experts, networks and inscriptions in the fabrication of accounting images: a study of the representation of three public hospitals. *Accounting, Organizations and Society*, 20 (2/3), 111–145.

Chua, W.F., 2007. Accounting, measuring, reporting, and strategizing – re-using verbs: a review essay. *Accounting, Organizations and Society*, 32 (4/5), 487–494.

Contrafatto, M. and Burns, J., 2013. Social and environmental accounting, organisational change and management accounting: a processual view. *Management Accounting Research*, 24 (4), 349–365.

Cooper, D.J. and Hopper, T., 2007. Critical theorising in management accounting research. In: C.S. Chapman, A.G. Hopwood, and M.D. Shields, eds. *Handbook of Management Accounting Research*. Oxford: Elsevier, 207–245.

Cooper, D.J. and Morgan, W., 2013. Meeting the evolving corporate reporting needs of government and society: arguments for a deliberative approach to accounting rule making. *Accounting and Business Research*, 43 (4), 418–441.

Cooper, D.J., Ezzamel, M., and Willmott, H., 2008. Examining 'institutionalization': a critical theoretic perspective. In: R. Greenwood, C. Oliver, K. Sahlin and R. Suddaby, eds. *The Sage Handbook of Organizational Institutionalism*. Thousand Oaks, CA: Sage, 673–701.

Dillard, J.F., Rigsby, J.T., and Goodman, C., 2004. The making and remaking of organization context: duality and the institutionalization process. *Accounting, Auditing and Accountability Journal*, 17 (4), 506–542.

DiMaggio, P.J. and Powell, W.W., 1983. The iron cage revisited: institutional isomorphism in organizational fields. *American Sociological Review*, 48 (1), 147–160.

Edwards, J.R., Boyns, T., and Matthews, M., 2003. Costing, pricing and politics in the British steel industry, 1918-1967. *Management Accounting Research*, 14 (1), 25–49.

Englund, H. and Gerdin, J., 2008. Transferring knowledge across sub-genres of the ABC implementation literature. *Management Accounting Research*, 19 (2), 149–162.

Ezzamel, M., Hoskin, K., and Macve, R., 1990. Managing it all by numbers: a review of Johnson and Kaplan's 'Relevance Lost'. *Accounting and Business Research*, 20 (78), 153–166.

Fligstein, N. and Dauter, L., 2007. The sociology of markets. *Annual Review of Sociology*, 33, 105–128. doi:10.1146/annurev.soc.33.040406.131736

Flyvbjerg, B., 2001. *Making Social Science Matter. Why Social Inquiry Fails and How It Can Succeed Again*. Cambridge: Cambridge University Press.

Fourcade, M., 2007. Theories of markets and theories of society. *American Behavioral Scientist*, 50 (8), 1015–1034.

Fourcade, M. and Healy, K., 2013. Classification situations: life-chances in the neoliberal era. *Accounting, Organizations and Society*, 38 (8), 559–572.

Hall, C., Scott, C., and Hood, C., 1999. *Telecommunications Regulation: Culture, Chaos and Interdependence inside the Regulatory Process*. London: Routledge.

Hansen, A., 2011. Relating performative and ostensive management accounting research: reflections on case study methodology. *Qualitative Research in Accounting and Management*, 8 (2), 108–138.

van Helden, G.J., 2005. Researching public sector transformation: the role of management accounting. *Financial Accountability and Management*, 21 (1), 99–133.

van Helden, G.J. and Northcott, D., 2010. Examining the practical relevance of public sector management accounting research. *Financial Accountability and Management*, 26 (2), 213–240.

Hood, C., Scott, C., James, O., Jones, G., and Travers, T., 1999. *Regulation inside Government: Waste-Watchers, Quality Police and Sleaze-Busters*. Oxford: Oxford University Press.

Hood, C., James, O., and Scott, C., 2000. Regulation of government: has it increased, is it increasing, should it be diminished? *Public Administration*, 78 (2), 283–304.

Hopper, T. and Armstrong, P., 1991. Cost accounting, controlling labour and the rise of the conglomerate. *Accounting, Organizations and Society*, 16 (5/6), 405–438.

Hopper, T. and Major, M., 2007. Extending institutional analysis through theoretical triangulation: regulation and activity-based costing in Portuguese telecommunications. *European Accounting Review*, 16 (1), 59–97.

Hopper, T., Kirkham, L., Scapens, R.W., and Turley, S., 1992. Does financial accounting dominate management accounting – a research note. *Management Accounting Research*, 3 (4), 307–311.

Hopper, T., Otley, D.T., and Scapens, R.W., 2001. British management accounting research: whence and whither. *British Accounting Review*, 33 (3), 263–291.

Hopwood, A.G., 2008. Management accounting research in a changing world. *Journal of Management Accounting Research*, 20 (1), 3–13.

Hopwood, A.G., 2009. The economic crisis and accounting: implications for the research community. *Accounting, Organizations and Society*, 34 (6/7), 797–802.

Hopwood, A.G. and Miller, P. eds., 1994. *Accounting as Social and Institutional Practice*. Cambridge: Cambridge University Press.

Ittner, C.D. and Larcker, D.F., 2001. Assessing empirical research in managerial accounting: a value-based management perspective. *Journal of Accounting and Economics*, 32 (4), 349–410.

Johnson, H.T. and Kaplan, R.S., 1987. *Relevance Lost: The Rise and Fall of Management Accounting*. Cambridge, MA: Harvard Business School Press.

Jönsson, S., 1991. Role making for accounting while the state is watching. *Accounting, Organizations and Society*, 16 (5/6), 521–546.

Jørgensen, B. and Messner, M., 2010. Accounting and strategising: a case study from new product development. *Accounting, Organizations and Society*, 35 (2), 184–204.

Joseph, N., Turley, S., Burns, J., Lewis, L., Scapens, R., and Southworth, A., 1996. External financial reporting and management information: a survey of U.K. management accountants. *Management Accounting Research*, 7 (1), 73–93.

Justesen, L. and Mouritsen, J., 2011. Effects of actor-network theory in accounting research. *Accounting, Auditing and Accountability Journal*, 24 (2), 161–193.

Kaplan, R.S., 2011. Accounting scholarship that advances professional knowledge and practice. *The Accounting Review*, 86 (2), 367–38.

Lantto, A.-M., in press. Business involvement in accounting: a case study of International Financial Report Reporting Standards adoption and the work of accountants. *European Accounting Review*.

Latour, B., 1987. *Science in Action*. Cambridge, MA: Harvard University Press.

Lawrence, S. and Sharma, U., 2002. Commodification of education and academic labour – using the balanced scorecard in a university setting. *Critical Perspectives on Accounting*, 13 (5/6), 661–677.

Lawrence, S., Alam, M., and Lowe, T., 1994. The great experiment: financial management reform in the NZ health sector. *Accounting, Auditing and Accountability Journal*, 7 (3), 68–95.

Llewellyn, S. and Northcott, D., 2005. The average hospital. *Accounting, Organizations and Society*, 30 (6), 555–583.

Lukka, K. and Granlund, M., 2002. The fragmented communication structure within the accounting academia: the case of activity-based costing research genres. *Accounting, Organizations and Society*, 27 (2), 165–190.

Lukka, K. and Suomala, P., 2014. Relevant interventionist research: balancing three intellectual virtues. *Accounting and Business Research*, 44 (2), 204–220.

MacKenzie, D., Muniesa, F., and Siu, L., eds., 2007. *Do Economics Make Markets? On the Performativity of Economics*. Princeton: Princeton University Press.

Malmi, T. and Granlund, M., 2009. In search of management accounting theory. *European Accounting Review*, 18 (3), 597 620.

McAdam, R. and Walker, T., 2003. An inquiry into balanced scorecards within Best Value implementation in UK local government. *Public Administration*, 81 (4), 873–892.

McNulty, T., Zattoni, A., and Douglas, T., 2013. Developing corporate governance research through qualitative methods: a review of previous studies. *Corporate Governance: An International Review*, 21 (2), 183–198.

van der Meer-Kooistra, J. and Vosselman, E., 2012. Research paradigms, theoretical pluralism and the practical relevance of management accounting knowledge. *Qualitative Research on Accounting and Management*, 9 (3), 245–264.

Merchant, K.A., 2012. Making management accounting research more useful. *Pacific Accounting Review*, 24 (3), 334–356.

Meyer, J.W. and Rowan, B., 1977. Institutionalized organizations: formal structure as myth and ceremony. *American Journal of Sociology*, 83 (2), 440–463.

Miller, P., 1991. Accounting innovation beyond the enterprise: problematizing investment decisions and programming economic growth in the U.K. in the 1960s. *Accounting, Organizations and Society*, 16 (8), 733–762.

Mitchell, F., 2002. Research and practice in management accounting: improving integration and communication. *European Accounting Review*, 11 (2), 277–289.

Modell, S., 2009. Institutional research on performance measurement and management in the public sector accounting literature: a review and assessment. *Financial Accountability and Management*, 25 (3), 277–303.

Modell, S., 2012a. The politics of the balanced scorecard. *Journal of Accounting and Organizational Change*, 8 (4), 475–489.

Modell, S., 2012b. Strategy, political regulation and management control in the public sector: institutional and critical perspectives. *Management Accounting Research*, 23 (4), 278–295.

Modell, S. and Wiesel, F., 2008. Marketization and performance measurement in Swedish central government: a comparative institutionalist study. *Abacus*, 44 (3), 251–283.

Moll, J., Burns, J., and Major, M., 2006. Institutional theory. In: Z. Hoque, ed. *Methodological Issues in Accounting Research: Theories and Methods*. London: Spiramus Press Ltd, 183–205.

Moore, D.R.J., 2013. Sustainability, institutionalization and the duality of structure: contradiction and unintended consequences in the political context of an Australian water business. *Management Accounting Research*, 24 (4), 366–386.

Mörth, U. ed., 2004. *Soft Law in Governance and Regulation*. Cheltenhem: Edgar Elgar.

Mouritsen, J., Thorsgaard Larsen, H., and Hansen, A., 2002. "Be critical!" Critique and naivete – Californian and French connections in critical Scandinavian accounting research. *Critical Perspectives on Accounting*, 13 (4), 497–513.

Neu, D., Cooper, D.J., and Everett, J., 2001. Critical accounting interventions. *Critical Perspectives on Accounting*, 12 (6), 735–762.

Nicolai, A. and Seidl, D., 2010. That's relevant! Different forms of practical relevance in management science. *Organization Studies*, 31 (9/10), 1257–1285.

Northcott, D., and France, N., 2005. The balanced scorecard in New Zealand health sector performance management: dissemination and diffusion. *Australian Accounting Review*, 15 (3), 34–46.

Ogden, S.G., 1997. Accounting for organizational performance: the construction of the customer in the privatised water industry. *Accounting, Organizations and Society*, 22 (6), 529–556.

Parker, L.D., 2012. Qualitative management accounting research: assessing deliverables and relevance. *Critical Perspectives on Accounting*, 23 (1), 54–70.

Power, M., 1997. *The Audit Society. Rituals of Verification*. Oxford: Oxford University Press.

Power, M., 2007. *Organized Uncertainty: Designing a World of Risk Management*. Oxford: Oxford University Press.

Preston, A.M., Chua, W.-F., and Neu, D., 1997. The diagnosis-related group-prospective payment system and the problem of the government of rationing health care to the elderly. *Accounting, Organizations and Society*, 22 (2), 147–164.

Quattrone, P., 2009. 'We have never been post-modern': on the search for management accounting theory. *European Accounting Review*, 18 (3), 621–630.

Roslender, R., 1996. Relevance lost and found: critical perspectives on the promise of management accounting. *Critical Perspectives on Accounting*, 7 (5), 533–561.

Roslender, R., 2013. Stuck in the middle with whom? (Belatedly) engaging with Laughlin while becoming (re-) acquainted with Merton and middle range theorising. *Critical Perspectives on Accounting*, 24 (3), 228–241.

Roslender, R. and Dillard, J.F., 2003. Reflections on the interdisciplinary perspectives on accounting project. *Critical Perspectives on Accounting*, 14 (3), 325–351.

Samuel, S., Dirsmith, M.W., and McElroy, B., 2005. Monetized medicine: from the physical to the fiscal. *Accounting, Organizations and Society*, 30 (3), 249–278.

Seal, W., 2012. Some proposals for impactful management control research. *Qualitative Research on Accounting and Management*, 9 (3), 228–244.

Soin, K. and Collier, P., 2013. Risk and risk management in management accounting and control. *Management Accounting Research*, 24 (2), 82–87.

van der Stede, W.A., 2011. Management accounting research in the wake of the crisis: some reflections. *European Accounting Review*, 20 (4), 605–623.

Tinker, T., 2005. *The withering of criticism*. A review of professional, Foucauldian, ethnographic, and epistemic studies in accounting. *Accounting, Auditing and Accountability Journal*, 18 (2), 100–135.

Tucker, B. and Parker, L., 2014. In our ivory towers? The research-practice gap in management accounting. *Accounting and Business Research*, 44 (2), 104–143.

Vollmer, H., Mennicken, A., and Preda, A., 2009. Tracking the numbers: across accounting and finance, organizations and markets. *Accounting, Organizations and Society*, 34 (5), 619–637.

Vosselman, E., 2014. The 'performativity thesis' and its critics: towards a relational ontology of management accounting. *Accounting and Business Research*, 44 (2), 181–203.

Westphal, J.D. and Zajac, E.J., 2013. A behavioural theory of corporate governance: explicating the mechanisms of socially situated and socially constituted agency. *Academy of Management Annals*, 7 (1), 607–661.

Whittle, A. and Spicer, A., 2008. Is actor-network theory critique? *Organization Studies*, 29 (4), 611–629.

Wiesel, F., Modell, S., and Moll, J., 2011. Customer orientation and management control in the public sector: a garbage can analysis. *European Accounting Review*, 20 (3), 551–581.

Wooten, M. and Hoffman, A.J., 2008. Organizational fields: past, present and future. In: R. Greenwood, C. Oliver, K. Sahlin, and R. Suddaby, eds. *The Sage Handbook of Organizational Institutionalism*. Thousand Oaks, CA: Sage, 130–147.

Zald, M.N. and Lounsbury, M., 2010. The wizards of Oz: towards an institutional approach to elites, expertise and command posts. *Organization Studies*, 31 (7), 963–996.

Zawawi, N.H.H. and Hoque, Z., 2010. Research on management accounting innovations: an overview of its recent development. *Qualitative Research on Accounting and Management*, 7 (4), 505–568.

In our ivory towers? The research-practice gap in management accounting

BASIL TUCKER[a] and LEE PARKER[b]

[a]School of Commerce, University of South Australia, Adelaide, Australia
[b]School of Accounting, RMIT University, Melbourne, Australia

This study reports on an investigation of 64 senior management accounting academics from 55 universities in 14 countries about the extent to which academic management accounting research does, and should inform practice. Drawing on the diffusion of innovations theory as a point of departure, and based on evidence obtained from a questionnaire survey and subsequent interviews, our findings reveal the prevalence of two broad schools of thought. One school, represented by the majority of senior academics, holds that there is a significant and widening 'gap' between academic research and the practice of management accounting, and that this gap is of considerable concern. In contrast, the other school holds that a divide between academic management accounting research and practice is appropriate, and that efforts to bridge this divide are unnecessary, untenable or irrelevant. From this empirical evidence, we advance a conceptual framework distinguishing between the 'type' of academic research undertaken, and the 'users' of academic research, and on the basis of this framework, contend that framing the relationship between academic research and practice as a 'gap' is potentially an oversimplification, and directs attention away from the broader but fundamental question of the role and societal relevance of academic research in management accounting.

Keywords: research-practice gap; the diffusion of innovations theory; management accounting research; relevance

1. Introduction

Apprehension about the contribution that academic research should make to practice has been repeatedly voiced in the academic literature. This concern has been expressed in special issues in leading academic journals, editors' forums and conference themes, by scholars in fields in which there are both researchers and practitioners (Rynes *et al.* 2001, Van de Ven and Johnson 2006, Shapiro *et al.* 2007). More specifically, recent research assessment exercises, particularly in Australia and the UK, have pressured academics and universities to deliver more relevant outcomes in their external engagement by linking research to practice (Parker *et al.* 2011).

Such concerns about the contribution that academic research – particularly accounting research – might or should make to practice have been accentuated in the wake of the 2008 banking fiasco, ensuing credit crunch and global financial crisis (Unerman and O'Dwyer 2010). Although a lament emerging from across the spectrum of accounting research areas (Parker *et al.* 2011), management accounting research is particularly vulnerable to charges of irrelevancy because of the fundamentally applied nature of the discipline (Ittner and Larcker 2002), and resultant expectations that may arise because of the direct engagement with practitioners that such research often necessitates (Chapman and Kern 2012). Described variously as a 'divide', 'schism' or 'gap' between research and practice, common to the exhortations of many senior academics (Kaplan 1986, Baxter 1988, Lee 1989, Mitchell 2002, Ittner and Larcker 2002, amongst others) are at least two observations. First, this gap is important. The nature and extent of any divide between academic management accounting research and practice has, apart from the obvious ramifications for funding, implications for the credibility, legitimacy, usability and usefulness of what for a large part of their time, accounting academics actually do.

The second observation of the conversations and commentaries about how academic research speaks to management accounting practice is that despite the intuitive appeal of these scholars' sentiments, the extent to which academic research *does* inform, or *should* inform practice has not been extensively canvassed or empirically substantiated. Implicitly framing the question of 'relevance' by reference to its use or usefulness to 'practice' or 'practitioners' is a position that can by no means be assumed to be unanimous or uncontested from a collective disciplinary perspective. For example, although the recent debate conducted in the *European Accounting Review* (Malmi and Granlund 2009a, 2009b, Quattrone 2009) provides an indication of the extremes of opinions on the question of relevance, the extent to which these quite disparate positions are ascribed to within the management accounting academy has yet to be established. However, identifying the predominant stance has important ramifications for management accounting research and management accounting researchers in terms of their identity, role and contribution to society (Wiesel *et al.* 2011).

Motivated by a desire to respond to these two observations, the current study seeks to provide empirical evidence about the extent to which the much-vaunted research-practice 'gap' is of significant concern within the academy. Further, this study aims to unpack academics' underlying conceptions of relevance and associated rationales for their attitudes to any such divide between research and practice. Our a priori position in this study proceeds from the 'traditional' view that regards academic research as a necessary companion to 'practice'. However, consistent with the aim of this study, we deliberately leave definitions of 'practice', 'practitioners' and 'relevance' open-ended, in order to avoid making unquestioned assumptions about some of these phenomena (Quattrone 2009). This approach facilitates our exploration of academics' perceptions of these terms in a relatively unconstrained way to permit our induction of the nature, coherence and variability that may exist in these understandings and the implications that may be drawn from them.

Obviously, there are at least two parties to the conversation about how academic research might inform practice,[1] and as Scapens (1994) argues, the 'gap' is a criticism not only of academics, but of accounting practice as well. As the producers of research, the views of academics on the relevance of their research would appear to be a logical starting point if we are to better understand the impediments preventing management accounting research influencing practice in meaningful ways (Baxter 1988).

We initiate our investigation by capturing the views of a cross-section of the senior academic management accounting community in order to identify and evaluate such impediments. However, merely tabling views and opinions of a sample, however representative, runs the risk of generating fragmentary diagnoses and conflicting remedies (Lee 1989, Rynes *et al.* 2001). The employment of a theoretical framework is likely to better enable a systematic view of the 'research-practice gap', by providing a means by which factors contributing to the gap may be identified, specified and evaluated. In this paper, we adopt an organising framework based on the diffusion of innovations theory (DT; Rogers 2003, Green et al. 2009), and use this theoretical standpoint as a lens through which to interpret a perspective of the research-practice gap as it may apply to management accounting. This theoretical stance has been used in other disciplines, notably medicine (Denis and Langley 2002), psychotherapy (Wiltsey Stirman et al. 2004), public health (Brownson et al. 2006), agriculture, technology, and substance abuse prevention (Rogers 2003), nursing (Hutchinson and Johnston 2004), and management (Rynes et al. 2001) as a framework to identify, analyse and evaluate the barriers obstructing a more effective engagement of research with practice. Clearly, appreciable discipline-specific differences characterise these diverse academic provinces. Nevertheless, importing the DT as it has been applied to the research-practice gap in these fields provides one point of departure from which to more rigorously explicate our understanding of the perceived relationship between management accounting academic research and practice.

Our selection of senior management accounting academics as the sample for this investigation is deliberate. Such individuals may be regarded as 'gatekeepers', who arguably exercise a major influence upon the type of academic research that is undertaken (Lee 1997), by virtue of their positions as departmental heads, editors and members of editorial boards, reviewers for leading academic journals, advisors and assessors of applications for academic appointment, tenure and promotion, and as supervisors and mentors to junior management accounting academics (Parker et al. 1998). Therefore, their perceptions of what they regard as constituting 'acceptable' research implicitly signals to the academic community, the nature and extent to which academic research should relate to practice, and indirectly influences the academic management accounting community's engagement with practice.

The remainder of this paper is structured as follows. First, we provide a synopsis of some of the discussion this topic has generated in the management accounting literature. We then discuss our choice of the DT as the basis of the analytic framework we draw on to organise, construct and explain barriers that may contribute to this schism. Next, we outline the research methods for the empirical portion of the study, and then present our quantitative results and qualitative findings. This is followed by a discussion of the implications of these results and findings. Finally concluding reflections, limitations of the study and possible directions for further research are presented.

2. The research-practice gap in management accounting

Because of its practice-based-nature (Luft and Shields 2002), charges of a gap between research[2] and practice in management accounting[3] have a particular sting in the tail as, 'in an applied field such as management accounting, research should provide explanations that are useful for those we study – managers, organizations and society' (Malmi and Granlund 2009a, p. 597). Moreover, the failure of management accounting research output 'to be used by someone to accomplish something' (Malmi and Granlund 2009a, p. 598) represents an important opportunity cost for the profession, academics, practitioners and the broader societal context in which accounting operates (Hopwood 1987). For researchers, a strong research-practice nexus serves to legitimise their academic pursuits by addressing relevant questions that contribute to the solution of practical problems (van Helden and Northcott 2010). For practitioners, academic research can usefully inform the performance implications of decision-making (Malmi and Granlund 2009a), by explaining, describing, developing and improving practice (Mitchell 2002), and thus play a potentially important role in informing the development of new practices that meet changing business needs (Unerman and O'Dwyer 2010).

However, as academic researchers and practitioners are located in inherently different communities of practice (Vermeulen 2005, Van de Ven and Johnson 2006), a certain amount of tension in engagement must be expected (Bricker and Previts 1990).

Researchers recognise the trade-offs among generality, simplicity and accuracy in theorising (Weick 1989), often opting for accuracy and generality, whereas practitioners prefer simplicity above all else (Malmi and Granlund 2009a). On the one hand, practitioners will incorporate academic research findings only if they are seen to be relevant (Mohrman *et al.* 2001), or provide clear and practical solutions to an immediate problem (van Helden *et al.* 2010). On the other hand, the necessary adoption by academic researchers of rigorous social science methods, and their focus on a limited set of research questions that can be 'addressed by a narrow set of generally accepted research methods' (Kaplan 2011, p. 369), are generally incompatible with the needs or interests of practitioners. An increasing preoccupation with rigour, epistemology and methodology by management accounting scholars (MacDonald and Richardson 2011), has also been argued to devalue research that seeks to speak to practitioners (Hopwood 2008, Otley 2001, van Helden and Northcott 2010), driving practical relevance from accounting research so that studies of practice have fallen out of favour in management accounting research in the last few decades (Kaplan 2011).

It is, therefore, hardly surprising that under such circumstances, a gap between academic research and practice is likely to exist. In the words of Laughlin (2011), academia and practice may be 'worlds apart' – so much so, that some observers are sceptical about whether a closer relationship is possible (Garland 1999), or even desirable (Earley 1999).

In reflecting on the research-practice gap as it has been presented in the academic management literature, Markides (2010, p. 122) observes, 'Wherever there is a problem, there must be (proposed) solutions, and over the years, academics have not shied away from offering their remedies to the problem'. Certainly, beyond the discipline of management accounting, numerous commentators on the research-practice gap have voiced a range of opinions on how this gap may be bridged (Table A1). These examples of such bridging strategies are not an exhaustive list of initiatives proposed to bridge the gap. Other ideas and proposals have been advanced by academics across a range of disciplines. However, as reasonable as many of these remedies appear, and despite the prescriptions offered, the divide between academic research and practice continues to persist and according to some (Swieringa 1998, Short *et al.* 2009, van Helden *et al.* 2010), it is even increasing.

Insofar as our understanding of the research-practice gap is concerned, our body of knowledge appears characterised by fragmentation rather than consolidation. Absent from much of the writings on the relationship between academic research and practice is an analytic structure or framework (Whetten 1989) that attempts to explain a particular set of empirical phenomena (how research engages with practice); or what Shapira (2011) calls 'theory'. Rather than 'putting the cart before the horse' by offering solutions without first adequately defining the problem, pursuing an understanding of how research relates to practice from a theoretical vantage point may serve to more clearly identify the fundamental reasons underlying the existence of the research-practice gap, and to provide a means by which the practicality of remedies can be evaluated.

One such theoretical framework that has been utilised in other applied disciplines to more systematically identify why academic research may fail in better informing practice has been the DT. The DT has yet to be extensively explored within a context of academic management accounting research informing practice, but its application may possess the potential to provide insights in identifying which barriers may be perceived to be instrumental in preventing the promulgation of academic research to practice. It is towards a consideration of this theoretical vantage point that the attention of this paper is now directed.

3. A diffusion of innovations perspective

As we have seen, concerns about a closer connection between research and practice are typical of the applied social sciences in general (Nicolai and Seidl 2010), and the reasons advanced, and solutions suggested across social science disciplines for the purported gap are strikingly similar (Stehr 1992). It is, therefore, not improbable that fundamental reasons for the apparent persistence of the relevance problem are common to many social science fields. Despite the idiosyncrasies between disciplines, one challenge in moving research to practice is the need to connect or engage different and distinct communities of practice (Green *et al.* 2009). One theoretical vantage point that may provide insights into how this connection or engagement may be facilitated is the DT. This frame of reference argues that new beliefs, ideas, knowledge, programmes, practices and technologies are communicated between members of a social system over time through a process known as diffusion (Rogers 2003). Of particular relevance to the current study, however, DT has been argued to apply not only *between* members of a distinct social system, but also *across* disparate social systems, such as those of academics and clinicians (Brownson *et al.* 2006), healthcare managers (Gautam 2008), social work practitioners (Murray 2009) and autism intervention workers (Dingfelder and Mandell 2011). The diffusion of academic research to such practice contexts involves negotiating four potential barriers that may prevent academic research from more effectively engaging with practice. These barriers: discovery, translation, dissemination and change, are depicted in Figure 1.

Figure 1 maintains that diffusion is not an instantaneous act, but rather, dependent upon successfully addressing four mutually related, yet independent potential barriers.

Discovery, 'the creation of knowledge through rigorous research that provides the scientific foundation of a discipline' (Gautam 2008, p. 156), can represent an important impediment to the closer integration of research and practice. Often represented as a 'knowledge production' problem (Van de Ven and Johnson 2006), the discovery barrier often manifests as a failure to pose questions of interest to management (Rynes *et al.* 2001, Vermeulen 2005), ignoring basic questions about the purpose of scholarly work (Pettigrew 2005), or knowledge 'lost before translation' (Shapiro *et al.* 2007). An underlying explanation offered for this knowledge production problem is that a research-practice divide occurs because practitioners face daily pressures that are disconnected from research questions posed by academics. The need for management accounting researchers to therefore, 'ask the right questions' in the first place, is a fundamental prerequisite if our research efforts are not to become isolated from practice.

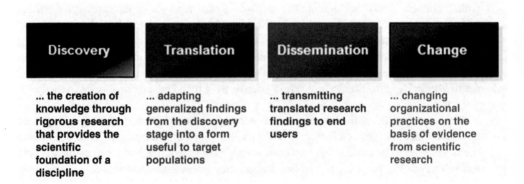

Figure 1. Barriers to research diffusion.
Source: Gautam 2008.

Overcoming the translation barrier requires academic research be presented in a form that is coherent and digestible for practitioners. In the management accounting literature, academic translation has been regularly cited as a major obstacle to bridging the research-practice gap. For instance, over three decades ago, Mautz (1978) condemned researchers as incompetent in communicating research matters to practitioners, Werner (1978) argued that practitioners will only give research a 'fair chance' if it is offered to them as interesting, readable and understandable, and Baxter (1988, p. 3) attributed a failure in translation as a primary cause of the gap between research and practice. These observations have apparently endured to the present day, being similarly observed within an MA context. van Helden and Northcott (2010) for instance, argue that the understandability of research findings is often hindered by poor presentation, such as excessive attention to methodology and theory, or by ignoring any research implications of potential relevance and interest to practitioners.

Dissemination involves exposing practitioners to research findings via appropriate media, distribution or communication channels (Gautam 2008). Concerns that management accounting research does not engage with practice often focus on this barrier. A number of causes have been attributed. They include a predilection towards communicating with academic colleagues in preference to practitioners (Malmi and Granlund 2009a), the time lags involved in academic publishing versus the practitioners' short-term decision requirements (Inanga and Schneider 2005), the general reluctance of practitioners to attempt reading management accounting research journals (Inanga and Schneider 2005, Scapens 2008) and, their disinterest in research outputs, preferring other presentation modes (Mitchell 2002).

Change is one of the key goals of applied academic research, involving the implementation of practices triggered by research-based evidence (Gautam 2008). This particular barrier is arguably independent of the diffusion process (Green *et al.* 2009), being largely related to the more general management of change. The area of change management has been extensively researched in the organisational, strategic and general management literatures, and a summary of these findings is far beyond the scope of this paper. Nevertheless, as Brownson *et al.* (2006) observed, common to much of this literature is the recognition that parties to the change need to be 'ready, willing, and able' to embrace new ways of operating if the adoption of the change is to be successful and sustainable. If meaning is, to a large extent, derived from context (Laughlin 2011), consequential and convincing connection of research with specific organisational settings is important. Thus, this barrier to the diffusion of academic research to practice is in effect about contextualising research to demonstrate to practitioners its amenability to adoption.

Each of these four barriers may potentially hinder the adoption of academic research findings by practitioners. Identifying the relative contribution of each of the barriers in the apparent failure of practitioners to embrace research findings may in itself, however, represent a gap in our understanding. What DT offers is an organising framework that can be employed to identify the main impediments preventing the engagement of research and practice, and to evaluate their relative significance. In view of the considerable, but fragmented, conversations that have occurred within the so-called 'relevance literature', obtaining an indication of the more problematic obstructions represents a first step to an improved understanding of why a more engaged relationship between research and practice may not occur. Explanations advanced in the academic literature concerning reasons why research does not adequately engage with practice have been largely speculative. They have been articulated by various senior scholars, across a range of disciplines, and drawn mainly from anecdotal perceptions. Such contributions, nonetheless, have been valuable in that they provide the motivation and platform for further empirically-based investigation to deconstruct the space between research and practice. The next logical step in this discourse is that of providing empirical research evidence in order to ascertain the extent to which such a gap is a relevant concern to academics, and then to understand why this may be so. Empirical studies capturing academics' views can equip scholars, policy-makers and indeed, practitioners with foundations for developing specific strategies, designed to narrow the gap (Parker 2011). This may also help avoid producing remedies that are more harmful than the disease (Markides 2007), and avoid 'the tendency for academics to express opinions about academic-practitioner relations in the absence of data' (Rynes *et al.* 2001, p. 343).

The current study, therefore, offers a first response to these observations by providing a theoretically informed, empirical base to explicate how management accounting academics perceive the relationship between academic research and practice. This, we argue, is a necessary perquisite to advocating remedies or solutions designed to enhance this relationship.

4.   Research methods

4.1   *Data sources*

Our target population comprised 'senior management accounting academics'. Unambiguously, specifying such an amorphous and dynamic population, however, is problematic. What constitutes a 'senior' management accounting academic is not readily obvious, and also open to debate. Moreover, by virtue of the process of appointment, promotion, retirement and resignation, this is a continually changing population. For these reasons, a nonprobabilistic, purposive approach was used to select the sample investigated in this study.

Although purposive samples can be drawn in different ways (Patton 2002), such samples are, by definition, selected according to predetermined criteria. The criteria we employed in selecting the 'senior management accounting academics' as respondents to this study were that they: (a) had attained the position of Professor, or Associate Professor (or its equivalent) at a recognised university; (b) publish or teach management accounting; (c) are or have at some time been a member of an Editorial Board of journals that publish quality, internationally recognised management accounting research[4] and (d) were either personally known to one or other of the authors, or, were recommended as participants by a respondent in the course of the study. Constructing the sample in this way inevitably introduces the possibility of potential selection bias as some population groups may be given disproportionately high or low chances of inclusion in the study. Rather than seeking a statistically representative sample, we have targeted a comprehensive international cohort of senior scholars capable of offering expertise and reflections most directly relevant to this study's objective, and of providing in depth conceptual understandings of the nature, dimensions and potential approaches to the management accounting research – practice gap.

As given in Table A2, our sample comprised 64 individuals, drawn from 55 Universities, located in 14 countries across four broad geographic regions: Australasia[5] (22), the UK (17), mainland Europe[6] (14) and North America (11). Journals in which these academics have published management accounting papers in the period 2007–2011 (inclusive) are depicted in Table A3. This profile of journals includes publication of the full range of generalist to specialist, quantitative to qualitative and positivist to interpretivist studies. It is notable also that interviewees' publications ultimately categorised in the majority or minority groups are distributed relatively evenly within each journal. Moreover, chi-square tests comparing majority and minority group publications by journal did not reveal statistically significant differences ($\chi^2 = 1.19$, df $= 10$, not significant at the 0.05 level). In segmenting the international management accounting academic community in this way, our intent was to enable some degree of comparison between locations by identifying common as well as contradictory views that may exist across geographic boundaries.

4.2 Data collection

The data for this study are derived from responses to a questionnaire survey and subsequent interviews undertaken with questionnaire respondents. The exploratory questionnaire survey (a copy of the questions comprising the questionnaire is provided in Table A4), represented the point of departure for this study. It is designed to identify the principal barriers perceived to inhibit academic research more effectively engaging with, and informing practice, and to evaluate their relative significance. These quantitative results are then used as a platform for the qualitative part of this study to consider the broader implications of how research does engage, and should engage with practice.

4.3 Questionnaire administration and response rates

The questionnaire was pilot tested with three senior management accounting academics (who were not subsequently included in the sample) in order to ensure that the variables of interest were relevant and that the questions used to measure each variable were unambiguous and captured the constructs of interest. In addition, input was also gained from two psychometricians to establish content and face validity of the instrument. These procedures resulted in minor changes being made to the questionnaire, primarily in terms of wording, format and presentation.

Questionnaires were emailed to 125 senior management accounting academics to ascertain their willingness to participate in the research. Over the course of a 5-month period, 67 academics (51% of the sample) responded, resulting in 64 usable responses. We compared the mean score of each measured variable for the first and last 20% of returns. No significant differences ($p > 0.05$) were identified, providing some support for the absence of any obvious response bias between early and late respondents. Although small, this sample size was considered appropriate and practicable for an exploratory study of this nature, given the seniority of respondents and our intention to capture empirical evidence about the perceived nature of the research-practice gap.

4.4 Measurement of constructs

Given the limited availability of established measures to assess the research-practice gap in a management accounting context, it was necessary to develop measurement instruments for the study. The questionnaire consisted of six sections. The first section comprised four questions designed to solicit demographic information about the respondent and their organisation. Sections 2–6 were presented as a 5-point scale, with anchors of 1 'strongly disagree' and 5 'strongly agree'. Section 7 comprised an open-ended question.

Section 2 comprised five general questions asking respondents' to rate their perception of the extent of the gap between academic research and practice, and how important they believed this gap to be. Sections 3–6 each comprised five questions, drawn directly from journal articles, books and book chapters that explicitly discuss the practical relevance of academic research – the 'relevance literature' – with each section corresponding to one of the four barriers to the effective diffusion of academic research to practice.

These measures were based largely on prior writings on the research-practice gap. We identified, in the relevance literature, the predominant arguments advanced for the failure of academic research to engage with practice, and then categorised these arguments according to each of the four barriers to diffusion. In so doing, our intent was to 'table' common barriers argued to prevent research from more effectively inform practice, in order to evaluate their veracity. While responses to the individual questions were themselves interesting, the scores for each of the five items comprising the discovery, translation, dissemination and change scales were summated into a composite score for further analysis. The literature origin of each question included in Sections 3–6 is discussed in turn.

4.4.1 *Section 3: Discovery*

The five questions comprising this section of the study reflected observations in the literature as important barriers pertaining to the discovery stage of the diffusion model. These questions related to academics' selection of research questions (Shapiro *et al.* 2007), the importance of research topics to practitioners (Van de Ven and Johnson 2006), the multidisciplinary nature of business research (Parker and Guthrie 2010), the immediate and short-term needs of the practitioners (Inanga and Schneider 2005) and the confidentiality of management accounting practices (Moehrle *et al.* 2009).

4.4.2 *Section 4: Translation*

Questions in this section of the questionnaire focused on observations identified in the literature relating to the understandability by practioners of academic research. Five issues were investigated: the extent to which research is orientated towards academics, rather than practitioners (Malmi and Granlund 2009a), the ability of practitioners to understand academic research relative to other kinds of information they may access (Wilkerson 1999), the development of consulting relationships between academics and practitioners as a means of more effectively facilitating knowledge transfer (Rynes *et al.* 2001), academics' taking sabbatical employment, short internships or secondments in industry to understand and learn more about business communication and practice (Swieringa 1998), and, the difficulty experienced by practitioners in reading academic publications (Baxter 1988).

4.4.3. *Section 5: Dissemination*

In the dissemination section of the questionnaire, five questions sought responses relating to the ease with which practitioners are able to access academic research (Shapiro *et al.* 2007), the necessity of transmitting research findings to practitioners (Scapens 2008), the role of professional associations in transmitting academic research findings to practitioners (Wilkerson 1999, Laughlin 2011), the overall awareness of practitioners of sources of academic research (Van de Ven and Johnson 2006), and the use of joint symposia between academics and practitioners in enhancing the communication of academic research to practitioners (Rynes *et al.* 2001).

4.4.4 *Section 6: Change*

Questions relating to this barrier to diffusion, sought to ascertain the extent to which management accounting research is perceived to influence practice. In particular, respondents were asked to rate how research makes a difference to practice in terms of proposing new techniques that meet changing needs and opportunities (van Helden and Northcott 2010), evaluating the effectiveness of existing techniques and approaches used by practitioners (van Helden and Northcott 2010), identifying the conditions necessary for the successful implementation of management accounting techniques (van Helden and Northcott 2010), explaining why particular management accounting techniques are used (Scapens 2008), and, the adequacy of training provided to practitioners in using research (Short *et al.* 2009).

4.4.5 *Section 7: Specific initiatives*

The one open-ended question comprising this section allowed respondents to elaborate upon the specific initiatives they perceived might help in bridging the gap between research and practice. Although the aim of the study was not to generate such prescriptive 'solutions', this question was deliberately included to stimulate further debate and trigger discussion in the interview stage of the study.

4.5 *Validity and reliability*

Reliability tests were conducted for each scale. Cronbach alpha coefficients obtained were 0.76, 0.82 and 0.73 for discovery, translation and dissemination, respectively. These results are acceptable according to Nunnally's (1978) guidelines. The Cronbach alpha coefficient for the change scale was 0.62, which although below the generally agreed upon lower limit for acceptability of 0.70, is above the lower limits of acceptability for exploratory research, generally considered to be around 0.50–0.60 (Nunnally 1978).

4.6 *Interviews*

Questions guiding the interviews were designed to enable interviewees to not only elaborate upon their responses to the questionnaire, but also to enable them to expound upon themes they chose to pursue, according to their observations, opinions and interpretations of the ways in which academic research does, and should, engage with practice (Kvale and Brinkmann 2009, Rubin and Rubin 2012). Thus, interviewer–interviewee discourses ranged from unstructured to semi-structured, according to interviewee identity and context (Roulston 2010, Hennink *et al.* 2011). Follow-up and probe questions were employed where we felt the need for clarification, examples, further detail and explanations from interviewees' initial responses (Bailey 2007). Rich additional information and understandings were gleaned from following up the interviewee's course of conversation with such qualitative interview probe questions (Ling and Horrocks 2010). The emphasis lay upon listening to the voices and perspectives of interviewees and allowing concepts and relationships to emerge from their responses, with reflections and spontaneous discussions prompted by the types of fundamental questions being posed. In particular, we were mindful of providing an environment in the discussions which permitted interviewees to raise issues to enable us to cite evidence not necessarily anticipated.

Given the logistics of interviewing senior academics from locations across the globe, interviewing by telephone or Skype was considered to be the most efficient means of direct contact when the participant was unable to meet personally. From a practical point of view, contacting and securing of appointments for face-to-face, telephone or Skype interviews with busy senior academics of professorial and head of school level took a considerable period of time, with time lags between first contact and eventual interview being as much as several weeks.

Interviews continued to the point of theoretical saturation, at which no new information or themes were observed in the data. Even though it is difficult to exactly measure when the condition of theoretical saturation is achieved (Guest *et al.* 2006), it was apparent that after analysis of 42 interviews, new thematic dimensions or characteristics emerged less frequently as data collection continued. After this point, issues raised were not novel in substance but rather were variations on already existing themes, and interviewees' articulations and perceptions ceased to offer new insights (Ahrens and Dent 1998). Nevertheless, for a period we continued with our interviews in order to satisfy ourselves that our understanding and interpretations of the evidence advanced was consistent and unambiguous. This was considered particularly important given the three modes used to capture the qualitative data. In total, 64 interviews were conducted; 11 in person, 35 via telephone and 18 using Skype.

The duration of the interviews was determined by how much the interviewee had to say, and their time constraints. The duration of interviews was between 45 and 80 minutes. Detailed notes were taken in each interview, and data were analysed following methods recommended by Eisenhardt (1989), and as recently employed by Ahrens and Chapman (2004). This approach uses an iterative process involving validation of data, identification of emerging themes, and interpreting data. Areas of agreement and disagreement with our theoretical stance were noted, with contrasting views identified.

5. Results and findings

5.1 *Questionnaire results*

We report the results of our quantitative analysis in two parts. First, questions 5–9 which relate to broad perceptions about the extent to which academic research engages with practice. Second, questions 10–29, which examine the four barriers to the more effective diffusion of academic research to practice. These results are expanded upon below.

5.1.1 *Existence of a gap*

Descriptive statistics for responses to questions 5–9 are presented in Table 1. Overall, results suggest that a divide between research and practice was perceived to exist, but this perception can only be interpreted as moderate. Responses did not exhibit strong support or opposition on the question of whether or not academic research is too isolated from practice (question 5). Generally, the belief that academic research should be based upon practice was acknowledged (question 6), but responses were somewhat divided on this, as were perceptions as to the extent to which academic research is based on practice (question 7). Respondents were fairly consistent in their perception that although practice should take into account of the findings of academic research (question 8), it does not (question 9).

Analysis of variance (ANOVA) comparisons between the four geographic regions from which our sample was drawn indicated no significant difference ($F = 3.77$; $p > 0.10$) in responses to

Table 1. Descriptive statistics: the extent to which academic research engages with practice ($n = 64$).

Question no.	Item	Range[a]		Mean	Standard deviation
		Minimum	Maximum		
5.	Academic research in management accounting is too isolated from practice	1	5	3.13	1.05
6.	Academic research should be based upon practice	1	5	3.09	1.08
7.	Generally, academic research is based upon practice	1	5	2.88	1.05
8.	Practice should take account of the findings of academic research	2	5	3.81	0.96
9.	Practice does take account of the findings of academic research	1	4	2.41	1.96

[a]The theoretical range for all items is 1–5.

these questions. In addition, we tested for differences in responses to all questionnaire items between respondents on the basis of what we considered to be dominant methodological affiliation. The methodological affiliation was identified by accessing the websites of each of the 64 academics participating in this study, and then inspecting the publications listed for the past 5 years. Academics were categorised as either positivist (19 academics) or interpretivist (45 academics), according to our interpretation of these publications. Although this dichotomous classification was admittedly subjective and broad, no significant difference ($F = 4.76; p > 0.10$) in responses between the two groups was found. On this basis, we cannot conclude that methodological persuasion or geographic location is a significant determinant on academics' perceptions of the ways in which academic research engages with practice.[7]

This initial window into the perceptions of senior academics presents a somewhat equivocal picture about how they believe research should and does speak to practice, as well as how practice should and does engage with academic research. On first inspection, the mean responses to the questions, as presented in Table 1 ($\pm 12\%$ of the midpoint), are by no means emphatic or unambiguous. A visual inspection of skewness and kurtosis statistics, combined with Shapiro–Wilks tests of each item ($S{-}W [64] = 0.91, 0.90, 0.91, 0.86, 0.87; p < 0.01$) indicated the data were normally distributed[8] (Hair et al. 2006). However, a closer scrutiny of the distribution of responses to questions 5–9 reveals a central tendency of the data. This convergence may be attributable to a general apathy or indifference by academics about the relationship between academic research and practice. However, it may also be explainable in terms of the somewhat polarised views on this topic. This polarity warrants additional consideration.

Overall, perceptions of the extent to which academic research is isolated from practice are fairly evenly divided. However, around 30% of the sample indicated that research is *not* too isolated from practice, whilst almost 40% perceived it *is*. Similarly, whilst approximately 30% of respondents believed that research *should be* based on practice, 40% *did not*. Further, almost 30% of academics perceived research *is* based upon practice, yet around 37% held a *contrary* view. Questions 8 and 9 revealed a more definite trend of the sample with nearly 60% of academics agreeing practice *should* be based on research, and roughly 60% also suggesting that *it is not*. These results reflect disparate views on the perceived extent of the gap between academic research and practice, and its importance, and were flagged for further investigation in the qualitative part of this study.

5.1.2 *The relative significance of barriers contributing to the research-practice gap*

In order to evaluate the relative importance of the discovery, translation, dissemination and change barriers, a repeated measures' ANOVA test with a post hoc Bonferroni test (alpha levels of $0.0125 = 0.05/4$) was conducted on the composite scales corresponding to each of the four barriers to diffusion, as reflected in Sections 3–6 of the questionnaire.

The results of this test, descriptive statistics for which are presented in Table 2, indicated a significant difference between the four means ($F = 32.439, p < 0.05$).

The Bonferroni post-hoc test indicated that, based on the contrasts, the difference between dissemination and translation was not significant, but both dissemination and translation were significantly greater than change, and discovery was significantly less than translation, dissemination and change. On the basis of these results then, translation and dissemination were perceived to be the most significant barriers to research engaging with practice.

In summary then, our quantitative results indicate that irrespective of country, or methodological persuasion of the academics surveyed, a gap between academic research and practice is indeed perceived to exist. Further, the barriers of translation and dissemination are seen to be the primary obstacles preventing academic research more effectively informing practice.

Table 2. Descriptive statistics: barriers to the more effective diffusion of academic research to practice ($n = 64$).

| Item | Range[a] | | Mean | Standard deviation |
	Minimum	Maximum		
Discovery	1	5	3.07	0.53
Translation	1	5	3.83	0.72
Dissemination	2	5	4.00	0.59
Change	1	5	3.29	0.72

[a]The theoretical range for all items is 1–5.

5.2 *Interview findings*

Interviews provided the opportunity to further explore in depth, the beliefs, opinions and perspectives of the senior management accounting academic community sampled in this study. This enabled us to obtain additional insights into the quantitative results, penetrating senior academics' meanings and rationales as well as elucidating their intentions and agendas. More than merely providing a complementary perspective on the results of the quantitative analysis, however, our qualitative investigation was particularly pertinent in view of the central tendency and polarisation of responses as presented in Table 1. Augmenting the quantitative analysis with interviews then, provided an opportunity to offer potential explanations of these results.

5.2.1 *Tension in the academy?*

Apparent from our interviews, and consistent with the story presented in Table 1, was the emergence of two distinct 'schools of thought' about the necessity for academic research to engage with practice; the first, that academic management accounting research is indeed divorced from practice, and that this divide should be bridged. As this perception was held by the majority (around 70–75%) of senior academics interviewed, we have termed it the 'majority' view. A contrasting view, however, was presented by the remaining (25–30%) of senior academics interviewed. This opinion, which we have identified as the 'minority' view held that an academic research disconnect from practice is not necessarily a cause for concern.

Rather than representing discrete, dichotomous 'states of fit', our classification of 'majority' to 'minority' should be thought of as representing two extremes on a continuum. Many academics in this study expressed views which acknowledged and recognised the legitimacy of the opposite school of thought, and others expressed moderated or qualified views. Nevertheless, it was very apparent in the interviews that one or other view predominated in their thinking, and this is what we have attempted to capture in our classification.

We illustrate these opposing schools of thought by presenting direct quotes from our discussions. In Table 3, the majority view as expressed in the interviews is outlined; the minority view is articulated in Table 4. These quotes are intended to illustrate the main thrust of these two themes and not to provide statistical evidence on the research question. They have been selected as capturing and representing a sense of the prevailing views of the sample. We elaborate on these views below.

5.2.2 *The majority view: there is a research-practice gap*

As illustrated in Table 3, three primary observations collectively define what we have termed the 'majority view'. First and foremost is the widespread belief that academic research *should* engage with practice. One common justification advanced for this argument was that management accounting is an inherently applied discipline. In the words of some interviewees; management

Table 3. Interview quotes illustrating the majority view.

Characteristics of the majority view	Illustrative quotes
Academic research should engage with practice	'Management accounting is a very, very, very applied discipline. We must have an impact on practice' (M1) 'We're an applied field – every research paper and study should have implications for practice' (M2) 'Somehow, our research needs to make it back to practice – we're an applied discipline. Our role is to help, improve, and create knowledge for practitioners' (M3) 'Our research should revolve around developing, adapting and applying new tools and techniques to practice, and providing practitioners with normative approaches' (M4) 'Management accounting research is about management accounting. Therefore, if we don't engage directly with practitioners, our research is pointless' (M5) 'Management accounting is an applied profession, so I find it hard to disconnect my research from practical problems' (M6) 'Our research should improve or contribute in some way to practice. Theorisation is no excuse for isolationism' (M7) 'It's of fundamental importance because we are an applied discipline. We wouldn't have academics if there was no practice' (M8) 'Although a lot of our research is conceptual, we have an obligation to show society what value we provide; we have a lot of freedom in what we do, but we need to keep in mind for whom we are doing it' (M9) 'We have a moral obligation to contribute to practice – we're consuming people's time – asking them to complete surveys, interviewing them and so forth – it's only fair we give something back to them' (M10) 'A large proportion of funding for Universities is consumed by academic salaries; only a part of this goes towards teaching, the rest of our time is spent on research. The Government, parents of our students – whoever is footing the bill – will eventually want to see what value our research provides. So unless we get our own backyard in order by demonstrating the value our research provides, someone else will do it for us' (M11) 'We're pretty much funded by the taxpayer – we therefore have every reason to be questioned by the government and by the public about what we do and to acknowledge the fact that they need and deserve a return on investment' (M12) 'Practice is our alpha and our omega – they should be the source of our research questions and be the beneficiaries of our findings' (M13) 'I want to be accused of being an academic and a consultant – that's the ideal' (M14)
Academic research does not engage with practice sufficiently	'I would have expected us to have more of an impact, but we're still a relatively young discipline' (M15) 'When was the last time we developed something new in the lab, so to speak? You have to go back over 20 years to the Balanced Scorecard for that. We don't deliver on what practitioners require' (M16) 'Some papers don't even engage with other academics, let alone practitioners!' (M17)

(Continued)

Table 3. Continued.

Characteristics of the majority view	Illustrative quotes
	'The gap is like the grand canyon! What we do is largely irrelevant to practitioners – our research is written by academics for academics. It's like medical researchers dreaming up cures for illnesses that do not exist and then publishing the results in an A* journal' (M18)
	'The gap is huge. The research we do is devoid of reality. Management accounting is an applied field. In reality though, management accounting research is typically a vehicle for social theory, when what we should be doing is using social theory to illuminate accounting' (M19)
	'Academia is about rigour, practice is about relevance. Making research relevant and rigorous is difficult; it requires different skill sets, and a different ether through which to transmit the story. But it is achievable. The two are not necessarily mutually exclusive' (M20)
	'If we don't provide practitioners with tools and techniques, what's the value of our research? What's contribution do we as researchers make?' (M21)
	'The gap is there – there's no question about it. It's a gap right across accounting – not just management accounting. You give our papers to practitioners, and they roll their eyes' (M22)
	'Most of our research is up itself; we don't engage or relate to the real world' (M23)
The 'gap' between research and practice is widening	'It's very large, getting larger, and has been over the past 30 years. It is the same all over the world. It will continue' (M24)
	'There's definitely a gap, and I think it will increase further in the future. Since the 90s, it's been virtually impossible to enter the world of academia directly from practice. The new breed of academics has a very poor appreciation of practice, and our credibility with practitioners is pretty low. They see us more like artists who do our own thing' (M25)
	'A lot of people think academics don't add value. Many practitioners and people not in academia hold the belief that 'those who can, do; those that can't, teach; the rest, research' (M26)
	'Academics are less "visible" nowadays because their performance is measured now on the basis of numbers of publications in "high-ranked" journals. In most universities an academic will not receive any "research points" for submissions to professional journals, professional organizations or practitioners. The character of the academic papers also changed because of the need to focus on theory, research methodology, innovative/complex quantitative methods, etc., and this is probably not what is most interesting to practitioners. No need to be nostalgic, but this might contribute to explaining the gap between the academia-practice (although probably not directly to closing it, unless performance measurement systems in universities change' (M27)
There are clear reasons or explanations for this gap	'We need to be practice-relevant, but it might be over a period of time and not immediately; it's like mining for that gem – much of what we research may have relevance to practitioners, but they need to dig to get to it. It's a long-term game. We change things slowly and incrementally' (M28)
	'The way in which academic research is conducted – where we make incremental advances building upon the work of others does not suit the immediate, short-term needs of practitioners' (M29)
	'It's very clear that all research is about illuminating – but not all research leads to nice packaging, however. It's often not easy to package – and we don't do it well – that's one of our problems' (M30)
	'The "gap" is not about research, it's about how we communicate the findings from our research' (M31)

'The way we talk and write is hard for practitioners to understand. (And) also, our papers aren't accessible to practitioners; it's too complicated and expensive and practitioners have no access to University libraries' (M32)

'The gap gets talked about a lot, but it's probably more of an expectations gap rather than a gap between what we research and how it's adopted' (M33)

'Academics talk in a language understood only by other academics, not by practitioners' (M34)

'Incentives from the performance measurement systems in universities really seem to influence the behaviour and activities of academics. Perhaps an intrinsic motivation to be engaged with practice did exist in the "past" (and in a way still exists), but the introduction of stricter performance measurement systems in universities might have put pressure on it (and articles in professional journals often are not "counted" in the performance measurement system). Perhaps several academics don't have much time anymore to work in practice or – now that performance measurement plays such an important role – they don't want to do activities anymore that are not measured (perhaps they lose ' intrinsic motivation' because of the strict measures). In the past the performance measurement was sometimes more qualitative and quite vague, and in that situation people perhaps did not feel like focusing on a limited number of indicators and seemed to be more engaged with practice' (M35)

'Academics write for other academics, in journals that aren't read by practitioners. This is likely to continue – who's going to stop us? Not the journal editors, not our colleagues, not the Universities, not practitioners' (M36)

'The pressure is on academics to publish in academic journals and these journals don't concern themselves with relevance to practice. The call that many of them have to include an 'implications for practice' section in the paper is superficial, rhetorical and pays lip-service to the need to be seen to relate theory to practice' (M37)

'From the academic side, there's no incentive to deliver to practice, all that matters is what gets published in academic journals; from the practitioner side, they are really time poor, focus on profit and cash-flow, have immediacy problems. They don't really have the time to read AOS' (M38)

'Nobody cares; academics play their own game and practitioners don't care about what we do' (M39)

'We expose our students to research, but unlike other fields like medicine, they don't see the need for research after they get their degree. They don't need to keep up to date with research as practitioners after they've got their entrance ticket' (M40)

'To use the terminology of a gap assumes that practitioners understand what we do – that's not necessarily so. Many laypeople understand how research can be done in medicine and science, but they don't understand how anyone can do research in accounting' (M41)

'The main cause of the gap is because practitioners don't understand what we do; they understand the need for research in medicine and science, but not in management accounting' (M42)

Table 4. Interview quotes illustrating the minority view.

Characteristics of the minority view	Illustrative quotes
Academic research does engage with practice	'By definition, management accounting researchers do research issues of interest to practitioners; we bring scholarly insight to issues that have ramifications for practice' (m1)
	'We can be as critical or as theoretical as we like, but the raw material – management accounting – is an inherently applied discipline. Like it or not, our research is based upon practice, if only in an indirect way' (m2)
	'The sum total of our research is not only what gets published in academic journals. We also introduce our findings in our teaching, in textbooks, through speeches, and consulting. Academic journals are not the only medium by which we transmit our research outcomes. I think we grossly underestimate the extent to which our research informs practice' (m3)
	'This business about 'the real world' is really annoying. Is there an unreal world out there? We're all practitioners: academics, professional bodies. I don't understand how research can be thought of as being isolated from practice' (m4)
	'The two worlds do influence each other, but I don't think we can isolate how this happens. In fact I don't even think we are aware of it happening, so we term this lack of understanding, a "gap"'. 'It depends upon how you define 'practice'. For me, practice, research and policy-makers all make up the profession; there is a symbiotic relationship between the three; ideally we'd see academics, practitioners and professional bodies as forming an 'ecosystem'. I think the problem is framing this relationship as a "gap"' (m5)
	'If you're talking about management accountants reading our papers, then yes, there is a gap. But if you're talking about our research informing practice, a gap does not exist because there are different avenues by which we get our messages out there; teaching (especially MBAs), executive presentations, textbooks, being in the field, consulting …' (m6)
Academic research cannot engage with practice	'Academics bring scholarly insight to practice – not solutions to practitioners. That should be left to consultants' (m7)
	'You could say that our role is to find things out and leave it for the world to work out what to do with it. Our role is not to engage directly, but to describe, explain and understand the world' (m8)
	'What we contribute is not the solution to problems, but the approach or mindset needed to solve problems. We teach people to fish that means teaching techniques to cast the line, determining how to select the best bait, evaluating the fish that's caught. This is where the value of our research lies, and how we engage with practice' (m9)
	'There are only certain things you can do with research; we can teach people to fish or give them a fish. When talking about a 'gap' most commentators are referring to the latter. For me, research is all about the former' (m10)
	'For me, research is about expanding theory and opening up new ways of thinking. Most of this is relevant to practice; but some of it is not' (m11)
	'Academics and practitioners live in two entirely different worlds – parallel universes if you like. We have different aims, objectives, time frames, and priorities. It's almost as though we speak two different languages. We have little to offer each other' (m12)

'Management accounting is quite different from other applied disciplines like the physical and health sciences – and even economics and finance. They are highly routinized and focused on techniques. We're a social science and therefore we're less able to transfer much of our research findings, our research does not lend itself to techniques with immediately relevant application. It's not appropriate to view our research as a list of recommendations. That's what consultants do' (m13)

'To suggest academic research in management accounting needs to engage with practice presupposes that managers act in an economically rational manner. They don't. There's a whole lot of political, institutional and social factors which generally drive what they do. Our role is to ask the questions; the role of practitioners is to determine the best answer' (m14)

Academic research need not engage with practice

'It really depends upon whether we're talking about practice (praxis) or practices. We need to differentiate between the two. Practices are about tools and techniques that are used in industry. Practice (or praxis) is a much broader term – it's about how those techniques are used, how they are interpreted and understood, what they mean in the field. There is certainly a 'gap' between research and practices, but I'm not convinced that there is a gap between research and praxis – that's what research is or should be all about' (m15)

'The "gap" between research and practice is really about the difference between basic research and applied research. There's a space for both. We need to do both, so when we talk about the gap between research and practice, it really depends on what type of research we mean' (m16)

'We need to dispel the myth that if it's not consulting, it's not relevant, and we need to expand the notion of relevance. Practitioners are one important audience for our research – but only one. Other researchers, policy-makers, students, regulators can and do benefit from our research efforts. What practitioners would like is only applied research – but our agenda is far wider than that' (m17)

'You don't need to be a good actor to criticise plays – likewise, we don't need to be immersed in practice to commentate on it' (m18)

Academic research should not engage with practice

'Some practitioners think that academic research should support their needs – but actually we're not there to get things right for practice. Unlike medicine or pharmacy, we don't generate a product – nor should we. Our research should describe, evaluate, illuminate and conceptualise practice, not to solve their immediate problems' (m19)

'There will always be a gap between research and practice – in fact it makes sense to have a gap. If there was no gap, it would suggest researchers are not doing their job. ...our job is to critique, challenge, conceptualise and debate the status quo – not to come up with a set of implementable recommendations. When you look at it this way, a gap is desirable, even necessary' (m20)

'There should be a gap between research and practice; academic research is not a commodity, driven by the wants of practitioners. There is a need to remain independent and autonomous – this is the business of Universities' (m21)

'If there were no gap, we'd run the risk of becoming irrelevant' (m22)

The research-practice gap is not an important 'so what' question

'The "gap" between research and practice is an emotive term. What does it mean? It makes for a dramatic headline' (m23)

(Continued)

Table 4. Continued.

Characteristics of the minority view	Illustrative quotes
	'What is it that is not happening? I don't get practitioners knocking on my door telling me my research is not engaging with practice. The so-called research-practice gap is just that – a perception that does not reflect reality. I'm not convinced, and it's not something I lose sleep over at night' (m24)
	'A lot of our research is not timely for practitioners right now, their horizon is the short-run, ours is the long-run. Just because research doesn't have a payoff today doesn't mean it's irrelevant. It takes a long time for academic research to trickle down to practice' (m25)
	'Policy-makers seem to have bought into this and may be overly-obsessed with a need to deliver something useful in the short-term. The concern that we (academics) are losing touch with reality is exaggerated – it's this perception we need to be mindful of, not "the gap"' (m26)
	'There's a fundamental difference between academe and practice; practitioners are busy fighting fires and delivering short-run results. Academics – by training if you like – are better able to concentrate on underlying forces affecting phenomena. We're much more than just scribes who are there to describe what's happening in practice. We have the luxury of time – to reflect, to build and test theory, to explain, to predict – this is our stock-in-trade, our competitive advantage. The talk of a gap I think confuses academics with consultants' (m27)
	'The research-practice gap has become something of a catch-all or caricature of the academic-practitioner relationship. I'm not sure it has a basis in reality' (m28)
	'We have no real empirical evidence, so we can only be speculative about this' (m29)
	'It (the relation to practice) doesn't worry me. There will always be a gap. It's not that important' (m30)
	'I don't really care whether there is engagement or not – it's not on my radar' (m31)
	'Compared with climate change, nuclear proliferation and world poverty, the claim that our research doesn't really impact the world isn't really that important' (m32)

accounting research should be '*performed in the service of some immediate end*', '*dedicated to the solution of practical problems in the field*', '*contribute to the solution of specific practical problems*' or '*directed primarily towards a practical aim or objective*'. Another prominent argument advanced for a close nexus between academic research and practice was that as universities were funded by external stakeholders (the government, and/or private tuition fees), academics needed to be accountable for the type of research they undertook, and the value it could provide. As one interviewee commented:

> We have a good life and are able to choose what we wish to research. Nevertheless, we shouldn't lose sight of our need to be accountable – stakeholders expect a return on their investment.

Although some majority academics saw a role for research as extending beyond the needs of practitioners (as typified by comment M20 in Table 3), this view was not widely articulated, and the needs of other stakeholders apart from practitioners certainly appeared to assume a secondary priority for these academics expressing this majority view.

The second observation characterising the majority view was the perception that academic management accounting research *does not* sufficiently engage with practice. Table 3 illustrates this sentiment, but not the (considerable) strength with which it was expressed in the interviews. Comments reflected the perception of a 'gap' between research and practice as, 'huge', 'enormous' or 'like the grand canyon'. This state of affairs was seen as undesirable. Sentiments indicating a need to 'bridge the gap', 'engage more with practitioners', 'reduce the schism', 'get closer to practice' or 'add more value to industry', were widespread in these interviews.

The third observation expressed by this group of academics was that the 'gap' between research and practice has widened over time, and shows every indication of continuing to do so: 'it's wide and it's been getting wider over the past 20 to 30 years – I can't see anything changing in the foreseeable future'. When asked to elaborate upon why this might be so, interviewees cited the way in which published research was written, the accessibility of academic journals to practitioners, the limited practical management accounting experience of younger academics, and a lack of incentives to engage with practice. These explanations were common to the majority of academics holding the 'majority view', however, their perceptions of academic research questions as being, 'divorced from "the real world"', and claims of 'the "long gestation period" for research to find its way to practice', were also advanced. An interesting reflection as to why academic research was seen to diverge from practice of management accounting related to the evolution of management accounting research. This theme was mentioned on several occasions, as one interviewee suggested:

> From its highly practical beginnings in the 70's and 80's, academic management accounting research has "mutated into a largely theoretical exercise; reflecting our need to legitimise our research and place in universities.

The comments of another interviewee expanded upon this point:

> We write for other academics, not for practitioners. Journals encourage this. Theorising is more important than practical use or usefulness, despite the rhetoric. We're rewarded for what we get published, not for how we inform practice.

In summary, advocates of the majority view perceive a definite gap between academic research and management accounting practice, and believe the existence of such a gap is undesirable and needs to be narrowed. The ways in which academic research is communicated; difficulties in practitioners accessing research findings; and, a lack of incentives for academics to engage with practitioner's were repeatedly stressed as factors primarily responsible for this (perceived lamentable) state of affairs.

5.2.3 *The minority view: 'What gap? So what?'*

Although representing the greater number of academics sampled in this study, the majority view was by no means the only perspective advanced on the ways in which academic research engages – or should engage – with practice. A number of interviewees voiced a quite contrasting view, and although numerically in the minority, proponents of this view were similarly emphatic in their opinions.

As presented in Table 4, academics holding this 'minority view' see that academic management accounting research: (a) need not; (b) should not or (c) cannot, engage with practice. To these academics, paramount considerations facing management accounting researchers included the issues of independence in research choices, autonomy and objectivity in how research was conducted, and the identification of further stakeholders in addition to practitioners as 'consumers' or potential beneficiaries of academic research. Common to them all is the belief that the 'gap' has limited significance for the academic research agenda, or as one academic put it, 'has minimal "so what" value'. Indeed, the responses of two senior academics[9] who declined to participate in this study were illustrative. In the words of one:

> I am not so sure that I have strong opinions on this other than that the debate on the relationship between theory/academe and practice is not the best allocation of scarce resource time.

And the other:

> I do not agree with the direction of the questions – suggesting that gaps between 'research' and 'practice' ought to be bridged. So, I am not sure including me in your sample will be particularly useful.

It is unfortunate that the views of these two particular academics were unable to be pursued in greater depth, as their sentiments as expressed, appear consistent with the 'minority view'.

A closer look at the views of the minority group, however, reveals a more nuanced view of academic management accounting research existing within this broad, generic classification. Prevailing within the minority view are subtly different standpoints that stem from the different opinions held by these academics in relation to two primary criteria: the type of academic research undertaken in management accounting, and; the consumers or users of academic research findings. These deeper insights, illustrated by a selection of representative comments of these particular academics are exhibited in Table 5.

5.2.4 *Nuances within the 'minority view'*

The broad theme apparent from the first column in Table 5 is the wide ranging orientation of academic management accounting research and diversity in its aims. As illustrated in Table 5, in addition to considerations of immediate application, academic research is variously motivated by a desire to 'improve understanding', 'describe, explain and understand the world', or, more pragmatically, 'publish in academic journals', which interviewees perceive to require a focus on 'theorising at the expense of relevance to the real-world', necessitating a 'theoretical rather than practical engagement'. These perceptions establish the focus of academic management accounting research – at least from the frame of reference of academics holding the minority

Table 5. A closer look at the 'minority view'.

Type of academic research undertaken	Range of consumers or 'users' of research findings
'Our role is to provide an unbiased view, to discover things, to improve understanding'	'Who says all management accounting research (or any research for that matter) should be directed at practitioners? There are a host of other stakeholders that our research informs: other disciplines, students, policy-makers, society. A focus only on practice is, I feel, myopic'
'The knowledge landscape is what academics are responsible for crafting. Our work should be based on rigour, reflection and reflexivity – not immediate short-term gratification'	'Not all research questions have a practical implication. A lot of research should, quite appropriately, develop and refine theory'
'There's a danger in equating research with consulting – some of our research needs to be of direct application, some of it is more ethereal'	'"Practice" is not an objective truth. By furthering theory, our research engages with knowledge firstly, and practice, secondly'
'The really interesting stuff is beyond the tools and techniques – for me, research is about context and conceptualisation'	'I prefer to think of research as looking at management accounting as a social phenomenon, where management accounting practice is part of a far wider context'
'Management accounting is a far more eclectic, conceptual and abstract than most other applied disciplines. Accounting is more "in the head"'	'I'd be really surprised if any of my research has ever been used in practice – I've never written for practitioners. I write for an academic audience'
'Academics do not want to be regarded as engineers who solve practical problems. We've been preoccupied with being informed by theory, because journals require a theoretical rather than a practical engagement. It's the world we live in; we have to play the game. It's hard to drain the swamp when you're up to your armpits in alligators'	'Practitioners are only one of our customers – our research probably resonates more with professional bodies and policymakers than practitioners'
'Unlike philosophy, science or the arts, as a recent addition to Universities management accounting sees the need to legitimise itself as an academic endeavour – we try to mimic philosophy and the natural sciences using their rules, perspectives, and ways of thinking – so we theorise – at the expense of relevance to the real world'	'Our role is not to only follow what practitioners want; if we did, we'd be little more than consultants'
'My job is to profess – not to consult. I demonstrate my value by publishing in academic journals. There's no incentive for me to engage with practitioners. It's of no assistance to my career – so why would I do it?'	'Research is of no interest to practitioners. Our role is to inform knowledge, not practice'
'We're not here to inform practice. Our research is to expend and convey knowledge to students and other academics in the first instance'	'Not a lot of our research is used in practice, from what I can see. What we do is based on fiction – our assumptions are too simplistic to be useful to practitioners'
'I don't think we need to be apologetic about research not having a direct and immediate application. As an academic community, our research can quite legitimately and in fact should inform theory'	'In medicine or the sciences, there is an expectation that research should inform practice. And it does. The same expectation does not apply in management accounting. We write for a far wider audience'
'Abstract research is entirely appropriate – not everything we do needs to be directly applied 'out there' – if we didn't engage in theorisation, we'd be little more than consultants'	'We're not consultants, but our research should in the first place generate generalisable conclusions that can be of use to practice'
'As academics, we have a license – in fact an obligation – to conduct a range of research widener than that necessary for practical purposes. Theoretical research without immediate application is valuable in itself. Application may come later, or use the theoretical understandings generated by pure research ...'	'We're here to serve the community – especially industry – not to serve ourselves'

view – as extending beyond practical engagement to a proclivity towards 'context and conceptualisation'.

Similarly, the second column of Table 5 introduces an array of potential, if not actual consumers or users of academic research. Besides the broad grouping of 'practitioners', they identify policy-makers, professional bodies, other academics and students as all comprising the audience to whom the research efforts of academics speak. This is reflected in the assertions of academics in stating their research is actually or potentially designed to, 'inform knowledge not practice', underlying the view that 'management accounting research is part of a far wider context', written for a 'far wider audience'.

Thus, because of rather than in spite of these variances in the orientation of research and the constituencies to which it may be directed, the message emerging is that framing the relationship between academic research and practice as a 'gap' that needs to be bridged is a view not automatically accepted by an appreciable segment of the academic management accounting research community. It is towards a consideration of the implications of this message that our attention is directed in the following section.

6. Discussion

Our results and findings suggest that the question of how academic research should inform practice is both complex and one in which consensus – at least within the academic community – will be difficult to achieve. In terms of the aims of this study, our evidence indicates that a majority of senior academics agree that academic research is indeed divorced from practice, and perceive this to be a less than optimal state of affairs. However, a minority, yet nevertheless significant number of our colleagues, have indicated that the extent to which our research engages with practice is an inflated, even over-estimated concern. From their perspective, the very framing of this relationship as a 'gap' is problematic.

How might this apparent tension be addressed and what are the implications for the broader management accounting research agenda? Rather than attempting to provide suggestions on how the 'gap' may be bridged, the central premise of this study is that a deeper conceptualisation of the relationship between academia and practice is a necessary starting point in this debate. To this end, we therefore provide a reflection on each respective position, and consequently proceed to considering how, if at all, these positions may be reconciled.

6.1 *Reconciling the majority and minority views – the search for the Holy Grail?*

The disparate positions represented by the 'majority' and 'minority' views as revealed in this study, appear to reflect quite distinct conceptualisations held by academics, of management accounting research. In view of the exploratory nature of this study, and our intent to *discover* and *understand*, we do not purport to adjudicate on or advocate the superiority of either perspective. However, we do see the minority perspective as offering a potentially productive extension to academics' introspection and configuring of their research intentions and target audiences. Nevertheless, it is apparent that in spite of their plausibility, both majority and minority views leave unanswered questions about how academic research should engage with practice.

6.1.1 *The majority view*

As we have seen, the prevalence of the majority view and why it is so apparently entrenched within the academic management accounting community is explainable in part, by the (perceived) inherently applied nature of management accounting as a discipline, leading to a need to demonstrate the relevance of academic research.

However, an unquestioned acceptance of what has seemingly become, at least for proponents of the majority view, 'conventional wisdom' on the role of management accounting research carries with it potential risks. First and foremost, the barriers of translation and dissemination as revealed from the perspective of DT, present the 'gap' between academic research with practice primarily as a technical problem; requiring more effective marketing. However, the persistence of the perceived distance between research and practice has invoked repeated calls for academic research to more closely engage with practice (Baxter 1988, Mitchell 2002, Moehrle *et al.* 2009, Malmi and Granlund 2009a, Baldvinsdottir *et al.* 2010, Parker *et al.* 2011). The apparent intransigence of the problem – or as a minimum, the perception of the problem – suggests that DT provides at best, only a partial diagnosis of the causes of the disconnect. As has been demonstrated by the results of the current study, by acting as an antecedent to the diffusion of academic research to practice, incentives tied to the University performance assessments that reward publications in international refereed journals (van Helden *et al.* 2010), which, in turn, typically downgrade studies that deliberately set out to encourage publication of research that engages with policy and practice (Laughlin 2011) appear to represent a barrier, equal to, if not greater than *translation* or *dissemination*, that serves to prevent academic research from engaging with practice.

Second, the conviction that academic research should serve practitioners in a direct way, may position academics as little more than consultants. Although the demarcation between these two groups is by no means clear-cut, the knowledge created by consultants and academics and the motives underlying the creation of these respective forms of knowledge is markedly different in a number of respects (see van Helden *et al.* 2010 for a more extensive discussion). The knowledge created by consultants is typically initiated by problems in practice and customised for application in practice. In contrast, academic research is typically directed towards answering more fundamental (i.e. theoretical) questions (Foster and Young 1997), and as we have seen, is often initiated by the pressure to publish in research journals (van Helden and Northcott 2010). If one competitive advantage possessed by academic researchers over consultants is their training in developing theories that explain or predict the effects of management accounting on individual, team and organisational performance (Foster and Young 1997), it would seem to make little sense for the research efforts of academics to assume a quasi-consultant role by merely reproducing the expectations of practitioners (McKelvey 2006). A third caveat in taking for granted the predominantly practical nature of academic management accounting research is that it may fail to recognise that the engagement of research with practice is an evolutionary process which occurs over time. Sometimes, this 'time-to-market' can be considerable, with the practical benefits of research not being immediately apparent. Thus, a failure to acknowledge the incremental advancement of knowledge generated through the academic research process, and its adoption by practice by osmosis rather than as a quantum leap, may obscure its underlying practical relevance and ultimate usefulness.

These potential risks in ascribing to the majority view do not purport to be exhaustive, and our intent on highlighting them is not to devalue or dismiss the legitimacy of viewing academic research as a necessary companion to practice. Rather, it serves to emphasise fundamental considerations of the role of academic management accounting research. Clearly, engagement with practice is, and is seen to be a major priority for academic management accounting research. But it is not the only one. The opinions of academics who ascribe to what we have termed, the minority view suggest a broader perspective of both the type of research that is undertaken, as well as the potential consumers of academic research findings.

6.1.2   *The minority view*

In failing to attach a high degree of significance or importance to the research-practice 'gap', proponents of the minority view stand in sharp contrast to what may be regarded as conventional thinking about the necessity of academic research engaging with practice. This view, or rather the frequency and intensity with which it was proclaimed was for us, in many respects, surprising. It flies in the face of the exhortations of respected members of the management accounting academic community who have emphasised the need to direct greater attention to the practical relevance of academic research (for example, amongst others, Mitchell 2002, Merchant and Van der Stede 2006, Scapens 2006, 2008, Hopwood 2007, Parker and Guthrie 2010, Scapens and Bromwich 2010, Kaplan 2011, Laughlin 2011).

The minority view offers an alternative perspective on the research-practice gap debate by potentially arguing the irrelevance of any such narrowly defined gap. Instead, it reconstitutes the underlying intention of management accounting research as being directed towards the production of fundamental long-term knowledge tailored specifically for the research literature and research community. This represents a foundation-laying argument reminiscent of those used to justify basic and theoretical research in the sciences. It is concerned with establishing a broad base of contextual knowledge and critique, the building of fundamental theory and the establishment of a literature that will condition more applied research that may follow. Its focus is upon generating foundational disciplinary knowledge that provides a basis for both researchers' and professionals' ideas and understandings in the field of management accounting. From this perspective, theorising and foundation building become the order of the day, as will be highlighted in Figure 2 shortly.

Why then, might such a view prevail, and how are we to interpret it? Does it reflect an emergent and considered reformulation of the management accounting researcher role? While being articulated by one segment of the management accounting research community, it may offer productive new ways of conceiving and developing the management accounting research focus and role. Alternatively, it may also reflect a preference of these particular academics for undertaking research that they perceive gives scientific respectability and eliminates the vocational stigma that (management accounting) research once bore (Kaplan 2011). Could it be that academics holding this minority view are examples of what Hopwood (2002) cites as careerist rather than curiosity-

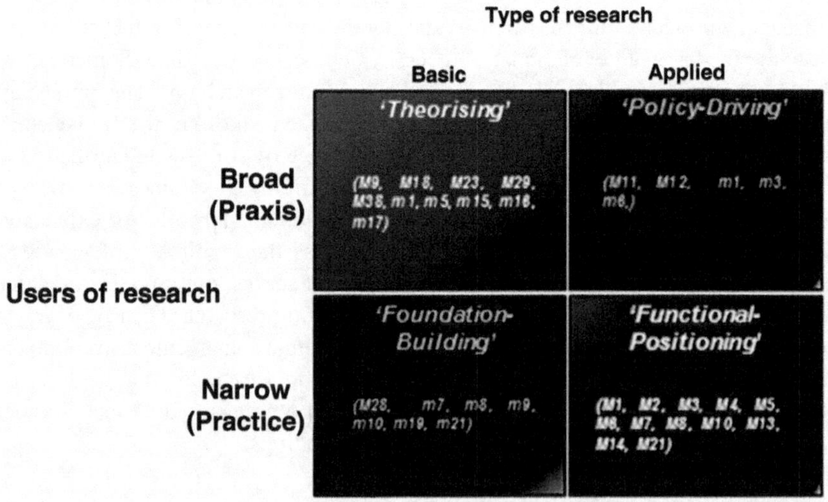

Figure 2.   Management accounting research: a conceptual framework.
Note: The bracketed references within this figure's quadrants refer to data presented in Tables 3 and 4.

oriented researchers, whose research choices primarily reflect their perceptions of the paradigms established by highly ranked journals? Is the minority view as enunciated in this study, the embodiment of a research tradition that 'fosters the attainment of academic credibility of the discipline at the expense of deriving guidance for practice' (Baldvinsdottir *et al.* 2010, p. 82), creating 'an environment dominated by sophisticated methodology, which although academically acceptable, lacks substance' (Inanga and Schneider 2005, p. 228)? Or, have the 'separate worlds' of the academic and practitioner as advanced by Laughlin (2011) become so divorced such that academic management accounting research is effectively restricted to the 'practice of theorising' (Quattrone 2000), in which research becomes 'an academic exercise that is useful to academics while *they* practice what *they* normally do, that is building theories?' [italics added] (Quattrone 2009, p. 627).

6.1.3   *Reflecting both perspectives*

In view of these questions, we contend that despite its broader and more inclusive position on the role of academic management accounting research, and the possibilities it offers for augmenting our understanding of how research may more adequately inform practice, as with the majority view, the minority view in and of itself cannot be considered as a complete or definitive explanation of the schism between academia and practice.

Collectively, however, the stances of both the majority and the minority views may provide a response to the central aim of the current study; to provide, from the perspective of senior academics, foundational insights into the impediments preventing academic research from more effectively engaging with practice. They also, however, beg the question of how – if at all – such almost contradictory viewpoints may be reconciled, or at least related.[10] The following section attempts such reconciliation through accommodating and locating what are clearly diverse perspectives on the role of academic management accounting research.

6.2   *Towards a taxonomy of management accounting research*

Our discussion of the majority and minority views has to this point, focussed primarily on the differences that distinguish these two standpoints. In very broad terms, the two primary characteristics that discriminate between these two views are first, the type or orientation of academic research that is conducted and second, the attributed actual or potential consumers or users of research findings. If we take these two characteristics as our point of reference, an initial start towards reconciling the majority and minority positions may be made. On a very general level, the type or orientation of academic research conducted may be thought of not as the ontological or epistemological positions adopted by management accounting researchers, but rather, as the form of research that may be undertaken. An important conceptual distinction in this regard is the categorisation of research as to whether it is conducted in a quest for fundamental understanding (basic research) and/or whether it is motivated by considerations of use (applied research). Basic research relates essentially to theory building and testing (Foster and Young 1997), whereas applied research is primarily directed to contribute to a change in practices (Scapens 2006).

Similarly, the second conceptual difference between majority and minority groups relates to the 'consumers' or 'end users' of research to whom the research findings are directed, and who may potentially use the outcomes of research. Our deliberately open-ended approach in both the questionnaire as well as the interviews in not explicitly 'defining' what constitutes 'practice', and what we meant by 'practitioners', permit this distinction to be made.

These two conceptual differences have implications for the question of what research is designed to do, for whom, and why. They relate to the inherent assumptions underpinning the research-practice discourse, and their clarification is, we maintain, a necessary precursor to any attempt to advance solutions or ways in which the 'gap may be bridged'. Importantly, distinguishing between the types and users of academic research can serve to locate the majority and minority academic groups identified in this study, and how the research focus of these groups may relate to each other. Our distinction between the 'type' of academic management accounting research on the one hand, and the 'users' of academic management accounting research on the other, is presented in the conceptual framework portrayed in Figure 2.

Figure 2 suggests that the nexus between academic research and management accounting practice comprises four broad viewpoints, represented by the interaction between whether the research may be conceived as basic or applied, and the usefulness of research outcomes to various consumers. Rather than conceptualising research as discrete types, the horizontal axis regards basic and applied research as two ends of a continuum.

In contrast, the vertical axis depicts the range of users or potential users of academic research findings, ranging from a primary and narrow group (practitioners) to a broader and more diverse array of constituencies (such as practitioners, regulators, government agencies, other academics, students, 'society'). In many ways, the vertical axis in Figure 2 can be likened to the division between practice and praxis, where the former emphasises the adoption and implementation of techniques and their use, whilst the latter can be thought of as the embedded contextual social, political and institutional determinants driving the use of such techniques.[11]

The conceptual framework presented in Figure 2 suggests the 'research-gap' debate is in fact, part of a far broader conversation encompassing the array of research orientations adopted by management accounting researchers as applicable to a diverse range of users, of which practitioners are but one. More than just a theoretical abstraction, this conceptual framework is empirically supported in the evidence collected in this study. Indeed, the voices of the academics holding both majority and minority views inform each of the four quadrants of Figure 2. By way of illustration, a selection of these views is included within the quadrants, as denoted by the codes assigned to the quotes presented in Tables 3 and 4. For example, comments, M1, M2, M3, M4, M5, M6, M7, M8, M10, M13, M14 and M21, reflect the position represented by the south-east quadrant ('Functional-Positioning'), in which research is most appropriately perceived to be applied, with a focus on practitioners as the ultimate beneficiaries of applied research findings. The quotations, M9, M18, M23, M29, M38, m1, m5, m15, m16 and m17, reflect a belief as implied by the north-west quadrant ('Theorising'), advocating the value of basic academic research and a broader range of consumers of the results of such research. Similarly, the sentiments pertaining to quotes, M28, m7, m8, m9, m10, m19 and m21, seemingly refer to the south-west quadrant ('Foundation-Building'), where academic research is primarily basic, but which has practitioners as its foremost audience. Finally, the observations associated with comments, M11, M12, m1, m3, and m6, broadly resonate with the north-east quadrant ('Policy-Driving'), in which applied research has appeal and relevance for practice as well as a broader range of constituents right through to the full suite of members and representatives of the broader society.

This conceptual framework contributes to the conversation about how academic research should engage with practice in two ways. First, by respectively positioning the majority and minority views of how research engages with practice, it provides a means by which the contrasting views articulated by senior management accounting academics participating in this study may be reconciled. In so doing, it eschews a one-dimensional view of academic research, and how such research 'should' relate to practice. The second contribution of this conceptual framework is that it serves to bring some context to the research-practice 'gap' conversation by dispelling what appears to be an inherently entrenched view that the primary role of academic research is to engage with practice.

Arguably, part of the challenge in developing a greater understanding of the nature of the apparent divide between academic research and the practice of management accounting is the homogeneity in the classification of 'management accounting research'. Although useful as an aggregate descriptor of a particular field of research activity, there exists a diverse variety of theoretical, epistemological, ontological, methodological approaches, traditions and frames of reference that together constitute the body of literature potentially available to practitioners. Moreover, collectively, management accounting research investigates a vast diversity of topics, undertaken by numerous researchers, in different temporal, geographical and contextual sites.[12] A presupposition that such a vast corpus of knowledge has, or should have as its sole aim, the intent to effectively engage with or inform practice is arguably somewhat unrealistic.

As posited by Figure 2, distinguishing between the types of research and users of academic research emphasises the potential diversity in research use as well as usefulness. While some might contend that a substantial proportion of academic management accounting research should directly inform practice, this framework proposes that there is space for both applied as well as basic research in the management accounting research agenda, and that practitioners should by no means be regarded as the sole consumers or potential beneficiaries of academic research. Such research has potential benefits not only for practitioners, but also for a broader range of additional stakeholders and constituencies. The relative weighting of basic and applied research is by all means contestable, but to assume *all* our research efforts should have in mind an application to practice is fallacious. In addition to practitioners, policy-makers, other academics, professional bodies and regulators are all potential beneficiaries or consumers of academic research findings. These positions have rarely been overtly explicated in research-practice gap conversations to date (Scapens 2006 and Laughlin 2011 are exceptions), but this framework accommodates their presence as 'players' in this broader conversation.

It is important to recognise that the four categorisations of research comprising our framework are presented only as archetypes. There are still likely to be inconsistencies in the conceptualisation of particular types of research and users to whom this research is primarily directed. Therefore, use of this framework will inevitably open up debate about 'what research should be placed within which quadrant'. Moreover, the categorisation of research as applied or pure, and users as narrow or broad is admittedly, somewhat simplistic. Nevertheless, these research archetypes could be very useful since conceptualising research in this way brings a different perspective to 'the gap', and indeed, introduces a degree of context to the debate by emphasising that in terms of research, 'one size does not indeed fit all'. When viewed through the lens of this framework, criticisms (such as 'practitioners do not read our journals' or 'we do not talk to practitioners to develop research questions') may be seen as making academic research appear less relevant than it really is. In turn, by providing a novel and broader perspective on the relationship between academic research and practice, this conceptual framework suggests that in reality, the 'gap' between research and practice diverts attention from the (arguably) more fundamental and broader discussion about the ends of research, and the means employed to reach them.

6.3 *The societal relevance of management accounting research*

In arguing for the expansion of the research-practice gap debate through adopting a much broader view of the types and users of management accounting research, this study responds directly to the central aim of this special issue; 'to consider the societal relevance of management accounting'.

The need for accounting in general, and management accounting in particular to contribute to society has been repeatedly voiced (Parker *et al.* 1998, Hopwood 2007, 2008, Scapens 2008, van Helden and Northcott 2010, Unerman and O'Dwyer 2010, Laughlin 2011, Kaplan 2011). While it is always difficult to talk of 'society', the findings of our study clearly identify a range of stakeholders for whom both applied and basic research may be relevant. This is exemplified by the 'Theorising' and 'Policy-Driving' quadrants of Figure 2. Students, regulators, decision- and policy-makers, academics, universities, professional and accreditation bodies have all been cited by the senior management accounting academics participating in this study, as groups comprising 'society', each with a quite legitimate and vested interest in academic management accounting research.

Similarly, as with the term, 'society', an unequivocal understanding of what is meant by 'relevance' is not without its challenges (Scapens 2008). Indeed, based on an analysis of 450 articles in three leading academic management journals, Nicolai and Seidl (2010) present a taxonomy of eight different forms of relevance, concluding 'relevance' can quite legitimately be considered a 'research topic in itself, rather than just an issue for presidential addresses or editorials' (Nicolai and Seidl 2010, p. 1279). Conceptualising 'relevance' as the impact of academic research on practice is very common in the relevance literature (e.g. Cohen 2007, Kieser and Wellstein 2008). However, on the basis of our findings, we contend that such a definition is overly narrow and gives the impression that the relevance of academic research is much less than it really is. If a broader meaning is afforded to the term, relevance and a broader target societal constituency attributed to the term, then 'relevant research' is an activity that develops insights that help 'society' understand itself better. Adopting such an understanding of the relevance of (academic) research resonates with the observation that relevance, 'is key for what academics do, their identity and role in society, although clearly many do not share the same idea of what counts as relevant' (Quattrone 2009, p. 622). As Scapens (2008) asserts,

> The ways of seeking relevance could, however, be very diverse; with some researchers seeking to intervene in individual organisations through interventionist research, while others might be more concerned to draw out the social and political consequences of accounting in modern organisations. (p. 915)

Although Scapens' observation was made in relation to interpretive accounting research, our findings suggest it is equally applicable to management accounting research from positivist through to more interpretivist traditions.

7. Concluding reflections

Over several decades, considerable disquiet about the extent to which management accounting research is relevant to practice has been expressed in the management accounting literature. This study offers an analysis of the debate by drawing on management accounting academics' diagnoses of the numerous reasons, sources and causes advanced for the research-practice gap. In so doing, our attention has been primarily directed towards defining the problem rather than generating solutions.

The quantitative part of this study sought to first, identify the predominant obstacles impeding research from more effectively engaging with practice, and then, to gauge their relative significance. The qualitative part of our study subsequently sought to provide a deeper and broader understanding of the ways in which academic research is perceived to engage with practice, and why this may be so. Together, this design has resulted in a broader conceptualisation of the phenomena commonly described as a 'research-practice gap', and illustrated the complexity and divergence of views held by senior members of the management accounting academy.

7.1 Contributions to the conversation

This study contributes to the 'research-practice gap' conversation in two ways. First, it is one of the few inquiries that have adopted a distinct theoretical vantage point to examine this much-discussed issue in management accounting. Second, this theoretical vantage point has permitted perhaps a more disciplined empirical investigation on what to-date have been largely reflective observations about the relationship between management accounting research and practice. The adoption of a theoretically informed, empirically based investigation, therefore, lays a foundation for more extensive future research; particularly as such issues have been (arguably) the subject of anecdotal academic discussion, rather than disciplined empirical enquiry.

Three insights emerge from this study as salient to the research-practice gap conversation. First, the majority of senior academics perceive a definite gap between research and practice, and that the existence of such a gap is important and should be bridged. This viewpoint sees management accounting research by virtue of its intrinsically applied nature, as a necessary companion to practice. In a sense, advocates of this 'majority' view see research as a means to the end of improving management accounting practice. The DT informs this majority view by identifying the translation and dissemination of research findings as the principal barriers impeding this engagement. However, an indispensable precondition for such engagement to occur is the existence of incentives provided to academics to engage with practice. Current incentives are not perceived to be adequate, thereby relegating the diffusion argument of dissemination and translation to a position of secondary importance.

The second insight contributed by this study is that a minority, yet nonetheless, sizeable proportion of senior academics believe that there is no 'gap', that this gap is unimportant, or that bridging this gap is untenable or unnecessary. This view collectively sees management accounting research as appropriately or unavoidably distinct and divorced from the practice of management accounting. To this minority group of scholars, the impact of research on practice is subordinate to the 'quest for new knowledge', the value of which is seen to extend to a range of stakeholders beyond that solely that of practitioners.

In attempting to reconcile these two somewhat disparate positions, our third contribution to the relevance conversation has been to advance a conceptual framework that albeit simplistic, distinguishes between the types and the users of research, thus enabling the location of majority and minority views as empirically identified in this study. From this conceptual framework, it is contended that if different forms of research are likely to speak to a range of potential users, academic research that engages with practice is but one of four broad directions along which researchers may embark. Indeed, the majority of senior academics participating in this study have within their publication portfolios, papers which could quite reasonably be classified in more than one quadrant. Therefore, to frame the relationship between research and management accounting practice as a 'gap' is somewhat misleading. Much of the discourse that conceptualises this relationship as a 'gap' has concentrated upon the, 'Functional-Positioning' quadrant as depicted in our conceptual framework. Although this quadrant may, as the majority view holds, be regarded as *the* most important, to dismiss or ignore the broader research portfolio as represented by the remaining three quadrants runs the risk of distorting and misrepresenting the contribution academic research can potentially provide. Not all research can, should or is designed to engage directly with practice. To assume otherwise is, we contend, unrepresentative and one-dimensional.

7.2 Limitations and opportunities for further investigation

Several limitations inherent in the design of this study are acknowledged. Clearly, the selection of the sample (senior management accounting academics) and its relatively small size were not designed to generate empirically generalisable statistical outcomes but rather to develop a provisional understanding of 'what is going on' from the perspectives of the actors involved. Our inferences focus on senior academics' views on how management accounting research should or does 'speak' to practice. Consequently, the minority view as articulated here may very well constitute a 'silent' and previously unrepresented minority perception that nonetheless exerts a pervasive influence on the management accounting research agenda. Still, we recognise that caution should be exercised in attempting to extrapolate the findings of this study to the collective academic management accounting community. Instead, the findings of this study should be regarded as a foundational basis for further empirical enquiry.

Another limitation of this investigation is that it has relied on data generated from a questionnaire and interviews that both carry their methodological limitations (Cook and Campbell 1979, Birnberg *et al.* 1990). While considerable care was taken in the development, testing and assessment of the psychometric properties of the instrument, further work is required to further validate it. The credibility and authenticity of qualitative data analysis and interpretation was enhanced as far as possible by protocols for data collection and analysis.

Despite these limitations, the current study represents an initial step in accumulating much needed empirical evidence on perceptions of the research-practice gap from the perspective of senior members of the academy. The results point to various avenues for future research. One obvious one is to test the extent to which the findings of the current study accurately reflect the perceptions of a greater proportion of management accounting academics including replication of this study to directly identify the views of younger as well as senior academics. In focusing only on senior academics – who are arguably less at risk from the 'publish or perish' research evaluation than their non-senior colleagues (Brinn *et al.* 2001) – the current study may well have understated the extent to which the minority view of research may, in reality, prevail.

Although one strength of the current study is its focus on perceptions from the academic perspective, it is unlikely that barriers between researchers and practitioners are attributable to only one side of the divide. Evidence capturing the views of practitioners as well as academic leaders and administrators would augment the insights gained from this study's focus on the 'supply' of academic research with evidence of the 'demand' of academic management accounting research.

The findings and conclusions presented here are not designed to constitute the final word on how management accounting research may or should more effectively contribute, connect with or influence practice. On the contrary, what we have hoped to demonstrate is the importance of recognising a broader dimension to this conversation. This is not a side-stepping of the issue. By all means, practitioners are clearly one important consumer of our research – but only one. Additional uses and users of our research efforts as management accounting academics both influence and are influenced by the collective configuration of our research portfolio. To be overly obsessed with a 'gap' carries with it a real danger for the future research agenda in our discipline. One size cannot fit all – at least within the confines of an ivory tower.

Acknowledgements

We express our appreciation to all the academics who participated in this study. Special thanks are made to Sven Modell, Jane Broadbent, Kim Langfield-Smith, Cheryl McWatters, Deryl Northcott, Bob Kaplan, Richard Laughlin, Ken Merchant, and Mark Young for their insightful and constructive comments on earlier drafts of this paper. We also gratefully acknowledge the valuable comments from participants in the paper's presentation at RMIT University, and School of Commerce Research Seminar, the University of South Australia.

Notes

1. That is, 'practice' as assumed or inferred by parties to this conversation.

2. The definition of management accounting research is consistent with that of Foster and Young (1997, p. 64): 'the process of using rigorous methods to explain and/or predict: (1) how changes to an existing management accounting system will affect management actions, motivation and organizational functioning, and (2) how internal and external organizational forces will affect management accounting system design and change'.

3. Following Malmi and Granlund (2009a, p. 640), the definition of management accounting as stated by CIMA (1996) is adopted in the current study: 'the process of identification, measurement, accumulation, analysis, preparation, interpretation and communication of information used by management to plan, evaluate and control within an entity and to assure appropriate use of and accountability for its resources'.

4. Following Chenhall and Smith (2010), these journals include A*-ranked journals (according to the 2010 Excellence in Research for Australia rankings of the Australian Research Council) in the general area of accounting that have published management accounting research. These are *The Accounting Review, Journal of Accounting Research, Accounting Organizations and Society, Contemporary Accounting Research, Journal of Accounting and Economics, Accounting, Auditing and Accountability Journal* and *Journal of Management Accounting Research*. In addition, four international journals that specialize in, or support management accounting research are included, namely, *Management Accounting Research, Behavioral Research in Accounting, Accounting and Business Research, and, Accounting and Finance*. Although necessarily restrictive, it was considered reasonable to select these journals, broadly regarded as the foremost international peer reviewed academic journals that publish management accounting research.

5. This included academics working in Universities in Australia, New Zealand, Japan or Singapore.

6. Although the UK is part of Europe, we base our distinction on research emanating from the UK and mainland Europe on cultural factors and historic differences (Hopper *et al.* 2001), resulting in the possibility of different definitions between these geographic reasons of what 'good' research is and how it should engage with practice (Amat *et al.* 1994, Bescos and Mendoza 1995, Chenhall and Langfield-Smith 1998).

7. The quantitative tests comparing geographic locations of respondents, and methodological affiliation were post hoc. They were undertaken *after* the completion of the interviews and were not taken into account in our selection of the sample. We point out that our qualitative findings were consistent with these quantitative results in that no readily identifiable trends or patterns in perceptions were discernible by geographic region or by methodological affiliation.

8. The detailed data are available upon request from the corresponding author.

9. These responses were conveyed to us through email communications with the particular academics.

10. Although intriguing, the aim of this study is not to predict such classification, but rather to understand the nature of what has been found to be a majority or minority view. What might predispose an academic to hold a majority or minority view is certainly a valid avenue for further research.

11. See Jarzabkowski *et al.* (2007) for a more extensive explanation of this distinction.

12. See Chenhall and Smith (2010) for a discussion of the evolution of Australian management accounting research as an example.

References

Ahrens, T. and Chapman, C.S., 2004. Accounting for flexibility and efficiency: a field study of management control systems in a restaurant chain. *Contemporary Accounting Research*, 21 (2), 271–301.

Ahrens, T. and Dent, J.F., 1998. Accounting and organizations: realizing the richness of field research. *Journal of Management Accounting Research*, 10 (1), 1–39.

Amat, J., Carmona, S., and Roberts, H., 1994. Context and change in management accounting systems: a Spanish case study. *Management Accounting Research*, 5 (2), 107–126.

Bailey, C.A., 2007. *A Guide to Qualitative Field Research*, 2nd ed. Thousand Oaks, CA: Sage, 95–112.

Baldvinsdottir, G., Mitchell, F., and Nørreklit, H., 2010. Issues in the relationship between theory and practice in management accounting. *Management Accounting Research*, 21 (2), 79–82.

Baxter, W.T., 1988. *Accounting Research–Academic Trends Versus Practical Needs*. Edinburgh: The Institute of Chartered Accountants of Scotland.

Bescos, P.L. and Mendoza, C., 1995. ABC in France. *Management Accounting* (UK), 76 (10), 33–41.

Billups, L.H., 1997. Response to bridging the research-to-practice gap. *Exceptional Children*, 63 (4), 525–527.

Birnberg, J.G., Shields, M.D., and Young, S.M., 1990. The case for multiple methods, in empirical management accounting research. *Journal of Management Accounting Research*, 2 (1), 33–66.

Bricker, R.J. and Previts, G.J., 1990. The sociology of accountancy: a study of academic and practice community schisms. *Accounting Horizons*, 4 (1), 1–14.

Brinn, T., Jones, M.J., and Pendlebury, M., 2001. The impact of research assessment exercises on UK accounting and finance faculty. *British Accounting Review*, 33 (3), 333–355.

Brownson, R., Kreuter, M., Arrington, B.B., and True, W., 2006. Translating scientific discoveries into public health action: how can schools of public health move us forward? *Public Health Reports*, 121 (1), 97–103.

Chapman, C.S. and Kern, A., 2012. What do academics do? Understanding the practical relevance of research. *Qualitative Research in Accounting and Management*, 9 (3), 279–281.

Chenhall, R.H. and Langfield-Smith, K., 1998. Adoption and benefits of management accounting practices: an Australian study. *Management Accounting Research*, 9 (1), 1–19.

Chenhall, R.H. and Smith, D., 2010. A review of Australian management accounting research: 1980–2009. *Accounting and Finance*, 51 (1), 173–206.

CIMA, 1996. *Official Terminology*. London: CIMA.

Cohen, D.J., 2007. The very separate worlds of academic and practitioner publications in human resource management: reasons for the divide and concrete solutions for bridging the gap. *Academy of Management Journal*, 50 (5), 1013–1019.

Cook, T.D. and Campbell, T.D., 1979. *Quasi-Experimentation: Design and Analysis Issues for Field Settings*. Chicago: Rand McNally.

Denis, J.L. and Langley, A., 2002. Introduction to the forum. *Health Care Management Review*, 27 (3), 32–34.

Dingfelder, H.E. and Mandell, D.S., 2011. Bridging the research-to-practice gap in autism intervention: an application of diffusion of innovation theory. *Journal of Autism and Developmental Disorders*, 41 (5), 597–609.

Earley, P.G., 1999. Creating value from scientific endeavor: can and should we translate research results for the practitioner? *In*: L. Larwood and U.E. Gattiker, eds. *Impact Analysis: How Research can Enter Application and Make a Difference*. Mahwah, NJ: Erlbaum, 97–104.

Eisenhardt, K.M., 1989. Building theories from case study research. *Academy of Management Review*, 14 (4), 532–551.

Foster, G. and Young, S.M., 1997. Frontiers of management accounting research. *Journal of Management Accounting Research*, 9 (1), 63–77.

Garland, H., 1999. Management research and management practice: Learning from our colleagues in economics. *In*: L. Larwood and U.E. Gattiker, eds. *Impact Analysis: How Research can Enter Application and Make a Difference*. Mahwah, NJ: Erlbaum, 129–135.

Gautam, K., 2008. Addressing the research-practice gap in healthcare management. *Journal of Public Health Management Practice*, 14 (2), 155–159.

Gopinath, C. and Hoffman, R.C., 1995. The relevance of strategy research: practitioner and academic viewpoints. *Journal of Management Studies*, 32 (5), 575–594.

Green, L.W., Ottoson, J.M., Garcia, C., and Hiatt, R.A., 2009. Diffusion theory and knowledge dissemination, utilization, and integration in public health. *Annual Review of Public Health*, 30, 151–174.

Guest, G., Bunce, A., and Johnson, L., 2006. How many interviews are enough? An experiment with data saturation and variability. *Field Methods*, 18 (1), 59–82.

Gulati, R., 2007. Tent poles, tribalism, and boundary spanning: the rigor-relevance debate in management research. *Academy of Management Journal*, 50 (4), 775–782.

Hair, J.F., Black, W.C., Babin, B.J., Anderson, R.E., and Tatham, R.L., 2006. *Multivariate Data Analysis*. 6th ed. Upper Saddle River, NJ: Pearson-Prentice Hall.

van Helden, G.J. and Northcott, D., 2010. Examining the practical relevance of public sector management accounting research. *Financial Accountability and Management*, 26 (2), 213–241.

van Helden, G.J., Aardemab, H., ter Bogtc, H.J., and Groot, T.L.C.M., 2010. Knowledge creation for practice in public sector management accounting by consultants and academics: preliminary findings and directions for future research. *Management Accounting Research*, 21 (2), 83–94.

Hennink, M., Hutter, I., and Bailey, A., 2011. *Qualitative Research Methods*. Los Angeles: Sage, 108–134.

Hopwood, A.G., 1987. The archaeology of accounting systems. *Accounting Organizations and Society*, 12 (3), 207–234.

Hopwood, A.G., 2002. If only there were simple solutions, but there aren't: some reflections on Zimmerman's critique of empirical management accounting research. *European Accounting Review*, 11 (4), 777–785.

Hopwood, A.G., 2007. Whither accounting research? *The Accounting Review*, 82 (5), 1365–1374.

Hopwood, A.G., 2008. Changing pressures on the research process: on trying to research in an age when curiosity is not enough. *European Accounting Review*, 17 (1), 87–96.

Hopper, T., Otley, D.T., and Scapens, R.W., 2001. British management accounting research: whence and whither? Opinions and recollections. *British Accounting Review*, 33 (3), 263–291.

Hutchinson, A.M. and Johnston, L., 2004. Bridging the divide: a survey of nurses' opinions regarding barriers to, and facilitators of, research utilization in the practice setting. *Clinical Nursing Issues*, 13 (3), 304–315.

Inanga, E.L. and Schneider, W.B., 2005. The failure of accounting research to improve accounting practice: a problem of theory and lack of communication. *Critical Perspectives on Accounting*, 16 (3), 227–248.

Ittner, C.D. and Larcker, D.F., 2002. Empirical managerial accounting research: are we just describing management consulting practice? *The European Accounting Review*, 11 (4), 787–794.

Jarzabkowski, P., Balogun, J., and Seidl, D., 2007. Strategizing: the challenges of a practice perspective. *Human Relations*, 60 (1), 5–27.

Kaplan, R.S., 1986. The role for empirical research in management accounting. *Accounting, Organizations and Society*, 11 (4/5), 429–452.

Kaplan, R.S., 2011. Accounting scholarship that advances professional knowledge and practice. *The Accounting Review*, 86 (2), 367–383.

Keefer, J.M. and Stone, S.J., 2009. Practitioner perspectives on the gap between research and practice: what gap? *Advances in Developing Human Resources*, 11 (4), 454–471.

Kieser, A. and Wellstein, B., 2008. Do activities of consultants and management scientists affect decision making by managers? *In*: G.P. Hodgkinson and W.H. Starbuck, eds. *The Oxford Handbook of Organizational Decision Making*. Oxford: Oxford University Press, 493–516.

Kvale, S. and Brinkmann, S., 2009. *Interviews: Learning the Craft of Qualitative Research Interviewing*. Los Angeles, CA: Sage.

Laughlin, R.C., 2011. Accounting research, policy and practice: worlds together or worlds apart? *In*: E. Evans, R. Burritt and J. Guthrie, eds. *Bridging the Gap Between Academic Accounting Research and Professional Practice*. Centre for Accounting, Governance and Sustainability, Sydney: University of South Australia and the Institute of Chartered Accountants of Australia, 23–30.

Lee, T.A., 1989. Education, practice and research in accounting: gaps, close loops, bridges and magic accounting. *Accounting and Business Research*, 19 (75), 237–253.

Lee, T.A., 1997. The editorial gatekeepers of the accounting academy. *Accounting, Auditing and Accountability Journal*, 10 (1), 11–30.

Ling, N. and Horrocks, C., 2010. *Interviews in Qualitative Research*. Los Angeles, CA: Sage.

Luft, J. and Shields, M.D., 2002. Zimmerman's contentious conjectures: describing the present and prescribing the future of empirical management accounting research. *European Accounting Review*, 11 (4), 795–803.

MacDonald, L.D. and Richardson, A.J., 2011. Does academic management accounting lag practice? A cliometric study. *Accounting History*, 16 (4), 365–388.

McKelvey, B., 2006. Response Van de Ven and Johnson's 'engaged scholarship': nice try, but. . . . *Academy of Management Review*, 31 (4), 830–832.

Malmi, T. and Granlund, M., 2009a. In search of management accounting theory. *European Accounting Review*, 18 (3), 597–620.

Malmi, T. and Granlund, M., 2009b. Agreeing on problems, where are the solutions? A reply to Quattrone. *European Accounting Review*, 18 (3), 631–639.

Markides, C., 2007. In search of ambidextrous professors. *Academy of Management Journal*, 50 (4), 762–768.

Markides, C., 2010. Crossing the chasm: how to convert relevant research into managerially useful research. *Journal of Applied Behavioral Science*, 47 (1), 121–134.

Mautz, R.K., 1978. Discussion. *In*: A.R. Abdel-Khalik and P.F. Keller, eds. *The Impact of Accounting Research on Practice and Disclosure*. Durham, NC: Duke University Press, Part III, 174–182.

Merchant, K.A. and Van der Stede, W.A., 2006. Field-based research in accounting: accomplishments and prospects. *Behavioral Research in Accounting*, 18 (1), 117–134.

Mitchell, F., 2002. Research and practice in management accounting: improving integration and communication. *European Accounting Review*, 11 (2), 277–289.

Moehrle, S., Anderson, K., Ayres, F., Bolt-Lee, C., Debreceny, R., Dugan, M., Hogan, C., Maher, M., and Plummer, E., 2009. The impact of academic accounting research on professional practice: an analysis by the AAA research impact task force. *Accounting Horizons*, 23 (4), 411–456.

Mohrman, S., Gibson, C., and Mohrman, A., 2001. Doing research that is useful to practice: a model and empirical exploration. *Academy of Management Journal*, 44 (2), 357–375.

Murray, C.E., 2009. Diffusion of innovation theory: a bridge for the research–practice gap in counseling. *Journal of Counseling and Development*, 87 (1), 108–116.

Nicolai, A. and Seidl, D., 2010. That's relevant! Different forms of practical relevance in management science. *Organization Studies*, 31 (9–10), 1257–1285.

Nunnally, J.C., 1978. *Psychometric Theory*. New York, NY: McGraw-Hill.

Otley, D.T., 2001. Extending the boundaries of management accounting research: developing systems for performance management. *British Accounting Review*, 33 (3), 243–261.

Parker, L.D., 2011. Qualitative management accounting research: assessing deliverables and relevance. *Critical Perspectives on Accounting*, 23 (1), 54–70.

Parker, L.D. and Guthrie, J., 2010. Editorial: business schools in an age of globalization. *Accounting, Auditing and Accountability Journal*, 23 (1), 5–13.

Parker, L.D., Guthrie, J., and Gray, R., 1998. Accounting and management research: passwords from the gatekeepers. *Accounting, Auditing and Accountability Journal*, 11 (4), 371–402.

Parker, L.D., Guthrie, J., and Linacre, S., 2011. Editorial: the relationship between academic accounting research and professional practice. *Accounting, Auditing and Accountability Journal*, 24 (1), 5–14.

Patton, M., 2002. *Qualitative Research and Evaluation Methods*. 3rd ed. Thousand Oaks, CA: Sage.

Pettigrew, A.M., 2005. The character and significance of management research on the public services. *Academy of Management Journal*, 48 (6), 973–977.

Quattrone, P., 2000. Constructivism and accounting research: towards a trans-disciplinary perspective. *Accounting, Auditing and Accountability Journal*, 13 (2), 662–708.

Quattrone, P., 2009. We have never been post-modern: on the search of management accounting theory. *European Accounting Review*, 18 (3), 621–630.

Rogers, E.M., 2003. *Diffusion of Innovations*. 5th ed. New York: The Free Press.

Roulston, K., 2010. *Reflective Interviewing: A Guide to Theory and Practice*. Los Angeles, CA: Sage.

Rubin, H.J. and Rubin, I.S., 2012. *Qualitative Interviewing: The Art of Hearing Data*. Los Angeles, CA: Sage.

Rynes, S.L., Bartunek, J.M., and Daft, D.L., 2001. Across the great divide: knowledge creation and transfer between practitioners and academics. *Academy of Management Journal*, 44 (2), 340–355.

Scapens, R.W., 1994. Never mind the gap: towards an institutional perspective of management accounting practice. *Management Accounting Research*, 5 (3/4), 301–321.

Scapens, R.W., 2006. Understanding management accounting practices: a personal journey. *The British Accounting Review*, 38 (1), 1–30.

Scapens, R.W., 2008. Seeking the relevance of interpretive research: a contribution to the polyphonic debate. *Critical Perspectives on Accounting*, 19 (6), 915–919.

Scapens, R.W. and Bromwich, M., 2010. Editorial. Practice, theory and paradigms. *Management Accounting Research*, 21 (2), 77–78.

Shapira, Z., 2011. Conceptual, empirical, and theoretical contributions to knowledge in organizational sciences. *Organization Science*, 22 (5), 1312–1321.

Shapiro, D.L., Kirkman, B.L., and Courtney, H.G., 2007. Perceived causes and solutions of the translation problem in management research. *Academy of Management Journal*, 50 (2), 249–266.

Short, D.C., Keefer, J.M., and Stone, S.J., 2009. The link between research and practice: experiences of different professions and implications for HRD. *Advances in Developing Human Resources*, 11 (4), 420–437.

Stehr, N., 1992. *Practical Knowledge: Applying the Social Sciences*. London: Sage.

Swieringa, R.J., 1998. Accounting research and policy making. *Accounting and Finance*, 38 (1), 29–49.

Unerman, J. and O'Dwyer, B., 2010. *The Relevance and Utility of Leading Accounting Research*. London: The Association of Chartered Certified Accountants, Research Report 120.

Van de Ven, A.H. and Johnson, P.E., 2006. Knowledge for theory and practice. *Academy of Management Review*, 31 (4), 802–821.

Vermeulen, F., 2005. On rigor and relevance: fostering dialectic progress in management research. *Academy of Management Journal*, 48 (6), 978–982.

Weick, K., 1989. Theory construction as disciplined imagination. *Academy of Management Review*, 14 (4), 516–531.

Werner, C.A., 1978. Discussion. *In*: A.R. Abdel-Khalik and P.F. Keller, eds. *The Impact of Accounting Research on Practice and Disclosure*. Durham, NC: Duke University Press, Part III, 183–187.

Whetten, D.A., 1989. What constitutes a theoretical contribution? *Academy of Management Review*, 14 (4), 490–495.

Wiesel, F., Modell, S., and Moll, J., 2011. Customer orientation and management control in the public sector: a garbage can analysis. *European Accounting Review*, 20 (3), 551–581.

Wilkerson, J.M., 1999. On research relevance, professors' 'real world' experience, and management development: are we closing the gap? *Journal of Management Development*, 18 (7), 598–613.

Wiltsey Stirman, S., Crits-Christoph, P., and DeRubeis, R.J., 2004. Achieving successful dissemination of empirically supported psychotherapies: a synthesis of dissemination theory. *Clinical Psychology: Science and Practice*, 11 (4), 343–359.

Appendix

Table A1. Strategies proposed on how academic research may more effectively engage with practice.

Author(s)	Suggested strategy
Keefer and Stone (2009)	Focusing on solving specific practice-based problems
Gulati (2007)	Relying on managerial sensibility to shape research questions
Rynes *et al.* (2001)	Taking sabbaticals in industry
Mohrman *et al.* (2001)	Developing consulting relationships with organisations
Van de Ven and Johnson (2006)	Confronting questions and anomalies existing in reality
Cohen (2007)	Practitioners reviewing for academic journals
Gopinath and Hoffman (1995)	Using consultants to bridge the gap
Vermeulen (2005)	Changing university incentive schemes to enable practitioner-based research to be afforded a higher credibility
Keefer and Stone (2009)	Holding joint symposia, bringing academics and practitioners together
Billups (1997)	Creating awards to recognise those who relate research to practice

Table A2. Characteristics of the respondents.

Region	Number of respondents	%
Australasia (Australia, New Zealand, Singapore, Hong Kong, and Japan)	22	34.3
UK	17	26.6
Mainland Europe	14	21.9
North America	11	17.2
Total	64	100
Position title		
Professor	56	87.5
Associate professor	8	11.5
Length of time working in academia		
Less than 1 year	0	0
1–2 years	0	0
3–4 years	1	1.5
5 years or more	63	98.5
Exposure of professional body to academic management accounting research	Mean[a]	Standard deviation
Publish in academic journals	4.29	1.19
Regularly read papers published in academic journals	4.47	0.98
Presentations/attend to academic conferences	4.06	1.24
Regularly accessing university websites to read research papers	3.85	1.28
Regularly meeting with academics	4.23	0.96
Editor/editorial board member (number of participants)	51	

[a]The theoretical range for all items is 1–5.

Table A3. Publications of respondents in internationally recognised journals publishing management accounting research (2007–2011).

Journal	'Majority' academics	'Minority' academics	Total
Accounting Organizations and Society	26	22	48
Management Accounting Research	22	19	41
Accounting, Auditing and Accountability Journal	20	14	34
Contemporary Accounting Research	13	10	23
Journal of Management Accounting Research	13	9	22
Accounting and Business Research	13	8	21
Behavioral Research in Accounting	9	7	16
Accounting and Finance	9	5	14
Journal of Accounting Research	7	4	11
The Accounting Review	6	4	10
Journal of Accounting and Economics	5	3	8
Total	143	105	248

Table A4. Survey questions used in the study.

Section 1: Background information

1. Name of University

....

2 What is your position title?

....

3. How long have you worked in academia?	*(Please tick appropriate box)*
Less than 1 year	
1 to 2 years	
3 to 4 years	
5 years or more	

4. What is your exposure to academic management accounting research? *(Please tick appropriate box)*

	Low				High
Publish in academic journals					
Regularly read papers published in academic journals					
Presentations to academic conferences					
Regularly accessing University websites to read research papers					
Regularly meeting with academics					

Other (Please specify)

Section 2: The research – practice gap in management accounting

This section of the questionnaire asks you to evaluate the extent of the gap between academic research and practice, and how important you believe this gap to be. (Please tick the appropriate box)

	Disagree				Agree
	1	2	3	4	5
5. Academic research in management accounting is too isolated from practice					
6. Academic research should be based upon practice.					
7. Generally, academic research is based upon practice					
8. Practice should take account of the findings of academic research.					
9. Practice does take account of the findings of academic research					

Section 3: Deciding what should be researched

This section of the questionnaire asks for your opinion about the selection of topics for management accounting research. (Please tick the appropriate box)

	Disagree Agree				
	1	2	3	4	5
10. Academics' selection of research questions is insufficiently influenced by business practitioners.					
11. Academics do not select research topics that are of importance to practitioners.					
12. Research topics in management accounting fail to take into account the influence of other disciplines.					
13. The time taken to undertake academic research is too long to meet the needs of practitioners.					
14. One important barrier facing academics wishing to base their research upon practice is that organizations prefer to keep their practices confidential.					

Section 4: The design of management accounting research

This section of the questionnaire asks for your opinion about the design of management accounting research. (Please tick the appropriate box)

	Disagree Agree				
	1	2	3	4	5
15. Academic research is typically oriented towards other academics, rather than practitioners.					
16. Academic research papers are more difficult to understand than other kinds of information available to practitioners.					
17. Development of consulting relationships between academics and practitioners are likely to enhance how research is designed.					
18. Academics taking time to work in industry is likely to enhance the ways in which research is designed.					
19. Practitioners find academic research papers hard to read.					

Section 5: Accessibility of management accounting research

This section of the questionnaire asks for your opinion about how effectively management accounting research is accessed by practitioners. (Please tick the appropriate box)

	Disagree Agree				
	1	2	3	4	5
20. Business practitioners do not access academic research.					
21. Improving how research findings are transmitted to practicing managers is not necessary.					
22. Professional associations have an important role to play in conveying academic research findings to practitioners.					
23. Practitioners are not aware of relevant academic research that might inform their practices.					

24. Joint seminars between academics and practitioners are likely to enhance the access of academic research to practitioners.

Section 6: Academic research influencing management accounting practice

This section of the questionnaire asks for your opinion about how management accounting research might more effectively influence practice. (Please tick the appropriate box)

	Disagree Agree				
	1	2	3	4	5
25. Academic research should propose new techniques that meet changing needs and opportunities facing practitioners.					
26. Academic research should focus on studying the effectiveness of existing techniques and approaches used by practitioners.					
27. Academic research should direct more attention to the successful implementation of management accounting techniques.					
28. Academic research should be more directed at explaining why particular management accounting techniques are used.					
29. Many practitioners receive insufficient training in using research.					

Section 7: Specific initiatives

30. What specific initiatives might in your view, help in bridging the gap between research and practice?

The societal relevance of management accounting innovations: economic value added and institutional work in the fields of Chinese and Thai state-owned enterprises

PIMSIRI CHIWAMIT[a], SVEN MODELL[b,c] and CHUN LEI YANG[b]

[a]Chulalongkorn Business School, Chulalongkorn University, Bangkok, Thailand; [b]Manchester Business School, University of Manchester, Manchester, UK; [c]NHH – Norwegian School of Economics, Bergen, Norway

This paper contributes to the ongoing debate about the relevance of management accounting. In doing so, we widen the definition of 'relevance' from the largely managerialist focus dominating this debate to examine how management accounting innovations get imbued with a broader range of societal interests and how actors representing vested interests go about entrenching and resisting such innovations. We explore these issues with reference to the institutionalisation of Economic Value Added (EVA^{TM}) as a governance mechanism for Chinese and Thai state-owned enterprises. Adopting a comparative, institutional field perspective, we theorise our observations through the conceptual lens of institutional work, or the human agency involved in creating, maintaining and disrupting institutions. We extend extant research on institutional work by exploring how the evolution of such work was conditioned by differences in field cohesiveness, defined in terms of how consistent and tightly coordinated key interests clustered around EVA^{TM} are. Our analysis also draws attention to how different types of institutional work support and detract from each other in the process of upholding such cohesiveness. We discuss the implications for future research on the societal relevance of management accounting innovations and institutional work.

Keywords: economic value added; institutional work; management accounting innovations; relevance; state-owned enterprises

1. Introduction

The relevance of management accounting has attracted ample attention in the accounting research literature. Close to three decades ago, Johnson and Kaplan (1987) raised concerns about the allegedly declining relevance of extant management accounting practices to management o.

contemporary organisations. Since then, we have witnessed a surge in research on management accounting innovations[1] devised to overcome this impasse (see Ittner and Larcker 2001, Zawawi and Hoque 2010). Empirical research on this topic has been dominated by investigations of organisations adopting and implementing such innovations but has paid scant attention to the long-standing observation that they may also extend their reach beyond individual organisations and form an integral part of broader, societal processes of governance and regulation (Miller 1991, Hopwood 1992, Miller and O'Leary 1993, 1994). However, some accounting scholars have recently drawn attention to how contemporary management accounting innovations, such as Activity-Based Costing and the Balanced Scorecard, influence such broader, societal phenomena and penetrate the spheres of policy-making and legislation (Hopper and Major 2007, Modell 2012a, 2012b). This calls for extending the prevailing view of the 'relevance' of management accounting as a primarily managerial issue of improving decision-making and control in individual organisations (cf. Tucker and Parker 2014) to explore its significance from a wider, societal perspective. Such broadening of the notion of relevance implies a commitment to examining how particular management accounting innovations get imbued with specific, societal interests and how actors representing vested interests go about entrenching and resisting such innovations. When viewed from this perspective, management accounting innovations can be said to obtain their relevance from their ability to further specific societal interests. The present paper explores the processes whereby such notions of relevance take shape.

One innovation with a long-standing pedigree in conventional management accounting thought, but also assuming wider societal relevance is *Economic Value Added* (EVA[TM]). Tracing its origins to traditional notions of residual income, the concept of EVA[TM] was devised and popularised by the US-based consulting firm Stern Stewart and subsequently heralded as a key innovation contributing to the contemporary reshaping of corporate control (see Bromwich and Walker 1998, Ittner and Larcker 1998, O'Hanlon and Peasnell 1998). As such, it evolved into a centrepiece of the broader shareholder value movement emerging since the 1980s (Froud *et al.* 2000a, Malmi and Ikäheimo 2003) and exercising a notable influence on management accounting and control practices in individual organisations (Ezzamel and Burns 2005, Ezzamel *et al.* 2008, Gleadle and Cornelius 2008, Kraus and Strömsten 2012). The shareholder value movement represents a social movement held together by the imperative of maximising shareholder wealth as an over-riding premise for the structuring of governance and control practices and has allegedly been furthered by the globalisation of modern capital markets and dissemination of economics-based conceptions of the firm (Davis and Thompson 1994, Fiss and Zajac 2004, Zajac and Westphal 2004). The relevance of EVA[TM] is here seen as primarily residing in the alignment of managerial interests and incentives with the preferences of dispersed shareholders who would otherwise be relatively powerless vis-a-vis management of large corporations (Bouwens and Spekle 2007). However, this disregards that notions of relevance are fragile, socially constructed outcomes that may vary considerably depending on whose interests are being buttressed by EVA[TM] and similar value-based management techniques. Support for this view can be summoned from the observation that such techniques may indeed serve wider interests as vehicles of political governance and regulation in contexts where capital markets pressures and notions of shareholder value have historically been less salient (Francis and Minchington 2002, Siti-Nabiha and Scapens 2005).

The discussion above raises the question of how the societal relevance of EVA[TM] as a governance mechanism takes shape in socio-economic contexts underpinned by a wider range of interests than those embedded in capital markets. We explore this question in the context of state-owned enterprise (SOE) reforms in the People's Republic of China (PRC) and Thailand unfolding over the past decade. The general relevance of pursuing a two-country comparison of the evolution of EVA[TM] in East Asia is underscored by the observation that the shareholder value movement has influenced governance reforms across this region whilst generating significant, country-specific variations in governance practices (Morgan and Takahashi 2002, Young et al. 2004, Wong 2005). More specifically, a comparison of governance reforms across Chinese and Thai SOEs sheds further light on how similarities and differences in the constellations of interests clustered around EVA^{TM} influence the process of rendering it societally relevant. As illustrated by our empirical analysis, such similarities and differences played a decisive role in the establishment and maintenance of EVA^{TM} as a governance mechanism and contribute to our theoretical understanding of the processes underpinning this development.

To theorise such developments, we adopt an institutional theory perspective.[2] In particular, we mobilise the notion of *institutional work*, defined as the human agency involved in creating, maintaining and disrupting institutions (Lawrence and Suddaby 2006, Lawrence et al. 2009), to enhance our understanding of how two institutional fields were gradually established and maintained around EVA^{TM} as a governance mechanism in the countries under examination. The institutional work approach signifies the most recent attempt to theorise change and stability in institutional fields. As such, it has proved useful for examining how actors representing diverse interests struggle to dominate particular fields and how an element of coordinated, collective action can be accomplished in the face of potentially fragile coalitions of interests (Zietsma and McKnight 2009, Zietsma and Lawrence 2010, Slager et al. 2012, Malsch and Gendron 2013).[3] It thus provides an appropriate analytical lens for examining how diverse actors with vested interests in EVA^{TM} strive to entrench it as a legitimate governance mechanism and how the struggles ensuing from such efforts determine its wider, societal relevance.

The remainder of the paper proceeds as follows. We start by introducing our conception of institutional fields and linking the notion of institutional work to prior research on EVA^{TM}. This is followed by an outline of the research contexts and design before providing a longitudinal analysis of the institutionalisation of EVA^{TM} as a governance mechanism for Chinese and Thai SOEs, respectively. We conclude the paper with a comparison of our findings across the two fields and delineate our contributions to the debate on the societal relevance of management accounting innovations and research on institutional work.

2. Theoretical approach

Institutional theory initially emerged as an attempt to explain the diffusion and stabilisation of relatively homogeneous organisational practices in institutional fields (DiMaggio and Powell 1983, Tolbert and Zucker 1983). The notion of institutional fields was advanced as an alternative to predominantly industry- or market-based classifications of organisations and was originally conceptualised as a widely recognised area of social life constituted by diverse constituency interests (DiMaggio and Powell 1983) or specific societal sectors dominated by firmly entrenched institutions (Scott and Meyer 1983). As such, institutional theorists recognised the importance of vested interests behind specific institutions (see Scott 1987), but arguably tended to bracket the processes whereby conflicting or misaligned interests become a source of resistance or institutional change. This led to charges that institutional theory was poorly equipped to explain the interest-driven human agency involved in the more or less ongoing processes of constructing institutions (Covaleski and Dirsmith 1988, DiMaggio 1988, Covaleski et al. 1993). However, considerable progress in addressing this limitation has been made over the past two decades and now constitutes a substantial corpus of research examining the agentic aspects of bringing about as well resisting institutional change (see Dorado 2005, Battilana et al. 2009).

In bringing stronger notions of agency back into institutional analyses, organisational theorists have increasingly recognised the potentially fragmented nature of institutional fields as made up of dispersed and heterogeneous actors with more or less competing interests (Kraatz and Block 2008,

Wooten and Hoffman 2008, Greenwood *et al.* 2011). Underpinning much of this research is a refined conception of institutional fields as structured around the specific *issues* at stake in institutional processes (Hoffman 1999, Wooten and Hoffman 2008). This has shifted the emphasis from the general configuration of societal sectors to the specific institutions (or innovations) constituting the object of institutionalisation. It also brings issues of conflict and resistance to the fore to explain how actors with vested interests in particular institutions vie for power and influence. This results in a view of the construction of institutional fields as an inherently indeterminate process. Any settlement resulting from such processes constitutes a potentially fragile outcome and makes institutionalisation an uncertain and contestable eventuality (Wooten and Hoffman 2008).

We adopt such an issue-based definition of institutional fields to examine the processes whereby EVA^{TM} was rendered relevant to diverse societal interests. The focal institution, or innovation, in this regard is the concept of EVA^{TM} and the concomitant systems applied to render it more firmly embedded in Chinese and Thai SOEs. However, the main object of theorisation in our analysis is the *process*, rather than the outcomes, of institutionalising EVA^{TM} as a governance mechanism (DiMaggio 1988, Abernathy and Chua 1996, Modell 2001). As such, we subscribe to an indeterminate view of institutional change and conceive of institutionalisation as a continuous process of 'experimentation' or adjustments to establish and maintain EVA^{TM} as a legitimate governance mechanism (cf. Andon *et al.* 2007, Modell 2009, Malsch and Gendron 2013). We do not see the ultimate embeddedness of EVA^{TM} in individual SOEs as a necessary criterion for evaluating the 'successfulness' of such processes as the maintenance of its relevance to some interests may entail important concessions to other, potentially conflicting interests reducing its influence on organisational practices. The balance between various interests resulting from such concessions may also be disrupted at any point in time and trigger further changes in institutional fields (cf. Yang and Modell 2013).

The institutional work approach is ideally placed for assisting in the theorisation of the processes of shaping institutions in the face of more or less competing interests. Growing out of the long-standing concerns with the lack of attention to interests and agency in institutional theory, it provides a fine-grained analytical lens for examining the ongoing processes whereby diverse actors shape institutions (Lawrence and Suddaby 2006, Lawrence *et al.* 2009). In doing so, it seeks to rescue institutional analyses from the deterministic tendencies prevailing in early advances in the area but also strives to avoid the pitfall of subscribing to overly rationalistic depictions of human agency as underpinned by relatively unbounded choice opportunities (cf. Lounsbury 2008). Institutional work is seen as an institutionally embedded activity, ultimately constrained by the social structures conditioning human agency,[4] although the main analytical thrust has tended to be on the deliberate and interest-driven efforts exercised by diverse actors (Lawrence *et al.* 2009, 2011, 2013). What distinguishes the institutional work approach from previous attempts to theorise such notions of embedded agency, however, is the more equal attention paid to the establishment of emerging institutions and the ongoing work involved in maintaining them as they start to stabilise (Lawrence and Suddaby 2006, Perkmann and Spicer 2008). Institutional work may also be undertaken by actors resisting institutional change and may thus contribute to preserve extant institutions (Rojas 2010, Currie *et al.* 2012). This emerging theorisation of institutional change and stability parallels similar efforts to examine the interplay between agency and structure in institutional research on accounting (Burns and Scapens 2000, Dillard *et al.* 2004, Englund and Gerdin 2011, Kilfoyle and Richardson 2011). However, the institutional work approach offers a more detailed classification of the various types of work, or agency, involved in the shaping of institutions (see Lawrence and Suddaby 2006). For the purpose of this paper, we build on Perkmann and Spicer's (2008) elaboration of Lawrence and Suddaby's (2006) original typology and distinguish between the political, technical and cultural work involved in the institutionalisation of EVA^{TM}.

Following Perkmann and Spicer (2008, p. 817), *political work* refers to the efforts of various actors to influence 'the development of rules, property rights and boundaries in the attempt to anchor an institution within the wider social system'. As such, it primarily entails the establishment of formal regulatory frameworks within which the users of a particular institution, or management innovation, need to operate through such mechanisms as legislation, policy formulation and standardisation. This often includes political negotiations between actors advocating and resisting focal innovations to ensure that interests remain reasonably aligned in institutional fields. This entails the establishment of agreements about the standards (e.g. organisational targets and performance evaluation standards) against which compliance with regulatory frameworks is assessed. However, it excludes the design of more detailed models required for the translation of such frameworks into practice. Such translations necessitate *technical work*, or crafting of specific innovations, and often involve considerable adjustments of their constitutive technical elements (e.g. specific techniques and procedures for measuring organisational performance) to make them fit particular institutional contexts. An important part of such work consists of educational activities aimed at training users of the focal innovation. This typically requires the employment of actors with greater technocratic expertise (e.g. consultants, professional bodies) working in close collaboration with the organisations adopting management innovations. *Cultural work*, by contrast, refers to the more symbolic actions undertaken to ensure that emerging institutions fit with the broader belief and meaning systems dominating a particular institutional field. In the context of the institutionalisation of management innovations this often entails mobilisation of normative discourses and rhetoric endorsed by various authorities (e.g. management 'gurus') or social movements. However, successful cultural work aimed at entrenching novel institutions also needs to ensure that such discourses and rhetoric are tailored to specific institutional contexts. As such, cultural work is fundamentally concerned with the framing of innovations in such a way that their meanings do not challenge those espoused by powerful interests. In contrast to political work, however, the primary vehicles to this end reside in the normative alignment and policing of broader meaning systems rather than formal regulation.

According to Perkmann and Spicer (2008), all these types of institutional work are often present in the institutionalisation of management innovations and may support or contradict each other. They also predict that innovations are more likely to become widely accepted in institutional fields where the three types of work are combined and build on each other in a cumulative manner as opposed to when they occur in isolation or are brought together at the same time. Moreover, they suggest that institutional work combining the skills of multiple actors is more likely to be successful than work that draws on a more limited range of expertise. What is lacking from Perkmann and Spicer's (2008) framework, however, is any consideration of how differences in the initial structuration of institutional fields formed around particular innovations influence the configurations of institutional work evolving over time. For instance, little attention was paid to how variations in extant regulation or meaning systems condition the prevalence and efficacy of different types of institutional work. Incorporating such considerations is important for overcoming the critique of the institutional work approach for bracketing the issue of how extant institutions shape the action repertoires of embedded agents (Khagan and Lounsbury 2011). Examining variations across institutional contexts is a potentially fruitful way of addressing this problem as it may illuminate which institutional arrangements are conducive to different types of institutional work (Hwang and Colyvas 2011).

Given our conception of institutional fields as more or less fragmented entities constituted by competing interests, it is particularly pertinent to examine how the structuration of such interests conditions the institutional work involved in developing EVA^{TM} as a focal innovation. To this end, we advance the notion of *field cohesiveness*, defined in terms of how consistent and tightly coordinated the interests clustered around a particular innovation are. Institutional fields may vary in their degree of cohesiveness at the outset of institutional processes. However, institutional work aimed at balancing between competing interests may also be required to uphold a degree of field cohesiveness and foster some consensus concerning particular courses of action. This is especially likely to be the case in fragmented institutional fields constituted by dispersed and heterogeneous actors with competing interests (cf. Zietsma and McKnight 2009, Slager *et al.* 2012). As noted by Dorado (2005), coordination in such fields often requires complex political negotiations aimed at balancing competing interests as opposed to situations where dominant actors may impose their interests on other constituencies in a more forceful and unilateral manner. However, little is known about how such differences in political work relate to other types of institutional work under different field conditions. Moreover, given the indeterminate view of institutionalisation underpinning the literature on institutional work it would be fallacious to assume that a given state of field cohesiveness will necessarily prevail over time. Following such an indeterminate view of change, we focus on the ongoing institutional work involved in creating and maintaining a degree of cohesiveness among the dominant interests clustered around EVA^{TM} as a governance mechanism in two institutional fields. However, we observe considerable caution in drawing more definite conclusions as to whether EVA^{TM} has become more or less firmly institutionalised in one or the other field.

Although the notion of institutional work has started to influence emerging accounting research (Goretzki *et al.* 2013, Malsch and Gendron 2013), it has not been explicitly used to examine the institutionalisation of EVA^{TM}. Nevertheless, a brief review underlines its general relevance to this end. The emergence of EVA^{TM} and similar performance metrics as cornerstones of the shareholder value movement has been underpinned by a considerable amount of cultural work. This is notably manifest in the mobilisation of powerful rhetoric linking this movement to broader, neo-liberal concerns with deregulation and the diffusion of capitalist modes of production (Froud *et al.* 2000a, Ezzamel *et al.* 2008). The normative discourse surrounding EVA^{TM} emphasises *inter alia* the need to adjust accounting profits for costs of capital and a range of financial accounting conventions to improve the alignment of managerial and shareholder interests. The linking of managerial incentives to such adjusted accounting metrics has also been presented as a prerequisite for the entrenchment of EVA^{TM} as a single, integrated financial management system in lieu of a broader range of disparate performance measures and control practices (Stewart 1991, Stern *et al.* 1995, 2001). However, the extent to which such ideals are achieved has been found to vary in organisations adopting EVA^{TM} (Malmi and Ikäheimo 2003). Such variations can partly be traced to the political and technical work involved in the process of implementation. Several studies show how actors with vested interests that conflict with notions of shareholder value engage in political work to resist the implementation of EVA^{TM} and other value-based management techniques (Francis and Minchington 2002, Ezzamel and Burns 2005, Siti-Nabiha and Scapens 2005). Other researchers have questioned the use of EVA^{TM} as an independent financial management system by drawing attention to the considerable amount of technical work undertaken to integrate it with other management innovations and render it firmly embedded in organisational control practices (Gleadle and Cornelius 2008, Woods *et al.* 2012).

Whilst the majority of the research reviewed above is based on organisation-specific experiences of EVA^{TM}, it is relevant to extend it to the institutional field level. There is some empirical evidence of the broader shareholder value movement struggling to gain momentum in specific institutional fields (Jurgens *et al.* 2000, Morgan and Takahashi 2002, Fiss and Zajac 2004, Meyer and Höllerer 2010). Similar to the emerging literature on EVA^{TM} implementation, these studies draw attention to how institutional processes are affected by the prevalence of multiple actors with more or less conflicting interests. Following the theoretical framework outlined in this section, we examine how the initial structuration of such interests around EVA^{TM} conditioned the evolution and combination of political, technical and cultural work in the fields under examination. In doing so, we pay particular attention to how key actors mobilised various types of institutional work to uphold a degree of field cohesiveness and balance between competing interests in their efforts to entrench EVA^{TM} as a governance mechanism. We now turn to describe the research design devised to this end.

3. Research context and design

Following the issue-based definition of institutional fields outlined in the foregoing, we examine the interactions between different types of institutional work and the key interests clustered around EVA^{TM} as a governance mechanism for Chinese and Thai SOEs. Whilst both fields encompass a large number of SOEs operating across a broad range of industries the emphasis of our analysis is on field-level differences and commonalities rather than industry- or enterprise-specific challenges emerging in the process of institutionalisation. Some similarities and differences across the two fields of particular relevance for our comparative analysis should be noted. In both fields, the main actors in charge of the development of EVA^{TM} as a governance mechanism are two regulatory agencies established as an integral part of broader governance reforms unfolding since the mid-1990s; the Chinese State Assets Supervision and Administration Committee (SASAC) and the Thai State Enterprise Policy Office (SEPO). Appendix 1 provides an overview of some regulatory guidelines for key technical aspects of EVA^{TM} as a performance management system advanced by these agencies. The two agencies are held accountable to the Ministry of Finance in their respective countries and have an over-riding responsibility for the development, maintenance and operation of corporate performance monitoring and incentive systems for individual SOEs. However, the clustering of other interests around EVA^{TM} as a governance mechanism differs considerably across the two fields as a result of country-specific variations in political systems, the development of capital markets and the varying reliance on private sector consulting firms in the process of institutionalisation. In the PRC, governance reforms have been heavily influenced by the long-standing dominance of the Chinese Communist Party (CCP) whose interests largely overlap with those of central government. This has fostered a cautious approach to the privatisation of SOEs. Even though a number of large SOEs have been listed on Chinese and international stock markets the State retains a controlling stake and has been reluctant to relinquish political control of their operations. The extent of stock-market listings of Thai SOEs has been even more restricted as a result of a lack of stable governments and political majorities in favour of such reforms although EVA^{TM} originally emerged as part of a reform initiative aimed at large-scale privatisation. The institutionalisation of EVA^{TM} in the Thai field has also been much more reliant on independent consulting firms than what has been the case in the PRC. Of particular significance in this respect are the Thai branch of Stern Stewart – Stern Stewart Thailand (SST) – and domestic consulting firms such as Thai Rating and Information Services (TRIS) working in close collaboration with the SEPO. Finally, the institutionalisation of EVA^{TM} in the Thai field entailed more extensive involvement of early adopters of this innovation, such as PTT Public Company Ltd (PTT), as an active partner in the dissemination of knowledge about this innovation.

The data informing our analysis were collected as part of two larger research projects unfolding between 2009 and 2012. These projects entailed extensive data collection at the overall field level as well as case studies within individual SOEs in the two fields. For the purpose of this paper, we primarily rely on data collected through interviews and extended discussions with representatives of the key field-level actors identified in the foregoing (see Appendix 2). The majority of interviews were conducted within the SASAC and the SEPO as this is where the main responsibility for the development of EVA^{TM} as a governance mechanism has resided.

However, especially in the Thai field, it was also necessary to extend interviews to capture the experiences of a broader range of actors, such as independent consulting firms and PTT. Access was facilitated by having two members of the research team of Chinese and Thai origin conducting the interviews in their respective countries. This was especially important to create an open and trusting interview climate and also facilitated interpretation of tacit social cues. An atmosphere of openness was also furthered by letting the interviewees 'lead' the interviews as far as possible whilst using a loosely structured interview guide as an unobtrusive prompt to ensure that important themes were covered in sufficient detail. The interviews followed a semi-structured format and targeted such themes as the rationale and consequences of the use of EVA^{TM} as a governance mechanism, its origin and chronological evolution, specific actions aimed at establishing and developing it as well as its broader role in the governance reforms affecting the two fields. In the Thai field, the majority of the interviews were voice recorded and transcribed. However, in the Chinese field, we chose not to do so as we expected interviewees to be unaccustomed and possibly uncomfortable with such practices.[5] Instead, notes were taken during the interviews and transcribed into extensive summaries immediately afterwards. In both fields, key informants were interviewed on more than one occasion, which provided ample opportunities for asking follow-up questions and respondent validation. The interviews were complemented with an analysis of policy documents and working material describing the positions and actions of key, field-level actors with respect to the development of EVA^{TM} and related governance reforms.

The institutional processes underpinning the evolution of EVA^{TM} in the two fields were first analysed independently of each other following a relatively open-ended, inductive approach. This

Table 1.   Relationships between different types of institutional work and field cohesiveness.

Types of institutional work	Relationships to field cohesiveness	
	Chinese field	Thai field
Political work	Initially limited due to alignment of economic and political interests of the State and bureaucratic interests of the SASAC	Initially significant to align dispersed economic and political interests of multiple actors (e.g. the Shinawatra government, Thai business interests, Stern Stewart) into cohesive field
	Gradually increasing vis-a-vis individual SOEs to balance economic and social interests and maintain field cohesiveness	Gradually increasing vis-a-vis individual SOEs to balance economic and social interests and maintain field cohesiveness
Cultural work	Initially limited but gradually increasing to support technical work vis-a-vis individual SOEs and maintain field cohesiveness	Initially significant to support political work aimed at creating cohesive field. Less pronounced as a vehicle of maintaining field cohesiveness vis-a-vis individual SOEs
Technical work	Dominated by bureaucratic interests of the SASAC. Limited collaboration with other actors although technical work gradually extended to individual SOEs	Entailing extensive collaboration between multiple actors (e.g. the SEPO, SST and other consultants, individual SOEs) and critical to the maintenance of field cohesiveness
	Emphasis on collaborative, technical work vis-a-vis individual SOEs reduced by political work required to balance economic and social interests and maintain field cohesiveness	Collaborative technical work necessitating political work vis-a-vis individual SOEs to maintain field cohesiveness

resulted in two extensive and rich narratives describing how the development of EVA[TM] was implicated in unfolding governance reforms. We then contrasted these developments following a comparative case study logic (Eisenhardt 1989) that sought to refine and extend the theoretical
framework informing our analysis (Keating 1995, Lukka 2005). In doing so, we re-analysed the
data across the two fields by seeking for indicators of different types of institutional work exercised
by diverse actors and how they mapped on to each other across different time periods. By comparing
the patterns of such accumulation of institutional work over time, we arrived at an initial understanding of key field-level differences. We then deepened this analysis by relating different types of institutional work to notions of field cohesiveness by seeking for explanations of how they contributed to
create and maintain such cohesiveness. To this end, we found it helpful to distinguish between the
economic, political and bureaucratic interests associated with the institutionalisation of EVA[TM] and
examine the degree of overlap and conflict between such interests conditioning and resulting from
institutional work. A limitation of our analysis is that our data provide little direct information about
how such work influenced broader, social interests that are potentially disadvantaged by EVA[TM].
Although the relative neglect of disadvantaged interests is an increasingly voiced critique of institutional research (Lawrence and Suddaby 2006, Modell 2012b), we partly tried to compensate for
it by examining how such interests have shaped over-riding governance reforms and how regulatory
agencies mediate between them and the imperatives of EVA[TM]. Table 1 summarises our analysis of
the relationships between different types of institutional work and the creation and maintenance of
field cohesiveness across the two fields under examination.

4.   EVA[TM] in the field of Chinese SOEs

4.1   *Institutional reform context*

The emergence of EVA[TM] constitutes one of the most recent initiatives in a long sequence of
SOE reforms in the PRC that have, in turn, formed a cornerstone of the country's transition
towards a socialist market economy since 1978. This process started with the Contract Responsibility System (CRS) in the early 1980s and continued with the Modern Enterprise System
(MES) from the mid-1990s. The CRS reform aimed at transforming SOEs from integral
parts of the state bureaucracy into independent legal entities and entailed substantial delegation
of decision-making rights. However, it largely failed to clarify property rights and led to
massive inefficiencies and a general loss of competitiveness which gradually resulted in esca-
lating financial losses (Hussain and Jian 1999, Chen *et al.* 2006, Hassard *et al.* 2007). The MES
reform was intended to rectify this situation and was more explicitly inspired by policy advice
from the World Bank and Chinese economists trained in the West (Steinfeld 1998, Hassard *et al.*
2007). In order to consolidate SOEs into larger and internationally competitive industrial
groups, the MES reform entailed an initial phase of divesting smaller SOEs to private and institutional investors followed by a period of increasing stock-market listings and formation of
Sino-foreign joint ventures. Rather than aiming at large-scale privatisation, however, stock-
market listings have mainly been pursued to support the country's broader economic reform
programme and the State has retained a controlling ownership stake in listed SOEs. Stock
market listings have primarily been used as a vehicle of raising capital to finance the aggressive
growth strategies pursued by many SOEs (Szamosszegi and Kyle 2011, World Bank 2012).
Over the last decade, central SOEs[6] have increasingly been listed on foreign stock exchanges
whilst embarking on state-backed strategies of expansion through international mergers and
acquisitions. This has, in turn, formed an important part of the broader economic and geo-pol-
itical ambitions of the PRC to influence global markets for strategically important resources
(McGregor 2011).

The MES reform also entailed changes in governance ostensibly aimed at enhancing the autonomy of boards of directors and their accountability to shareholders, whilst reducing the lingering element of state intervention. Such priorities formed key elements of the policy advice initially offered by the World Bank (World Bank 1995, 1997). However, central government and the CCP continued to control the appointment of key personnel and a range of other strategic decisions in order to execute government policies and have proved reluctant to give full sway to capital markets. This has led to allegations that the State is unduly exploiting the interests of minority shareholders in listed SOEs and overlooking the development of efficient capital markets (see Clarke 2003). Notions of long-term shareholder value have become largely synonymous with the economic and political interests of the State in preserving and enhancing the value of SOEs, whilst Chinese stock markets have allegedly remained relatively under-developed and highly speculative (Steinfeld 1998, Szamosszegi and Kyle 2011, World Bank 2012).

A long-standing concern in the reform of Chinese SOEs has been the need to balance these emerging economic and political interests in developing them into commercially viable and internationally competitive entities with the extensive social welfare obligations vested in this societal sector. Historically, many SOEs have provided a broad range of social welfare services to cater for their work force and local communities 'from the cradle to the grave' and have allegedly been heavily over-staffed as a result of the Government's policy of using them as vehicles of furthering social and political stability (Steinfeld 1998, Hassard et al. 2007). The MES reform, in particular, has stepped up the pressures on SOEs to scale back such welfare commitments and lay off workers, which has increased the risks of social unrest (Hassard et al. 2008). The need to avoid social unrest is, in turn, intimately linked to the political interests of preserving the authority of central government and the hegemony of the CCP as a state-bearing party and has amplified the challenge of balancing between economic and broader, social interests.

The need to maintain such a balance is notably manifest in the systems of corporate oversight and performance monitoring established as part of the MES reform. In 2003, a number of previously dispersed governance functions were vested in the SASAC as a newly formed regulatory agency. Whilst the agency was given a clear mandate to further the economic performance of SOEs, it was also entrusted with the task of ensuring that vital social interests were not unduly jeopardised. A centralised system for performance monitoring was established to ensure that SOEs comply with politically charged performance aspects, such as safety and environmental standards, and control tendencies towards social unrest and instability whilst conforming to the economic reform agenda. Performance monitoring partly came to rely on league tables initially based on the ranking of central SOEs across such indicators as total profits, return on investment and a selection of operating-level measures capturing industry-specific characteristics. League table performance has an important impact on the promotion prospects of the 'responsible persons'[7] of individual SOEs and central resource allocation decisions. Highly ranked SOEs tend to receive preferential treatment from central government whilst chronic under-performers typically suffer a loss of reputation and may be subject to consolidation. However, league table performance is only part of a broader and highly complex governance system aimed at ensuring that social stability and political control are not being compromised. Individual SOEs face severe penalties if the pursuit of economic performance aspects is seen as leading to social unrest. To mitigate such tendencies, league tables are complemented with 'operational difficulty indexes' based on weighted performance scores for total and net assets, sales, total profits, total headcount and the proportion of retired staff to total headcount. Some SOEs are also given special 'policy allowances' for undertaking government-sanctioned tasks aimed at upholding social stability and executing specific policy initiatives. Moreover, performance evaluation entails a considerable element of subjectivity and enterprises of high political significance often receive favourable treatment in performance evaluation (Du et al. 2012). This enables the SASAC to exercise a considerable amount of discretion and moderate performance scores such that conflicts between economic and broader social interests can at least be partly accommodated. As explicated in our analysis of the institutionalisation of EVA^{TM}, however, it also opens up considerable opportunities for individual SOEs to engage in political work aimed at relaxing the regulatory framework underpinning performance evaluation.

The formation of the SASAC and the establishment of governance practices such as those described above may be seen as an attempt to create and maintain a degree of field cohesiveness in a socio-economic context historically characterised by strongly conflicting interests. Whilst the MES reform has not resolved the long-standing conflict between the economic and social interests served by SOEs, the role of the SASAC is to ensure that coordinated responses to such conflicts can be initiated such that more over-riding, political interests in preserving social stability are not being jeopardised. However, the strategy of consolidating central SOEs into larger and more autonomous entities has also enhanced their bargaining power in a manner that is not necessarily consistent with the bureaucratic interests of the SASAC in implementing specific governance mechanisms. As explicated in the following sections, this has created particular challenges of maintaining field cohesiveness with an important influence on the institutional work involved in establishing EVA^{TM} as a legitimate governance mechanism.

4.2 The emergence and early institutionalisation of EVA^{TM} (2003–2010)

The consecutive governance reforms in the PRC have fostered a climate where the ability to experiment successfully with various management innovations whilst complying with the broader, political interests in maintaining social stability has become a key career requirement for SOE managers at all levels. The typical career trajectory of SOE managers is to work their way up through the corporate hierarchy to then join the ranks of the state and party bureaucracy and, in many cases, reaching high-level political offices. Similar promotion principles apply to SASAC officials and have reinforced the incentives to comply with the modernising ethos of the MES reform and experiment with 'Western' management innovations. However, the adoption of such innovations has often followed a pattern of considerable adjustments, or what Mitter (2004) called 'China centrism', to fit the country's cultural and political circumstances. In particular, the Maoist legacy has made it pivotal for the experimenting with such innovations to be aligned with what is widely referred to as 'correct thinking' to signal their consistency with the broader belief and value systems underpinning the emerging, socialist market economy. This entails a pronounced propensity to frame allegedly 'capitalist' innovations as compatible with the collectivist ethos of Maoism. For instance, the very notion of privatisation was long a taboo subject and tended to be couched in the guise of 'corporatisation' and 'commercialisation'. The promotion system in place has also reinforced the bureaucratic interests of regulatory agencies such as the SASAC to adapt and contextualise foreign ideas to fit notions of 'correct thinking'. As a new government agency filling a highly public role, it has been especially important for it to demonstrate its capacity to oversee SOE reforms on an independent basis without relying too much on external advisors.

The emergence of EVA^{TM} as a governance mechanism for SOEs reflects this bureaucratic interest in being seen to innovate on an independent basis whilst drawing considerable inspiration from abroad. From its inception, the agency had a strong government mandate to develop novel means of enhancing the value of SOEs. This was notably epitomised by its mission to 'safeguard and increase the value of state assets' and can partly be understood against the backdrop of the growing concerns with the often low-yielding investment strategies pursued by many SOEs in the early phases of the MES reform. The reform initially created powerful incentives to pursue growth at any cost and often saw SOEs expanding into unrelated industries in ways that allegedly detracted from the creation of internationally competitive corporations. To reverse this develop-ment, the World Bank recommended the use of EVA^{TM} already in 2002 (World Bank 2002) and the first Secretary-General of the SASAC took a keen interest in developing it as a governance mechanism. More direct inspiration to this end was sought from the reputedly successful appli-cation of EVA^{TM} in Singaporean SOEs. After a visit to the SASAC's Singaporean counterpart Temasek in 2003, the Secretary-General officially proposed the use of EVA^{TM} and a board decision was subsequently made to adopt it as a key governance mechanism for central SOEs. The task of developing an EVA^{TM} system suitable to Chinese SOEs was initially assigned to one of the performance review divisions[8] within the SASAC. Over the following two years, this organisational unit undertook a considerable amount of technical work including the calcu-lation of EVA^{TM} metrics for individual SOEs and the development of handbooks and instruction manuals describing how to develop and implement the system. To support this technical work, the SASAC initially sought some assistance from Stern Stewart by organising overseas training activities and dispatching several executive teams to its New York headquarters and Singaporean branch to learn about EVA^{TM}.[9] Consistent with the bureaucratic interest in being seen to innovate on an independent basis, however, it soon distanced itself from any dependence on foreign con-sultants. Instead, the technical work largely progressed as an internal project within the SASAC and initially entailed little involvement of SOE managers.

One important reason for the limited involvement of SOE managers in the initial technical work on developing the EVA^{TM} system was the considerable scepticism harboured by many SOEs. Even though the decision by the SASAC to adopt EVA^{TM} signalled an intention to embed it in the regulatory framework guiding governance practices, the emphasis on enhanced financial returns underpinning the initiative was often in direct conflict with the far-reaching social welfare obligations burdening many SOEs. For instance, the initial calculations of EVA^{TM} tended to show negative results partly due to the costs of providing social welfare services and maintaining staff levels. This prompted the SASAC to refrain from officially reporting EVA^{TM} data for individual SOEs and delay its implementation as a governance mechanism. One of our interviewees recalled:

> The total EVA was a huge negative figure [in 2003]. It was simply out of the question to roll it out. To begin with, the responsible persons would not have it. Besides, back then we had more pressing matters at hand: we had yet to create a regulatory framework from scratch to establish the SASAC as the acting shareholder evaluating the performance of central SOE responsible persons. Since the infrastructure was not there, EVA remained an unofficial experiment. (Interview, Deputy Head of Per-formance Review Division 2, SASAC, 5-6/11/12)

Moreover, several SOEs arguably saw the creation of a new regulatory framework around EVA^{TM} as a potential intrusion into their new-found autonomy. This compelled the SASAC to engage in a considerable amount of political work as a complement to its ongoing technical work. An impor-tant part of this political work was the establishment of clearer division of responsibilities and role expectations to crystallise the enhanced emphasis on the State as a shareholder, or as one of our interviewees explained:

> The reform up until 2007 was a matter of establishing necessary rules [for EVA to come to the fore]. Previously there were no norms and the parties involved in SOE administration all had some sort of identity crisis [due to unclear property rights]. The methods were old, bureaucratic, volume-driven and they did not suit a market economy due to the lacking notion of the State as a shareholder . . . . It was not until the formation of the SASAC in 2003 that we began to have performance management in a real sense by considering indicators that the shareholders care about the most, such as profit, return on investment and began to link compensation to performance. (Interview, Deputy Head of Per-formance Review Division 2, SASAC, 5–6/11/12)

On the one hand, the introduction of EVA^{TM} may thus be seen as an important step in the political work aimed at strengthening the regulatory framework underpinning the governance of SOEs. On the other, this necessitated extensive concessions on the part of the SASAC to reassure SOEs that the reform did not infringe on their autonomy. This led to protracted negotiations aimed at establishing some acceptable balance between the interests of the SASAC and individual SOEs. Informal negotiations were first initiated with the 'responsible persons' of individual SOEs to prepare them for the introduction of EVA^{TM} and were gradually extended to broader categories of accounting staff. The Head of the Performance Review Division in charge of the initial development of EVA^{TM} described why such negotiations were an indispensable part of the political work associated with the introduction of EVA^{TM}:

> Central SOEs are a very unique context where, for EVA or any reform to take root, you need the support of the vast majority [of central SOE responsible persons]. By vast majority I do not mean 80% of the population. I am talking about 95% and higher. These companies are so powerful that even the small minority can be strong enough to topple the reform. That is why we undertook careful and patient preparations. (Interview, Head of Performance Review Division 2, SASAC, 5–6/11/12)

In other words, any attempt to introduce EVA^{TM} without a considerable element of political work might have threatened the interests of individual SOEs and reduced field cohesiveness. This prompted the SASAC to adopt a cautious approach to its implementation. Between 2003 and the official implementation of EVA^{TM} as a governance mechanism in 2007, the technical work on developing the system continued on an 'unofficial' basis alongside continued political negotiations and was gradually expanded to include accounting executives from individual SOEs in the drafting of instruction manuals. One SASAC official elaborated on how this combination of political and increasingly collaborative, technical work gradually enhanced the acceptability of EVA^{TM} and facilitated the process of contextualising it to fit Chinese SOEs:

> Our 'tactics' were to consult, consult again and consult more. By involving SOEs in the process, responsible persons came to endorse EVA at the conceptual level. Eventually they became our partners in the design of the EVA reform. Although we initiated a lot of overseas training, our work is firmly grounded in the Chinese context. The senior SOE accounting executives contributed a lot more to the reform than Stern Stewart. In the future we will continue to count on them to sort out remaining implementation issues. (Interview, Head of Performance Review Division 2, SASAC, 5–6 November 2012)

By the time EVA^{TM} was officially launched as a governance mechanism in 2007, the SASAC had built up considerable technical expertise in applying the system. This enhanced its confidence in using it as a governance mechanism and further reduced its dependence on external advisors. Even though Stern Stewart re-opened its Chinese branch around the same time, its influence on the continued evolution of EVA^{TM} in central SOEs has been limited. Our interviewees attributed this to the technical expertise already available within the SASAC but also to the considerable costs of relying on renowned Western consultants to carry out large-scale change projects. Nevertheless, the agency increasingly mobilised elements of the traditional, shareholder value-focused rhetoric espoused by Stern Stewart as a basis for the cultural work involved in persuading SOEs of the merits of EVA^{TM}. The introduction of EVA^{TM} was intimately linked to the government-backed strategy of stimulating so-called 'high-quality' (i.e. high return as opposed to merely profitable) growth for the benefit of shareholders and overcome the tendencies of SOEs to 'over-invest' in low-yielding projects. For instance, the agency's official motivation for the introduction of EVA^{TM} suggested that:

Recently, many central SOEs have invested in speculative financial products and real estate markets, rather than focusing on their core competence. This is an important background to the EVA^{TM} reform. The mission is to reinforce value creation, force managers to think on behalf of the shareholders, focusing on the main activities, avoiding the tendency to go for size, etc. (SASAC, Annual Review of Central SOE Performance, 2006)

To compel SOEs to change their investment strategies and reinforce managerial incentives to take EVA^{TM} to heart, the SASAC also made extensive appeals to its symbolic significance as an innovation adopted by many leading Western companies and emphasised the need to adopt the same 'language' as such companies. Repeated references were made to the use of EVA^{TM} as a key mechanism for enhancing shareholder value in many Fortune 500 companies and around the time of its official launch the Deputy General-Secretary of the SASAC proclaimed:

Our global strategy requires SOEs to compare with the West, with multinationals rather than compare with the domestic ... Comparing central SOEs with local companies in terms of market share, sales, or profitability is like comparing an adult with an infant for height, body weight and strength. The comparison is not meaningful. A meaningful comparison is against the World's best in terms of key financial indicators adopted by them. Central SOEs need to deepen the reform, create a reasonable value chain, avoid low level repetition and competition, enhance the notion of return on investment, improve the quality of merger and acquisitions, refrain from blind expansion and avoid loss-making image projects. (Official statement, Deputy Secretary-General of the SASAC, 2007)

However, the SASAC was also at pains to adjust its cultural work of associating EVA^{TM} with notions of shareholder value and international competitiveness to fit the idea of 'correct thinking'. Whilst emphasising the primacy of enhancing shareholder value, the rhetoric mobilised to this end entailed warnings against going down this path at the expense of traditional notions of political and social stability. For instance, the Deputy General-Secretary of the SASAC cautioned:

The Scientific Approach of Development requires central SOEs to establish correct thinking about performance, pay attention to the issues and contradictions arising from the reform ... issues such as innovation, safety, quality of growth and the balance between reform, change and stability .... But at present, there are still some practices that are incompatible with the Scientific Approach of Development, such as lack of innovation and sensitivity to the market, volatile performance results, heavy loss in a small number of SOEs, irrational decision-making, high D/A rate, etc. (Official statement, Deputy Secretary-General of SASAC 2006)

Such efforts to imbue the introduction of EVA^{TM} with notions of 'correct thinking' were reinforced by the mobilisation of traditional Maoist methods, such as the organisation of periodic 'political learning seminars' targeting the 'responsible persons' of individual SOEs. These seminars aimed at fostering some consistency in interpretations of EVA^{TM} as a mechanism supporting the development of the socialist market economy whilst encouraging SOE managers to adapt it to their unique circumstances. The SASAC saw such seminars as an important vehicle of 'uniting managers' thinking'[10] around its reform agenda and reinforcing the efforts of 'responsible persons' to disseminate knowledge about EVA^{TM} and extend training programmes to broader managerial cadres. The cultural work pivoting on efforts to foster 'correct thinking' was thus envisaged to support the technical work initiated by the SASAC and nurture field cohesiveness by aligning managerial interests with the emerging reform agenda.

To further such alignment and avoid jeopardising field cohesiveness, the SASAC initially encouraged SOEs to adopt EVA^{TM} on a voluntary basis and relied extensively on 'positive feedback' to enterprises with high EVA^{TM} results whilst refraining from exposing and punishing underperformers. Adopting SOEs were encouraged to link EVA^{TM} to internal management processes such as strategy formulation, budgeting, performance management, business process improvement and personnel management. The SASAC also continued to involve SOE staff in collaborative, technical work to refine EVA^{TM} instruction manuals. However, this work seemed to be insufficient to overcome some pertinent obstacles to implementation. Even though the proportion of SOEs adopting EVA^{TM} between 2007 and 2009 increased from about 50% to two thirds, its initial use was fraught with technical difficulties related to the translation of notions of cost of capital, insufficient staff training and problems of integrating EVA^{TM} with internal business processes. In 2009, the SASAC officially recognised that:

> Most SOE accounting staff felt that EVA was just another performance measure and failed to see its fundamental significance ... in many companies that have joined the experiment, EVA was an isolated process detached from incentives and the business process. (SASAC, Annual Review of Central SOE Performance, 2009)

As explicated below, these difficulties in rendering EVA^{TM} more firmly embedded persisted throughout the following years despite mounting efforts to make it an integral part of the performance management practices of SOEs.

4.3 Continued development and institutionalisation of EVA^{TM} (2010 onwards)

Having secured some initial acceptance of EVA^{TM} among SOEs, the SASAC stepped up its efforts to turn it into a more dominant governance mechanism from 2010 onwards. The five-year plan for SOEs covering the period 2010–15 signalled the start of the so-called 'EVA era' and turned the use of EVA^{TM} into a compulsory requirement for all central SOEs. EVA^{TM} replaced return on investment as a key financial performance indicator in the league tables drawn up by the SASAC. The weight attached to EVA^{TM} in the league tables has been about 40% and SOE managers have been urged to step up their technical work to turn it into an integral part of performance management practices. Between 2010 and 2012, SOEs have been required to not only report EVA^{TM} at the corporate level but also to increase the weight attached to it in internal league tables from five to 30%. Even though the SASAC has the power to make such practices mandatory, this was combined with continued political work pivoting on informal negotiations with the 'responsible persons' to enhance their commitment to EVA^{TM}. Such political work was supported by continued cultural work relying on high-powered rhetoric hailing EVA^{TM} as the epitome of improved performance management. For instance, in an official statement the new Secretary-General of the SASAC proclaimed:

> EVA is of signal importance in our [five-year] plan. We expect nothing short of the highest level of political commitment. Taking over from the previous Secretary-General, I feel tremendous personal responsibility .... The key to our success is that leaders of central SOEs unite in their thinking around the SASAC. Internal training must cover three levels down the managerial ranks. All central SOEs must incorporate EVA for internal performance management in a manner that suggests an appropriate understanding of the spirit of EVA, rather than simply copy-pasting the SASAC instruction. We encourage creative and context-specific solutions to implementation problems. For example, individual SOEs could establish more specific and more challenging cost of capital for internal performance management and link rewards/sanctions to EVA performance. (Secretary-General of the SASAC, speech at Annual Performance Conference, 2011)

The SASAC thus set a relatively ambitious official agenda for the further development of EVA^{TM} as a governance mechanism. Yet our interviews with SASAC staff and other actors with a stake in the reform suggested that a considerable amount of technical work remained to be done to render EVA^{TM} more firmly embedded as a governance mechanism. The manuals devised by the SASAC instructed individual SOEs to calculate risk-adjusted, weighted average cost of capital (WACC) and undertake some financial accounting adjustments to derive simplified versions of EVA™ (see Appendix 1). However, our interviews with SASAC officials directly involved in the technical work of assisting SOEs to this end revealed how the agency continued to struggle to render such key aspects of EVA™ meaningful. A junior member of staff with extensive experience in dealing with such problems explained:

> Then there is the issue of the cost of capital. In theory, it is WACC. The debt capital was determined by the company's situation, equity cost needs to reflect the risk factors of the industry, using CAPM. But CAPM involves Beta, which can only be used in listed companies. And our stock market is far from mature, the pricing mechanism does not reflect the company's risk and value. (Interview, Officer, Performance Review Division 1, SASAC, 24 September 2011)

In the face of such technical problems, the SASAC specified a uniform but relatively arbitrary WACC rate for the majority of SOEs. Contrary to the ambition to use of EVA™ to stimulate 'high quality' growth, this uniform rate was also kept considerably lower (at 5.5%) than the rate of return required for listed, private sector companies in China (see Stern 2011). Even though the SASAC recognised that this reduced the pressures on SOEs to enhance shareholder value, our interviewees indicated that this was necessary to avoid resistance and keep up the momentum behind the reform. The Head of the Performance Review Division initially developing the EVA™ system argued that this cautious approach had been rather successful in changing managerial mindsets in favour of notions consistent with the idea of 'high quality' growth:

> EVA brought Chinese central SOEs to the world stage. It is reassuring for the international stakeholders that we are using the World's best system to capture SOE performance. It is an important achievement that we are now adopting the same sort of language [as Western multinationals] to describe SOE performance. Internally, the EVA reform re-shaped SOE investment decisions by changing the mindset of the responsible persons from the deep-seated 'let us do it' mentality to one that is more cost conscious. The core of the EVA reform is precisely to imbue these people with an understanding of the notion of cost of capital. We can safely say that this aim has been achieved and managerial behaviour has indeed been improved. (Interview, Head of Performance Review Division 2, SASAC, 5–6 November 2012)

However, this view was contradicted by other interviewees within and outside the SASAC who suggested that more far-reaching changes would be necessary to alter managerial mindsets to focus on EVA™ rather than accounting profits. One member of SASAC staff explained:

> EVA poses a significant challenge to existing senior managers. They not only need to accept the importance of EVA, but also need to understand the meaning of it .... Responsible persons need to switch from profit orientation to value orientation. You may think it is easy, some people think it is a matter of SOEs responsible persons talking about EVA day in day out. But I am not very optimistic because profitability has become the mentality, and most responsible persons associate economic performance with profit, so change is not just matter of rhetoric, but involves all-out changes in decision making rules, managerial methods and incentives. EVA needs to be infused in the process of budgeting, routine management, investment approval, etc. – that is what I call real EVA. (Interview, Deputy Head, Performance Review Division 1, SASAC, 5 September 2011)

Similarly, an observer within the Ministry of Finance explained how the embedded, profit-orientated mindset detracted from the ambition to turn EVA™ into an effective tool for internal performance management:

> The SASAC emphasised EVA as a value-based management system, the idea is good, but the SASAC's idea contrasts with the prevailing view among many SOEs that EVA is just a measurement tool. In practice, these SOEs carried on with the old, profit-orientated thinking and action. There has been no change in the managerial behaviour or leadership style. There simply is no space for the notion of value based management to be infused. If the responsible person does not change their understanding, how can you expect the functional department managers to change? The prevailing understanding is very simplistic – EVA is all about financial departments adjusting reports and come up with a new number. That is why I say despite of the [SASAC's] heavy advertising campaign, EVA works at the margins rather than the core of the SASAC's performance management system. (Interview, Senior Fellow of Research Centre, Ministry of Finance, 30 July 2012)

With the exception of key champions of EVA^{TM}, such as the Head of the Performance Review Division primarily in charge of its development, there was a widespread view that most SOEs continued to approach it as little more than a new performance metric evolving in isolation from other management practices. This contrasts sharply with the official SASAC rhetoric hailing it as the backbone of reformed performance management practices.

Our findings thus provide a contradictory picture regarding the achievements of EVA^{TM}. Although the SASAC officially projected a trajectory whereby EVA^{TM} would gradually be refined and turned into a firmly embedded management system as part of the five-year plan for 2010–2015, there were signs of insufficient technical work being expended to this end. In particular, there were widespread concerns among our interviewees that accounting staff within individual SOEs had not received adequate training and found the calculations required to derive EVA^{TM} overly complex. Interestingly, however, there are also restrictions to how far SASAC staff can go to assist individual SOEs in resolving such problems without disrupting the configurations of interests and field cohesiveness emanating from the earlier institutional work associated with EVA^{TM}. On the one hand, the SASAC has been careful to uphold its more clear-cut role as a shareholder in its dealings with SOEs. On the other, this posture has led it to refrain from taking an overly forceful approach to extending the collaborative, technical work within individual SOEs. One of our interviewees explained:

> The SASAC does not directly control the business operations and it only understands the business to a limited degree . . . . In addition, it does not want to be too intervening and wants to keep a certain distance and sense of authority. Thus, it is the central SOEs' responsibility to customise EVA and tailor it to the needs of each enterprise. The unspoken rule of the reform is to draw on the diverse experiences and experiments of each central SOE, then generalise and conclude . . . . Some SOEs were unhappy with the SASAC, arguing that [this approach] is no good. This is unfair – the responsibility is not that of the SASAC . . . . The SASAC could try to tailor the EVA method, but there is a limit to it, it is not possible to give individualised plans to over 100 central SOEs. (Interview, Deputy Director, Internal Performance Bureau, SASAC, 6 August 2010)

The efforts of the SASAC to strengthen the incentives of managers to undertake technical work aimed at refining and implementing EVA^{TM} systems have also been limited by the continuous need to maintain some balance between the economic and social interests served by SOEs. Several of our interviewees drew attention to how this continues to prompt a considerable amount of political work that effectively relaxes the monitoring of SOEs' ability to meet EVA^{TM} targets and reduces the pressures on managers to take the reform to heart. Most importantly, the introduction of EVA^{TM} has not changed the highly subjective performance evaluation practices employed by the SASAC and the concomitant practice of individual SOEs to negotiate for adjustments of performance scores before league table results are published. Many SOEs routinely advance requests for adjustments of performance scores for context-specific circumstances whilst the SASAC is keen on ensuring that wider, political objectives such as the need to prevent social unrest are not jeopardised. One SASAC official described how such political work formed a prerequisite for resolving potential conflicts and maintain a degree of field cohesiveness:

> We have a number of central SOEs specializing in projects concerning national security, we have a number of central SOEs carrying out national strategic agendas, we also have a number of central SOEs struggling with tremendous social and historical burdens. In addition, changes in central policy, the macro-economic environment and even unexpected natural disasters during the evaluation period all call for some sort of re-evaluation of the performance. Before publishing the results we consider all these factors and make standard adjustments for comparable companies. The key is to pre-empt causes of complaints and controversy to our best ability beforehand, as we need to ensure the fairness for all appraisees while maintaining the authority of the SASAC. (Interview, Deputy Head of Performance Review Division 2, SASAC, 5–6 November 2012)

The same interviewee also described how the continued reliance on subjective adjustments has weakened the efficacy of EVA^{TM} as a governance mechanism by rhetorically asking:

> How often do you see SOE responsible persons being fired for missing financial targets? The emphasis on financial performance is yet to create 'real' effects on the benefits of managers. (Interview, Deputy Head of Performance Review Division 2, SASAC, 5–6 November 2012)

Despite insisting on increasing the weight attached to EVA^{TM} in internal league tables, the SASAC has also been careful in encouraging SOEs to tie it to incentive plans at lower managerial levels for fear of disrupting the balance between economic and social interests. One of our interviewees explained how such deviations from key prescriptions typically offered by EVA^{TM} advocates such as Stern Stewart were related to political obstacles:

> From the experience abroad it is important to have a reward system in place and link it to EVA performance so that managers are treated as if they were owners of the business. There should be no upper limit of the financial reward, or there will be agency problems. At present, these types of incentives are impossible in central SOEs, as they need to consider issues such as equality and balance between different interest groups. (Interview, Policy Advisor, University of BeiJing, 26 September 2011)

The discussion above suggests that the ongoing political work aimed at balancing between competing interests and thus maintain a degree of field cohesiveness has so far over-shadowed the efforts to deepen the collaborative, technical work initiated by the SASAC and individual SOEs to render EVA^{TM} more firmly embedded in their performance management practices. This is indicative of how a lack of mutually supportive types of institutional work may hamper institutionalisation (cf. Perkmann and Spicer 2008). The relaxing of the regulatory framework established to monitor SOEs' compliance with the reform presents an instance of political work that has prevented EVA^{TM} from becoming overly dominant as a performance indicator. Two years into the 'EVA era', the SASAC officially acknowledged the lingering problems of rendering the reform more deeply embedded:

> Value based management is not well understood and poorly applied in practice. Value creation ability remains weak and return on investment remains low. Total performance management remains largely rhetorical. Deputies' evaluation in particular lacks depth and quantification. Boards of directors' experiments are rather uneven and there is a misalignment between the performance management organised by boards of directors and the performance management of the SASAC. (SASAC, Annual Review of Central SOE Performance, 2011)

Despite the compulsory use of EVA^{TM} as a performance metric and the increasing weight attached to it in league tables, it would thus be erroneous to conclude that it has yet become widely and firmly embedded within individual SOEs. This observation is largely confirmed by a recent, comparative field study of the use of EVA^{TM} in four SOEs (Bhimani *et al.* 2013). However, EVA^{TM} continues to epitomise the modernising ethos of ongoing governance reforms and is thus of significant relevance to other actors, such as the SASAC, with vested interests in pursuing such reforms. It would thus be premature to draw more definite conclusions regarding its fate in Chinese SOEs.

5. EVA^{TM} in the field of Thai SOEs

5.1 *Institutional reform context*

In comparison with the PRC, the introduction of EVA^{TM} in Thai SOEs was more intimately linked to privatisation efforts and stock-market listings although it was preceded by a relatively long period of unsuccessful advances to this end. Attempts to privatise SOEs first emerged in 1983 in response to requirements laid down in structural adjustment loans provided by the World Bank but had limited impact (Dempsey 2000). Between 1983 and 1996, only a few, insignificant SOEs were sold to private investors or part-privatised whilst more far-reaching privatisation plans met with considerable resistance from workers and trade unions due to fear of job losses. The momentum behind privatisation was also reduced by the country's steady economic growth throughout this time period (Dempsey 2000). Renewed pressures for privatisation arose in the wake of the East-Asian financial crisis in 1997 as the World Bank and the International Monetary Fund tied their provision of financial aid packages to pledges of industrial restructuring (Yindeepit 2010). However, these pressures were also warded off relatively quickly as a result of the country's rapid recovery and repayment of international loans. The vast majority of SOEs thus remained under complete state control whilst only a handful developed ownership structures entailing minority shareholders.

Notwithstanding this inertia, the World Bank had a notable impact on the reform of governance structures for Thai SOEs from the mid-1990s. Following its recommendations (see World Bank 1994), the Ministry of Finance devised the State Enterprise Performance Evaluation System (SEPES) which included a range of financial and non-financial indicators and replaced a more rudimentary system of performance monitoring mainly based on existing accounting data. The system entailed performance agreements and bonus programmes for each individual SOE and was designed to capture firm-specific performance characteristics. The tasks of monitoring SOE performance and developing systems to this end were vested in the SEPO. In contrast to the approach adopted by the SASAC in the PRC, however, much of the technical work associated with developing and maintaining performance monitoring systems has tended to be delegated to domestic consulting firms such as TRIS. This firm assists the SEPO in drafting performance agreements, defining performance indicators and determining targets and weights attached to individual indicators. Working alongside other consulting companies, such as Stern Stewart, it also came to play an active role in developing EVA^{TM} as an integral part of the extant performance management framework.

The development of performance management in the 1990s was complemented with other governance reforms aimed at enhancing the decision-making discretion and accountability of boards of directors and SOE management. However, it was only after the election of Dr Thaksin Shinawatra as Prime Minister in 2001 that more forceful efforts to privatise Thai SOEs emerged. The Shinawatra government came to power based on an ambitious programme of public sector reform and liberalisation that was partly inspired by the Prime Minister's experience as the head and majority shareholder of a large business group. Several influential cabinet members shared this experience and had long-standing social ties and business interests in common with the Shinawatra family. They allegedly also had strongly vested, economic interests in pursuing privatisation of SOEs and benefited from initial public offerings. This was notably manifest in the first major privatisation attempt of PTT Public Company Ltd in 2001, where four out of six major shareholders were business interests closely associated with Dr Shinawatra's political party. This was followed by a number of highly publicised attempts to float other SOEs on the Thai stock exchange over the following years and economic policy decisions with a favourable impact on share prices. Between 2002 and 2006, the Thai stock market index rose by 161% and Dr Shinawatra's main holding company experienced a surge in shareholder value before it was sold to foreign investors in 2006.

The discussion above is indicative of how specific economic interests gradually became conflated with political interests in privatising SOEs. The privatisation programme was also consistent with the recommendations of the World Bank and the International Monetary Fund and was accompanied by accelerated repayment of loans provided by the latter organisation which further inspired investor confidence. A relatively cohesive field was thus established around the idea of privatisation. As explicated in the following section, this field was further expanded through the institutional work associated with the introduction of EVA^{TM} as a governance mechanism for Thai SOEs.

5.2   *The emergence and early institutionalisation of EVA^{TM} (2001–2006)*

The emergence and early institutionalisation of EVA^{TM} as a governance mechanism entailed an initial period of mainly political and cultural work before the technical work required to develop it as a performance management system could be initiated. The idea of using EVA^{TM} as a governance mechanism reportedly originated from a business man affiliated with the Prime Minister Dr Shinawatra who eventually became the Chairman of the Thai branch of Stern Stewart (SST). Having familiarised himself with the concept as a consultant in the USA he approached the Government with a proposal to adopt it to support the process of privatisation and make SOEs more shareholder-focused. This led to some negotiations aimed at making EVA^{TM} a key part of continued governance reforms. To convince the Government of the merits of EVA^{TM}, particular emphasis was placed on how it might resolve long-standing efficiency problems in SOEs and further the privatisation programme by signalling a commitment to enhancing shareholder value. The average rate of return on assets among Thai SOEs at the time was around 4% and was singled out as a key area for improvement to facilitate stock market listings. However, the amount of political work required to convince the Government of mobilising EVA^{TM} to this end was reduced by the Prime Minister's readiness to accept the idea and experience of using it in one of his own companies or as the Chairman of SST explained:

> Thaksin told me that he could leave his company to become a politician without worrying, because the EVA system had made [one of his companies'] staff work effectively on behalf of him and [the Singaporean holding company] Temasek effectively used EVA to monitor Singaporean SOEs. Thus, he strongly supported our EVA project. He talked about EVA many times in cabinet meetings and he also taught the Council of Ministers the fundamentals of EVA. The EVA Challenge book was also included in his list of the books that Thai people should read. (Interview, Chairman of SST, 7 October 2010).

The Chairman of SST also described how the political work of building commitment to EVA^{TM} was supported by an element of cultural work. The Prime Minister explicitly mobilised the normative shareholder value discourse to convince cabinet members and SOEs of the usefulness of EVA^{TM}. On the Prime Minister's initiative, 60 copies of the book 'The EVA Challenge' (Stern *et al.* 2001) were distributed to senior SOE managers and other relevant authorities. In an official statement around the same time he also proclaimed:

> The CFO must truly understand the numbers and be a 'co-thinker' with the President. Otherwise, the President will be blind and have a misperception of the organisation. .... The CFO must be able to read financial statements and analyse what the Economic Value of the organisation is. If the Economic Value is negative, the organisation will not survive. (Official statement by Thaksin Shinawatra, 21 October 2002, SEPO Office)

This initial political and cultural work led to further expansion of the field created around EVA^{TM} through the invitation of Stern Stewart to Thailand. Its Thai branch – SST – was founded in 2002 with the Chairman owning 51% of the shares and Stern Stewart holding the minority stake. Around the same time, however, some SOEs had begun to experiment with the Balanced Scorecard which fostered some initial competition with EVA^{TM} and made some additional political work necessary. The Finance Minister, in particular, was initially lukewarm to the notion of EVA^{TM} as he had recently started to persuade SOEs to adopt the Balanced Scorecard as an alternative governance mechanism. However, his endorsement of the Balanced Scorecard as a superior performance management system was partly undermined by the emergence of serious liquidity problems in a major SOE adopting the system at an early stage. As a close personal affiliate of Dr Shinawatra,[11] the Finance Minister also found it difficult to resist the political pressures to accept the emerging reform agenda and was eventually won over to the idea that EVA^{TM} provided a superior means of aligning the interests of shareholders and managers. Some of our interviewees described how the political work underpinning this conversion was supported by an element of cultural work pivoting on the shareholder value discourse associated with EVA^{TM}. In particular, SST staff went to considerable length demonstrating how the Ministry of Finance would gain as a major shareholder from the alignment of managerial interests with those of owners. To overcome resistance, SST staff also engaged in cultural work aimed at negating the proposition that EVA^{TM} was incompatible with the Balanced Scorecard as a performance management technique. Citing key Balanced Scorecard advocates, such as Robert S. Kaplan, they repeatedly sought to demonstrate how he effectively endorsed EVA^{TM}:

> We start with the destination. What are we trying to achieve? We feel that what for-profit companies should be delivering is great financial performance .... We're certainly very comfortable with the newer financial metrics like EVA and other shareholder value-based metrics as the overarching objective. If you were just using earnings per share or net income, you'd run into problems of over investment-investing too much in capital to generate earnings or net income. (Extract from SST presentation material; Robert S. Kaplan, quoted in CFO Magazine, February 2001).

The combination of political and cultural work to win over the Finance Minister to the use of EVA^{TM} was also supported by a visit to Thailand by one of the co-founders of Stern Stewart, Joel M. Stern, who engaged in further, direct negotiations with him. These efforts finally bore fruit in 2003, when the Ministry of Finance officially agreed to use EVA^{TM} as a key financial performance metric for SOEs and instructed the SEPO to further develop it as an integral part of the extant governance system. The Ministry of Finance and senior SEPO official also started to reproduce much of the cultural work associated with the use of EVA^{TM} as a vehicle of enhanced shareholder value. For instance, the Director of the SEPO officially lauded it as a vehicle of enhancing the efficiency of SOEs by mobilising rhetoric echoing the Government's official, shareholder-focused discourse:

> The Thai Government has foreseen that increased efficiency in SOEs is of vital importance because SOEs is a powerful tool for developing the country's economic system. The current government policy specified that SOEs need to urgently enhance quality of service in response to customers' demand, and increase competitive capability. Importantly, SOEs must create increased economic value for the country's assets. In response to the government policy, SEPO is introducing EVA

concepts to SOEs. EVA is a popular management system that has been adopted and successfully used by the business sector as well as the state enterprise sector in several countries such as Singapore. (Official statement by the Director of SEPO, *Positioning Magazine*, 8 December 2005)

In comparison with the PRC, however, we observed much less cultural work aimed at adapting the shareholder-focused discourse to the specific social context of Thai SOEs. The introduction of EVA^{TM} was consistently underpinned by a rather uncritical endorsement of the conventional shareholder value rhetoric by the actors propagating its use by SOEs whilst few attempts were initially made to contextualise it.

In contrast to the PRC, the ensuing technical work aimed at developing EVA^{TM} as a governance mechanism also relied more heavily on close collaboration between the SEPO and independent consultants. The SEPO commissioned SST to conduct a feasibility study which entailed calculation of EVA^{TM} metrics for about two thirds of all SOEs and which was followed by the initiation of pilot projects in four of them. Study trips to Singapore were also organised to learn about the use of EVA^{TM} by Temasek and individual SOEs before EVA^{TM} adoption and reporting were made compulsory requirements for most SOEs participating in the feasibility study in 2006. Following the standard approach to EVA^{TM} implementation recommended by Stern Stewart, the SEPO drew up relatively ambitious plans for how individual SOEs should develop the system. This included a first phase of making the system operational and was to be followed by more concerted efforts to disaggregate and cascade corporate-level EVA^{TM} metrics to individual business units and, ultimately, making them an integral part of corporate decision-making and incentive plans. Nevertheless, the SEPO deviated from the prescription to use EVA^{TM} as a single, financial management system in lieu of a broader range of financial and non-financial performance indicators by concomitantly making the Balanced Scorecard a compulsory requirement for SOEs. According to the performance agreements drawn up for individual SOEs, the weight attached to EVA^{TM} was 15% of total performance scores. However, at the time, the SEPO affirmed its commitment to EVA^{TM} implementation by stating that this weight would increase over the coming years.

Consistent with Perkmann and Spicer (2008), the above analysis shows how the initial institutionalisation of EVA^{TM} as a governance mechanism hinged on the gradual accumulation of different types of institutional work mobilised by diverse actors. Through the accumulation of political and cultural work a relatively cohesive field was first created out of a set of dispersed economic and political interests represented by the Shinawatra government, members of the Thai business community and Stern Stewart. This field was subsequently expanded to include bureaucratic interests vested in the executive realm of government (through the SEPO) to add momentum to the technical work required to make EVA^{TM} operational. Taken together, this accumulation of institutional work initially resulted in relatively forced implementation of EVA^{TM} to spearhead the Government's privatisation programme, or as an ex-country manager of SST recalled:

I personally did not think that it was a good idea to implement EVA in all SOEs at the same time because I believed that it was easier and more convincing for most SOEs to implement EVA if they have successful examples to learn from. That approach was adopted by Temasek when they introduced EVA to Singaporean SOEs. However, the Finance Minister saw it as more beneficial if all SOEs started to understand their economic values and how to improve them as soon as possible. (Interview, Ex-Country Manager of SST, 29 December 2010).

However, the cohesiveness of the field created around EVA^{TM} and the plans to privatise SOEs was soon threatened by political work in the form of popular protests supported by trade unions and various non-governmental organisations representing broader social interests such as employment levels and affordable provision of public goods and services. The protests against the Government's privatisation plans were an integral part of the broader popular discontent fuelled by the mounting corruption charges levied at Dr Shinawatra and his associates. Over time, allegations grew that key members of Dr Shinawatra's political party had benefited substantially from privatisations as a result of securing preferential terms in conjunction with initial public offerings and through other business contacts with individual SOEs. These allegations dated back to the floating of PTT in 2001 and fuelled the development leading up to the 'bloodless coup' that ousted the Shinawatra government in 2006 and forced the Prime Minister into exile. Around the same time, a key episode effectively putting a halt to further privatisations occurred as a result of the Government's repeated attempts to float one of the largest public utility companies in the country. This led to massive popular protests culminating in a petition to the Supreme Administrative Court. The Court's subsequent ruling in favour of the petition established a powerful precedent and rendered it difficult for future governments to pursue privatisations of SOEs. Hence at the time of our study, only six out of 58 SOEs were part-privatised and listed on the Thai stock exchange. As explicated below, however, this successful mobilisation of political work to resist privatisation did not mean that the institutional work aimed at maintaining and developing EVA^{TM} as a governance mechanism dissipated.

5.3 *Continued development and institutionalisation of EVA^{TM} (2006 onwards)*

The demise of the Shinawatra government was followed by a period of political instability that reduced the pressures for further governance reforms. Instead, it was largely left to the SEPO to continue developing EVA^{TM} as a governance mechanism. In collaboration with SST, other consulting companies and individual SOEs, the agency launched a number of initiatives mainly geared towards refining the technical aspects of EVA^{TM} and supporting its implementation and use over the following years. The technical work on developing EVA^{TM} thus continued despite the reduced political momentum behind the reform. When queried about the reasons for this continued bureaucratic interest in using EVA^{TM}, a high-ranking SEPO official drew attention to how the earlier political work had established a regulatory framework supporting these efforts:

> The SEPO did not consider disbanding the EVA project because we think it was useful. Even if we would want to cancel the project, our bureaucratic process and regulations will not allow us to do so whenever we want. A cancelation of the project is not that easy because although the project originated from a push from powerful people at higher levels, government officials at various levels need to work out and document sound rationales as well as detailed plans for projects before implementing them. (Interview, Head of SOE Performance Evaluation Division, SEPO, 12 May 2012)

Similarly, a senior policy advisor within the Ministry of Finance emphasised how political regulation continued to support the development of EVA^{TM} as a governance mechanism despite the change in government:

> Although the EVA project was politically pushed by the Thaksin government, it was also in line with the broader government policy agenda of 'Thai public sector reforms'. In addition, the SEPO's strong support in terms of time and resources spent on the project was not only caused by the policy but also came from our expectations on the benefits that the EVA project seemed to bring to SOEs. (Interview, Senior Executive and Fiscal Advisor, Ministry of Finance, 12 October 2010)

The technical work undertaken in the years following the demise of the Shinawatra government relied heavily on feedback from individual SOEs as they began to experiment with the EVA^{TM} system and led the SEPO's to make considerable adjustments in response to emerging challenges.

An important initial step in the continued development of EVA^{TM} was to organise a series of weekly workshops whereby early adopters, especially PTT,[12] were asked to share their experiences with other SOEs. This company also continued to be used as a reference point for 'best EVA^{TM} practice' and was called on to support other initiatives to reinforce EVA^{TM} implementation over the following years. Several of our interviewees emphasised its usefulness:

> PTT is very helpful for us because they have been using EVA for a long time. So they understand practical problems that are not stated in the textbooks. In addition, as PTT is a SOE, its employees understand other SOEs as well as how EVA should be applied in those SOEs better than consultants. Importantly, PTT's staff can translate difficult concepts into easy language while training other SOEs. We have received very positive feedback about PTT's involvement in EVA implementation from SOEs. (Interview, Deputy Director, SEPO, 10 December 2010)

> Actually, it is very difficult to implement EVA to all SOEs at the same time, and this is not a normal approach we have used in other countries. Fortunately, we have PTT which started to develop an EVA system in 1995, and the Managing Director of PTT has an in-depth understanding of EVA. Therefore, the Managing Director and his team can effectively convince other SOEs to realise the benefits of the EVA system, and provide useful suggestions about EVA implementation in SOEs. (Interview, Ex-Country Manager of SST, 29 December 2010)

Nevertheless, several SOEs continued to struggle with key, technical aspects of the system. Similar to the PRC, most SOEs found it especially difficult to establish reliable estimates for WACC as a variable, risk-adjusted measure of costs of capital due to the significant problems of identifying adequate market benchmarks. Despite efforts to derive industry-specific WACC rates, this reduced the informativeness of EVA^{TM} as a performance indicator, or as a consultant to the SEPO explained:

> Calculating WACC for companies in emerging markets like Thailand is really difficult because we do not have sufficient data, and our capital market is not stable. Thus, the SEPO decided to standardise the WACC calculation by announcing key parameters for each industry. Although the SEPO updates such parameters every year, the values are quite stable. So, now, we have relatively fixed charges for capital. The quantitative measurement of EVA is not very different from analysing budget variances. Increases in EVA mainly come from net profit as WACC is frozen. (Interview, Vice Director of TRIS, 17 January 2011).

Individual SOEs also encountered major obstacles to the use of EVA^{TM} for internal performance management, such as difficulties in creating transfer pricing systems and EVA^{TM} responsibility centres to enable disaggregation of the metric to organisational sub-units and integrating it with the Balanced Scorecard and internal incentive plans. Following emerging complaints from SOEs over such issues, the SEPO took a number of additional initiatives to reinforce the technical work on developing EVA^{TM}. Among the more important steps were the establishment of an EVA^{TM} call centre and a project called the 'EVA^{TM} clinic', which were both aimed at helping SOEs resolving organisation-specific problems. The SEPO also organised best practice and mentoring programmes and singled out a smaller number of SOEs of particular economic importance as targets for intensive staff training. Several of these initiatives were supported by PTT and external consultants hired by the SEPO. Even though SST ceased to operate in 2007, a number of its former employees continued to assist the SEPO in the development of EVA^{TM}. However, the agency strived to gradually reduce its dependence on consultants in recognition of the substantial costs associated with their services and encouraged individual SOEs to share such services and rely more on PTT. Although this increased the workload of PTT staff, a key member of the team involved in assisting other SOEs with EVA^{TM} implementation corroborated the view that this had contributed to render the system more context-sensitive:

> Actually, we are happy to assist other SOEs. Those SOEs told us that our support was more practical than that from external consultants because we understood potential difficulties that SOEs might face from implementing EVA. However, we think that the EVA package initiated by SEPO does not fit many SOEs. Some SOEs never make a profit due to their revenue structure. In that case, how can EVA incentivise them to improve performance? In addition, SEPO did not really understand the core of EVA. Some of their evaluation criteria do not make sense for us. For example, we have used EVA for about ten years, and they selected us as the best practice, but they still required us to prepare unnecessary reports according to their checklist for initial stage of implementation. (Interview, Head and Analyst, Business Planning Department, Corporate Business Unit, PTT, 29 September 2010)

Consistent with Perkmann and Spicer's (2008) predictions, the sustained technical work based on collaboration between a broad range of actors with diverse expertise appears to have borne some fruit in terms of enhancing SOEs' understanding and acceptance of EVA^{TM}. A consultant with long-standing experience of working with the SEPO remarked:

> I think the SEPO's approach in governing and supervising the EVA project is very good. The SEPO works very closely with SOEs, providing a lot of services such as the clinic, call centre, and expert consulting. Otherwise, the project might fail because the EVA concepts are quite difficult and create several practical problems for SOEs. (Interview, Vice Director of TRIS, 17 January 2011).

However, the collaborative technical work also opened up opportunities for political work on the part of SOEs and eventually led the SEPO to relax the regulatory framework established around EVA^{TM}. Individual SOEs were particularly concerned that the initial plans to make EVA^{TM} a more dominant performance metric might conflict with broader social interests vested in their roles as providers of public goods and services and used the continuous solicitation of feedback as a vehicle of negotiating for some alleviation of financial pressures. Several SOEs raised concerns that the plans to gradually increase the weight of EVA^{TM} in league tables and implement a more aggressive performance management regime might jeopardise their public service ethos and ability to comply with other regulatory requirements (e.g. maintaining regulated prices). As such pressures mounted, the SEPO gradually started to renege on its initial plans to turn EVA^{TM} into a more dominant means of performance improvement as a senior agency official explained:

> We got a lot of complaints from SOEs about continuous improvement targets. Many SOEs disliked the EVA system because of the ambitious continuous improvement goal. So we reconsidered this and started to recognise that the continuous improvement target is not quite appropriate for most SOEs because their ultimate goals are not to maximise financial value and the operations of some SOEs are regulated. Therefore, we decided to change our approach to setting EVA targets to be based on SOEs business plans as well as budgets. (Interview, Head of SOE Performance Evaluation Division, SEPO, 2 August 11)

There was widespread agreement among our interviewees that this embedding of EVA^{TM} in extant systems of budgeting took some of the edge off the system as a vehicle of performance improvement. The SEPO was forced to make similar concessions with respect to the plans to tie EVA^{TM} more closely to managerial incentives. As the work on developing the EVA^{TM} system progressed, several SOEs raised concerns that more aggressive incentivisation of staff would conflict with long-standing cultural values such as the Thai tradition of *Krengjai*, which emphasises the need to nurture a harmonious and collaborative work environment and prevent employees from losing face. In contrast to the normative advice of Stern Stewart to couple EVA^{TM} to essentially uncapped bonus schemes (see Stern *et al.* 2001), this compelled the SEPO to restrict the funds set aside for bonuses and reconsider its initial plans of encouraging SOEs to push incentives down the corporate hierarchy. This reduced the pressures on individual

SOEs to develop EVA^{TM}-based incentive schemes beyond their compulsory inclusion in the compensation packages of Chief Executive Officers. According to a centrally placed informant within the Ministry of Finance:

> We do not want to be too aggressive about internal incentive plans because it can lead to conflicts among individual units. Since SOEs were established, profitable SOEs received fixed bonuses equal to nine per cent of profit but not more than five month's salary. We just changed to pay different corporate bonuses based on nine levels of performance in 1995. Thus, SOE employees still believe that bonuses are part of the salaries that they must receive and most managers dare not change it. Until now, although management has a right to apportion bonuses to their employees based on their individual performance, as far as I know only two SOEs do that. (Interview, Senior Executive and Fiscal Advisor, Ministry of Finance, 12 October 2010)

The discussion above illustrates how the extension of the collaborative, technical work to entail an element of political work detracting from more forceful implementation of EVA^{TM} contributed to balance conflicting interests and thus maintain a degree of field cohesiveness. The adjustment of the regulatory framework around EVA^{TM} to embedded, cultural values may also be seen as an example of how political work became intertwined with an element of cultural work to maintain such cohesiveness. The overall effect of this complex intertwining of different types of institutional work was a gradual relaxation of the use of EVA^{TM} as a governance mechanism. In addition to the reduced ambitions to use EVA^{TM} as a vehicle of aggressive performance improvement, the SEPO refrained from its initial plans to turn it into a more dominant performance metric. Over the time period 2006–2009, the average weight attached to EVA^{TM} in corporate league tables was around 10%. A senior SEPO official explained how such adjustments were due to the need to maintain some balance between the economic and broader social interests and avoid jeopardising the broader, societal objectives of SOEs:

> SOEs have several missions to complete. Thus, it is impossible to use EVA as a stand-alone system. Nevertheless, the current weight of 10% is not insignificant at all. We normally do not assign a weight higher than 10% to any individual performance indicator. (Interview, Head of SOE Performance Evaluation Division, SOE Performance Management and Evaluation Bureau, SEPO, 11 October 2010)

The relaxation of the regulatory framework established around EVA^{TM} is also manifest in the gradual change in performance evaluation practices applied by the SEPO. Rather than focusing on absolute EVA^{TM} performance in terms of the ability of SOEs to meet quantifiable targets, the agency has shifted its emphasis to a more flexible and qualitative approach where the development of managerial mindsets supporting value creation constitutes an increasingly important criterion. This development was accelerated after 2010 when a new performance monitoring system – the State Enterprise Performance Appraisal (SEPA) system – was introduced as a result of unfolding governance reforms. This reform was proposed by an independent policy review committee with representatives from the SEPO, the Thai Quality Institute and private sector consultants and had been introduced in five SOEs at the time of our field work. In contrast to earlier, results-orientated systems of performance monitoring, the SEPA system was modelled on a more process-orientated, total quality management-inspired approach placing considerable emphasis on organisational self assessment. Whilst EVA^{TM} is still a compulsory performance indicator for the majority of Thai SOEs there were some suggestions that it might require further adjustments to maintain its position as a key governance mechanism. Even though SEPO staff saw no major problems associated with reconciling the use of EVA^{TM} with the SEPA system, one of them concluded:

I think our support for the EVA project has reached its saturation point. From now on, we will not force SOEs to do any specific thing about EVA. We just provide some general advice as to how they should consider merging EVA into SEPA. Nevertheless, they cannot abandon EVA because in the SEPA evaluation framework, the use of the EVA system is one criterion. As some SOEs commented that standard criteria cannot match their organisation, and sometimes act as barriers to their performance improvement, I think that this more flexible approach should enable individual SOEs to reach their full potential. However, it will take some time to improve. SOEs might need to learn from their mistakes along the way. (Interview, Head of SOE Performance Evaluation Division, SEPO, 11 October 2010)

Hence by the time our field work ended the development of performance management practices in Thai, SOEs had entered a new phase posing some challenges to the EVA^{TM} system although it was not yet questioned as a governance mechanism. This is indicative of EVA^{TM} having achieved a certain degree of embeddedness in the formal governance system operating at the institutional field level although individual SOEs still have considerable discretion in applying it. However, our analysis suggests that such embeddedness was only achieved as a result of considerable adjustments resulting from the intertwining of especially technical and political work in the years following the demise of the Shinawatra government. An important trigger of such work was the need to balance the economic and social interests served by SOEs to maintain a degree of field cohesiveness. The ambition to maintain some balance between economic and social interests is also evident in the cautious approach adopted by the SEPO to the diffusion of EVA^{TM} beyond the two thirds of SOEs initially adopting it in 2006. By the time our field work ended, the agency had not forced any additional SOEs to adopt EVA^{TM} and had granted special exemptions to SOEs without extensive commercial operations to ensure that vital social performance aspects are not compromised. We may thus conclude that the continued relevance of EVA^{TM} as a governance mechanism to especially the SEPO has only been achieved through significant concessions to the wider range of interests served by SOEs.

6. Concluding discussion

We started this paper by questioning the assumption that the relevance of EVA^{TM} as a governance mechanism primarily resides in its capacity to align managerial interests and incentives with the preferences of dispersed shareholders in a modern and increasingly globalised capital markets context. Instead, we advance a notion of relevance centred on the propensity of management accounting innovations to get imbued with a broader range of societal interests and explore the institutional work undertaken by diverse actors with vested interests in EVA^{TM} to establish and maintain it as a legitimate governance mechanism. Whilst elements of the traditional, shareholder value-based discourse were mobilised as part of the cultural work aimed at legitimising EVA^{TM}, our analysis reveals how notions of shareholder value may be co-opted by interests other than those represented by the global investment community. In the Chinese field, the use of EVA^{TM} to enhance shareholder value primarily originated in the economic and political interests of the State in increasing the value of state assets and redirect SOE strategies to focus on high-return growth whilst the interests of minority shareholders have arguably been of lesser concern. Similarly, in the Thai field, EVA^{TM} was initially mobilised as a means of facilitating large-scale privatisation by a group of dominant political actors with strongly vested, economic interests in pursuing such a reform programme rather than favouring global, capital markets interests.

In both countries, the fields created around EVA^{TM} were also held together by bureaucratic interests vested in the regulatory agencies (i.e. the SASAC and the SEPO) in charge of undertaking and coordinating much of the technical work associated with making it operational. In the PRC, such bureaucratic interests are closely aligned with the economic and political interests of the State through the promotion practices in place for SOE managers and SASAC staff. Conversely, in Thailand, the bureaucratic interests in making EVA^{TM} operational persisted despite the waning of strong political pressures for privatisation after 2006 as it was seen as a potentially useful governance mechanism supported by the regulatory framework established through previous reforms. Regardless of such differences, however, the regulatory agencies in the two countries have also had to engage in a considerable element of political work to uphold a degree of field cohesiveness. This was not least evident in the continuous negotiations aimed at balancing between the economic and social interests served by SOEs in response to concerns that overly forceful applications of EVA^{TM} as a vehicle of performance improvement and incentivisation may skew interests too heavily in favour of the economic. This, in turn, contributed to relax the regulatory framework established around EVA although it was not rejected as an illegitimate governance mechanism and prevented notions of shareholder value from becoming overly dominant in individual SOEs. This illustrates how the maintenance of field cohesiveness entails intricate balancing acts preventing management accounting innovations from becoming firmly embedded in individual organisations. However, this does not mean that such innovations necessarily lose their relevance or that the institutional work geared towards establishing and maintaining them should be seen as some form of 'quasi-failure'. Rather, given that such work often entails maintenance of fragile coalitions of interests (cf. Zietsma and McKnight 2009, Slager et al. 2012), the relevance of management accounting innovations to some actors (e.g. regulators, the State) may only be achievable through compromises and concessions to other actors with partly diverging interests. Failing to recognise the need for such balancing between competing interests implies a risk of reifying a narrow conception of relevance where management accounting is seen as mainly serving one dominant category of (typically managerial) interests at the expense of other constituencies.

This revised conception of the relevance of EVA^{TM} goes a long way beyond the economics-based imperative of using it as a means of aligning managerial interests with those of dispersed shareholders and maximising shareholder value (cf. Bouwens and Spekle 2007). It also extends prior, sociologically informed analyses of EVA^{TM} and the concomitant shareholder value movement. The latter body of research has primarily traced the salience of these phenomena to differences in ownership structure and specific managerial characteristics (Jurgens et al. 2000, Morgan and Takahashi 2002, Fiss and Zajac 2004), the pervasiveness of consultancy rhetoric and competing discourses (Froud et al. 2000a, Meyer and Höllerer 2010) and intra-organisational power struggles (Ezzamel and Burns 2005, Siti-Nabiha and Scapens 2005, Ezzamel et al. 2008). Whilst our analysis does not negate the influence of such factors, it underscores the need to situate the institutionalisation of EVA^{TM} in a somewhat broader, societal context and take a wider range of actors and interests into account. In particular, it underlines the nature of such processes as more politically motivated projects relying on extensive government intervention and the alignment of a multitude of interests for their realisation. The institutionalisation of EVA^{TM} was obviously conditioned by the prevailing dominance of State ownership whilst the influence of independent consultants as mediators of EVA^{TM} implementation varied considerably across the fields under examination. However, it also relied heavily on the actions of regulatory agencies and the institutional work that they engaged in vis-a-vis individual SOEs. Moreover, our study provides some insights into the efforts undertaken to safeguard wider, social interests that risk being marginalised by notions of shareholder value (cf. Froud et al. 2000b, Fligstein and Shin 2007).

Our empirical analysis also deepens our understanding of how the interplay between different types of institutional work involved in establishing and maintaining EVA^{TM} as a governance mechanism varies depending on the structuration of institutional fields. Whilst our findings are broadly consistent with Perkmann and Spicer's (2008) prediction that successful institutional work tends to evolve in a cumulative manner, we extend their framework by drawing attention to how the specific types and sequencing of such work varied depending on the challenges of upholding a degree of field cohesiveness. In the PRC, a fairly limited amount of political and cultural work was initially required to create a reasonably cohesive field around EVA^{TM} and initiate some technical work aimed at making it operational. Indeed, elements of such a field were already in place through the close alignment of the interests of the State and the SASAC in enhancing the value of SOEs. The main challenges of embedding EVA^{TM} in extant governance structures without disrupting the configurations of interests established through previous reforms and jeopardising field cohesiveness rather arose from the extension of institutional work to individual SOEs. This led to a cautious and protracted reform path entailing a considerable amount of political and cultural work to support the involvement of SOE managers in the collaborative, technical work aimed at making EVA^{TM} a more integral part of their performance management practices. However, the political work prompting some relaxation of the regulatory framework established around EVA^{TM} also reduced the impetus behind such technical work.

The accumulation of institutional work in the Thai field followed a rather different trajectory. Despite the early formation of a field around the idea of privatisation, a greater element of political and cultural work was required to extend this to the notion of EVA^{TM} and bring together a dispersed set of actors, such as members of the Shinawatra government and the Thai business community and Stern Stewart, before the technical work involving individual SOEs could be initiated. Once this collaborative, technical work was under way, however, it seems to have been less dependent on forceful political support for its realisation. Indeed, it may even be argued that it was this continued technical work, involving a broad range of actors and expertise that maintained a degree of field cohesiveness and prevented EVA^{TM} from being rejected in the years following the demise of the Shinawatra government. This may explain the relative salience of collaborative, technical work aimed at embedding EVA^{TM} in the performance management practices of individual SOEs. Similar to the PRC, however, this could only be sustained over time as a result of considerable concessions and adjustments of performance evaluation standards mediated through a pronounced element of political work vis-a-vis individual SOEs.

This comparison of the relationships between various types of institutional work illustrates how the constellations of such work are contingent on the embeddedness of actors in different field conditions and starts to address the critique of prior research on such work for neglecting notions of embedded agency (Khagan and Lounsbury 2011). In particular, we draw attention to how differences in the initial states of field cohesiveness fostered different patterns of institutional work and how the maintenance of such cohesiveness subsequently required and detracted from different types of institutional work. What would seem to be of particular importance in this regard are the field conditions conducive to collaborative, technical work aimed at embedding EVA^{TM} in the performance management practices of individual SOEs. Whilst the extent of such work was limited by the considerable political work required to maintain the cohesiveness of the Chinese field, it arguably formed a more integral part of the very maintenance of such cohesiveness in the Thai field although it ultimately entailed similar concessions to the political work advanced by SOEs. These findings nuance Perkmann and Spicer's (2008) prediction that institutional work combining multiple actors and expertise into collaborative constellations is a necessary condition for successful institutionalisation. Indeed, in some fields such collaborative work may even be counterproductive as it may be seen as threatening the fragile balance between diverse interests and thus jeopardise field cohesiveness. As argued in the foregoing, such balancing acts may be necessary to prevent management accounting innovations from being rejected as illegitimate and thus preserve their relevance to particular interests. Hence the relative success of institutional work needs to be evaluated against its propensity to uphold fragile coalitions of interests rather than being confined to the question of whether particular innovations become more or less firmly embedded in organisational practices. This differs from Perkmann and Spicer's (2008) framework, which subscribes to a conception of successful institutional work as invariably entailing such embedding, or relatively firm institutionalisation, of innovations. More generally, it calls for further research into how institutional work is implicated in the process of sustaining more or less fragile coalitions of interests under different field conditions whilst avoiding the fallacy of viewing institutionalisation as a process with a definite end point. Studying institutional work implies paying close empirical attention to the unfolding efforts of diverse actors to maintain even firmly institutionalised practices whilst remaining alert to emerging conflicts and struggles as other actors try to disrupt them or create new institutions (cf. Lawrence et al. 2009). It also requires us to recognise that different coalitions of interests supporting or challenging particular practices may be disrupted at any point in time (cf. Yang and Modell 2013).

To conclude, we hope to have demonstrated how the institutional work approach may enhance our understanding of the processes whereby management accounting innovations assume broader, societal relevance and extend research beyond the largely managerialist concerns dominating much of the debate on the relevance of management accounting. The main contribution of this approach is that it draws attention to the broader range of interests and actors implicated in the evolution of such innovations whilst tapping into an established theoretical body of knowledge concerning how innovations evolve in institutional fields. Whilst institutional theory has been highly influential in research on management accounting change over the past decade, much of it has been relatively silent about broader, field-level processes such as those described in our analysis (but see e.g. Modell 2003, Dillard et al. 2004, Hopper and Major 2007, Modell et al. 2007). This may have cemented an unduly narrow emphasis on the responses of individual organisations to largely 'given', or exogenous, institutional pressures reinforcing an essentially managerialist perspective on the process of change (Modell 2012b). In contrast, we believe there is scope for extending the quest for the broader, societal relevance of management accounting innovations across multiple levels of analysis to explore the complex, recursive dynamics unfolding as institutional processes bridge organisations, fields and wider spheres of society (Dillard et al. 2004, Hopper and Major 2007). This may shed further light on how such innovations become implicated in everyday organisational practices as well as broader societal processes with potentially far-reaching implications for a wide range of constituencies.

We also believe that multi-level analyses of the institutional work involved in the development of accounting may contribute to bridging the gap between management accounting research and other areas of accounting scholarship. As noted by Vollmer et al. (2009), there is currently a distinct but potentially detrimental division of labour between management accounting scholars primarily focusing on the internal use of accounting in organisations and financial accounting research more concerned with external reporting and use of accounting information by various societal constituencies. The institutional work approach offers an opportunity to extend analyses of management accounting to examine the roles of actors often excluded from such research (e.g. auditors, financial analysts, regulators, societal pressure groups) and how their interactions with intra-organisational actors (e.g. management, trade unions) shape accounting practices. For instance, it may shed further light on how efforts to enhance the decision relevance of accounting to some actors influence the interests of other actors and how different coalitions of interests are formed and disrupted in the struggle for supremacy in interpreting accounting information. Such research may enhance our understanding of how the relevance of accounting is concomitantly construed within and beyond individual organisations and relax the somewhat contrived distinction between management and financial accounting scholarship as separate research projects.

Acknowledgements

We are grateful for the insightful comments on previous versions of the paper by two anonymous *ABR* reviewers and Vivien Beattie (Editor-in-Chief). Additional comments by Rafael Heinzelman, Bob Scapens and Samar Magdy Mohamad El Sayad are also acknowledged. The paper has been presented at the 6th workshop on Management Accounting as Social and Organisational Practice (MASOP), Copenhagen (2013), the 7th Asia Pacific Interdisciplinary Research on Accounting (APIRA) conference, Kobe (2013) and research seminars at the Norwegian School of Economics and Turku School of Economics.

Notes

1. Following Zawawi and Hoque (2010), management accounting innovations refer to novel or redesigned accounting techniques. EVA has been identified as one of the most significant management accounting innovations for the purpose of performance measurement and management emerging over the past decades (Ittner and Larcker 1998).
2. By institutional theory we primarily refer to neo-institutional sociology. Although institutional research on accounting has also drawn on other perspectives, such as old institutional economics, this research has mostly been undertaken within individual organisations (Burns and Scapens 2000, Dillard *et al.* 2004, Ma and Tayles 2009). Since our analysis is located at the institutional field level we adopt an analytical perspective emanating from a more substantial body of work at this level (cf. Wooten and Hoffman 2008).
3. This conception of institutional work as implicated in the maintenance of potentially fragile coalitions of interests is akin to the formation of continuously evolving actor-networks in actor-network theory (ANT). Whilst these conceptual similarities have been acknowledged by scholars of institutional work (Lawrence and Suddaby 2006), ANT differs from institutional theory in that it deliberately sets out to transcend dualisms such as those between agency and structure and privileges analyses of ongoing interactions between human and non-human actors (Justesen and Mouritsen 2011). We see a risk of such actor-centric analyses detracting from the need for more careful attention to institutional work as embedded in extant social structures (cf. Hwang and Colyvas 2011, Khagan and Lounsbury 2011).
4. The view of human agency as *conditioned* by institutional structures is not intended to denote a deterministic view of the process of institutionalisation. The concept of institutional work recognises that extant institutional structures always interact with an element of intentional human agency in such processes (cf. Lawrence *et al.* 2009).
5. Prior research on management accounting practices in the PRC have noted the difficulties in conducting qualitative research due to the lack of organisational familiarity with such research (see Duh *et al.* 2008). Our decision to refrain from voice recording interviews was part of a conscious strategy to lower such barriers.
6. Central SOEs are distinct from local SOEs in that the former are centrally controlled and administered whereas the latter are governed by local authorities. The latter have not been affected by the introduction of EVA and are not part of our analysis.
7. 'Responsible person' refers to an individual (e.g. Chairman or CEO) who is charged with the overall responsibility for running a central SOE and who is held accountable for its performance.
8. The SASAC is organised into several performance review divisions entrusted with largely similar tasks in monitoring the performance of SOEs across various industrial sectors.
9. The reasons for the choice of Stern Stewart rather than other consulting firms are unclear, although one of our interviewees claimed that it possessed superior expertise in devising EVA systems.
10. Quote from official SASAC document from 2009.
11. The Finance Minister used to be a board member of Dr Shinawatra's holding company.
12. PTT had adopted EVA on a voluntary basis before it became a compulsory requirement for Thai SOEs.

References

Abernathy, M.A. and Chua, W.F., 1996. A field study of control systems 'redesign': the impact of institutional processes on strategic choice. *Contemporary Accounting Research*, 13 (2), 569–606.

Andon, P., Baxter, J., and Chua, W.F., 2007. Accounting change as relational drifting: a field study of experiments with performance measurement. *Management Accounting Research*, 18 (4), 273–308.

Battilana, J., Leca, B., and Boxenbaum, E., 2009. How actors change institutions: towards a theory of institutional entrepreneurship. *The Academy of Management Annals*, 3, 65–107.

Bhimani, A., Dai, N.T., Tang, G., and Li, P., 2013. When strategy loses control: economic value added in Chinese state owned enterprises. Working paper, London School of Economics.

Bouwens, J. and Spekle, R., 2007. Does EVA add value? In: T. Hopper, D. Northcott, and R.W. Scapens, eds. *Issues in Management Accounting*. 3rd ed. London: Pearson, 245–268.

Bromwich, M. and Walker, M., 1998. Residual income: past and future. *Management Accounting Research*, 9 (4), 391–419.

Burns, J. and Scapens, R.W., 2000. Conceptualising management accounting change: an institutional framework. *Management Accounting Research*, 11 (1), 3–25.

Chen, G., Firth, M., and Rui, O., 2006. Have China's enterprise reforms led to improved efficiency and profitability? *Emerging Markets Review*, 7 (1), 82–109.

Clarke, D.C., 2003. Corporate governance in China: an overview. *China Economic Review*, 14 (4), 494–507.

Covaleski, M.A. and Dirsmith, M.W., 1988. An institutional perspective on the rise, fall and social transformation of a university budget category. *Administrative Science Quarterly*, 33 (4), 562–587.

Covaleski, M.A., Dirsmith, M.W., and Michelman, J.E., 1993. An institutional theory perspective on the DRG framework, case-mix accounting systems and health-care organizations. *Accounting, Organizations and Society*, 18 (1), 65–80.

Currie, G., Lockett, A., Finn, R., Martin, G., and Waring, J., 2012. Institutional work to maintain professional power: recreating the model of medical professionalism. *Organization Studies*, 33 (7), 937–962.

Davis, G.F. and Thompson, T.A., 1994. A social movement perspective on corporate control. *Administrative Science Quarterly*, 39 (1), 141–173.

Dempsey, J.R., 2000. Thailand's privatization of state owned enterprises during the economic downturn. *Law and Policy in International Business*, 31 (2), 373–402.

Dillard, J.F., Rigsby, J.T., and Goodman, C., 2004. The making and remaking of organization context: duality and the institutionalization process. *Accounting, Auditing and Accountability Journal*, 17 (4), 506–542.

DiMaggio, P.J., 1988. Interest and agency in institutional theory. In: L.G. Zucker, ed. *Institutional Patterns and Organizations: Culture and Environment*. Cambridge, MA: Ballinger, 3–21.

DiMaggio, P.J. and Powell, W.W., 1983. The iron cage revisited: institutional isomorphism in organizational fields. *American Sociological Review*, 48 (1), 147–160.

Dorado, S., 2005. Institutional entrepreneurship, partaking and convening. *Organization Studies*, 26 (3), 385–414.

Du, F., Tang, G., and Young, S.M., 2012. Influence activities and favouritism in subjective performance evaluation: evidence from Chinese state-owned enterprises. *The Accounting Review*, 87 (5), 1555–1588.

Duh, R.-R., Xiao, J.Z., and Chow, C.W., 2008. An overview and assessment of contemporary management accounting research in China. *Journal of Management Accounting Research*, 20, 129–164.

Eisenhardt, K.M., 1989. Building theories from case study research. *Academy of Management Review*, 14 (4), 532–550.

Englund, H. and Gerdin, J., 2011. Agency and structure in management accounting research: reflections and extensions of Kilfoyle and Richardson. *Critical Perspectives on Accounting*, 22 (6), 581–592.

Ezzamel, M. and Burns, J., 2005. Professional competition, economic value added and management control strategies. *Organization Studies*, 26 (5), 755–777.

Ezzamel, M., Willmott, H., and Worthington, F., 2008. Manufacturing shareholder value: the role of accounting in organizational transformation. *Accounting, Organizations and Society*, 33 (1), 107–140.

Fiss, P.C. and Zajac, E.J., 2004. The diffusion of ideas over contested terrain: the (non)adoption of shareholder value orientation among German firms. *Administrative Science Quarterly*, 49 (4), 501–534.

Fligstein, N. and Shin, T., 2007. Shareholder value and the transformation of the U.S. economy, 1984–2000. *Sociological Forum*, 22 (4), 399–424.

Francis, G. and Minchington, C., 2002. Regulating shareholder value: a case study of the introduction of value-based management in a water company. *British Journal of Management*, 13 (3), 233–247.

Froud, J., Haslam, C., Johal, S., and Williams, K., 2000a. Shareholder value and financialization: consultancy promises, management moves. *Economy and Society*, 29 (1), 80–110.

Froud, J., Haslam, C., Johal, S., and Williams, K., 2000b. Restructuring for shareholder value and its implications for labour. *Cambridge Journal of Economics*, 24 (6), 771–797.

Gleadle, P. and Cornelius, N., 2008. A case study of financialization and EVA. *Critical Perspectives on Accounting*, 19 (8), 1219–1238.

Goretzki, L., Strauss, E., and Weber, J., 2013. An institutional perspective on the changes in management accountants' professional role. *Management Accounting Research*, 24 (1), 41–63.

Greenwood, R., Raynard, M., Kodeih, F., Micelotta, A.R., and Lounsbury, M., 2011. Institutional complexity and organizational responses. *Academy of Management Annals*, 5, 317–371.

Hassard, J., Sheehan, J., Zhou, M.X., Tong, J.T., and Morris, J., 2007. *China's State Enterprise Reform: From Marx to the Market*. New York: Routledge.

Hassard, J., Sheehan, J., and Yuxin, X., 2008. Chinese state-enterprise reform: economic transition, labour unrest and worker representation. *Capital and Class*, 96 (3), 31–52.

Hoffman, A.J. 1999. Institutional evolution and change: environmentalism and the U.S. chemical industry. *Academy of Management Journal*, 42 (4), 351–371.

Hopper, T. and Major, M., 2007. Extending institutional analysis through theoretical triangulation: regulation and activity-based costing in Portuguese telecommunications'. *European Accounting Review*, 16 (1), 59–97.

Hopwood, A.G., 1992. Accounting calculation and the shifting sphere of the economic. *European Accounting Review*, 1 (1), 125–143.

Hussain, A. and Jian, C., 1999. Changes in China's industrial landscape and their implication. *International Studies of Management and Organization*, 29 (3), 5–20.

Hwang, H. and Colyvas, J.A., 2011. Problematising actors and institutions in institutional work. *Journal of Management Inquiry*, 20 (1), 62–66.

Ittner, C.D. and Larcker, D.F., 1998. Innovation in performance measurement: trends and research implications. *Journal of Management Accounting Research*, 10, 205–238.

Ittner, C.D. and Larcker, D.F., 2001. Assessing empirical research in managerial accounting: a value-based management perspective. *Journal of Accounting and Economics*, 32 (4), 349–410.

Johnson, H.T. and Kaplan, R.S., 1987. *Relevance Lost: The Rise and Fall of Management Accounting*. Cambridge, MA: Harvard Business School Press.

Jurgens, U., Naumann, K., and Rupp, J., 2000. Shareholder value in an adverse environment: the German case. *Economy and Society*, 29 (1), 54–79.

Justesen, L. and Mouritsen, J., 2011. Effects of actor-network theory in accounting research. *Accounting, Auditing and Accountability Journal*, 24 (2), 161–193.

Keating, P.J., 1995. A framework for classifying and evaluating the theoretical contributions of case research in management accounting. *Journal of Management Accounting Research*, 7, 66–86.

Khagan, W. and Lounsbury, M., 2011. Institutions and work. *Journal of Management Inquiry*, 29 (1), 73–81.

Kilfoyle, E. and Richardson, A.J., 2011. Agency and structure in budgeting: thesis, antithesis and synthesis. *Critical Perspectives on Accounting*, 22 (2), 183–199.

Kraatz, M.S. and Block, E., 2008. Organizational implications of institutional pluralism. In R. Greenwood, C. Oliver, K. Sahlin, and R. Suddaby, eds. *The Sage Handbook of Organizational Institutionalism*. Thousand Oaks: Sage, 243–275.

Kraus, K. and Strömsten, T., 2012. Going public: the role of accounting and shareholder value in making sense of an IPO. *Management Accounting Research*, 23 (2), 186–201.

Lawrence, T.B. and Suddaby, R., 2006. Institutions and institutional work. In: S.R. Clegg, C. Hardy, T.B. Lawrence, and W.R. Nord, eds. *The Sage Handbook of Organization Studies*. 2nd ed. Sage: Thousand Oaks, 215–254.

Lawrence, T.B., Suddaby, R., and Leca, B., 2009. Introduction: theorizing and studying institutional work. In: T. Lawrence, R. Suddaby, and P. Leca, eds. *Institutional Work. Actors and Agency in Institutional Studies of Organizations*. Cambridge: Cambridge University Press, 1–27.

Lawrence, T., Suddaby, R., and Leca, B., 2011. Institutional work: refocusing institutional studies of organizations. *Journal of Management Inquiry*, 20 (1), 52–58.

Lawrence, T.B., Leca, B., and Zilber, T., 2013. Institutional work: current research, new directions and overlooked issues. *Organization Studies*, 34 (8), 1023–1033.

Lounsbury, M., 2008. Institutional rationality and practice variation: new directions in the institutional analysis of practice. *Accounting, Organizations and Society*, 33 (4–5), 349–361.

Lukka, K., 2005. Approaches to case research in management accounting: the nature of empirical intervention and theory linkage. In: S. Jönsson and J. Mouritsen, eds. *Accounting in Scandinavia – The Northern Lights*. Malmö: Liber and Copenhagen Business School Press, 375–399.

Ma, Y. and Tayles, M., 2009. On the emergence of strategic management accounting: an institutional perspective. *Accounting and Business Research*, 39 (5), 473–495.

Malmi, T. and Ikäheimo, S., 2003. Value-based management practices – some evidence from the field. *Management Accounting Research*, 14 (3), 235–254.

Malsch, B. and Gendron, Y., 2013. Re-theorizing change: institutional experimentation and the struggle for domination in the field of public accounting. *Journal of Management Studies*, 50 (5), 870–899.

McGregor, R., 2011. *The Party: The Secret World of China's Communist Rulers: 1.3 Billion People, 1 Secret Regime*. London: Penguin.

Meyer, R.E. and Höllerer, M.A., 2010. Meaning structures in a contested issue field: a topographic map of shareholder value in Austria. *Academy of Management Journal*, 53 (6), 1241–1262.

Miller, P., 1991. Accounting innovation beyond the enterprise: problematizing investment decisions and programming economic growth in the U.K. in the 1960s. *Accounting, Organizations and Society*, 16 (8), 733–762.

Miller, P. and O'Leary, T., 1993. Accounting expertise and the politics of the product: economic citizenship and modes of corporate governance. *Accounting, Organizations and Society*, 18 (2/3), 187–206.

Miller, P. and O'Leary, T., 1994. Accounting, 'economic citizenship' and the spatial reordering of manufacture. *Accounting, Organizations and Society*, 19 (1), 15–43.

Mitter, R., 2004. *A Bitter Revolution: China's Struggle with the Modern World*. Oxford: Oxford University Press.

Modell, S., 2001. Performance measurement and institutional processes: a study of managerial responses to public sector reform. *Management Accounting Research*, 12 (4), 437–464.

Modell, S., 2003. Goals versus institutions: the development of performance measurement in the Swedish university sector. *Management Accounting Research*, 14 (4), 333–359.

Modell, S., 2009. Bundling management control innovations: a field study of organisational experimenting with total quality management and the balanced scorecard. *Accounting, Auditing and Accountability Journal*, 22 (1), 59–90.

Modell, S., 2012a. The politics of the balanced scorecard. *Journal of Accounting and Organizational Change*, 8 (4), 475–489.

Modell, S., 2012b. Strategy, political regulation and management control in the public sector: institutional and critical perspectives. *Management Accounting Research*, 23 (4), 278–295.

Modell, S., Jacobs, K., and Wiesel, F., 2007. A process (re)turn? Path dependencies, institutions and performance management in Swedish central government. *Management Accounting Research*, 18 (4), 453–475.

Morgan, G. and Takahashi, Y., 2002. Shareholder value in the Japanese context. *Competition and Change*, 6 (2), 169–191.

O'Hanlon, J. and Peasnell, K., 1998. Wall Street's contribution to management accounting: the Stern Stewart EVA financial management system. *Management Accounting Research*, 9 (4), 421–444.

Perkmann, M. and Spicer, A., 2008. How are management fashions institutionalized? The role of institutional work. *Human Relations*, 61 (6), 811–844.

Rojas, F., 2010. Power through institutional work: acquiring academic authority in the 1968 Third World Strike. *Academy of Management Journal*, 53 (6), 1263–1280.

Scott, W.R., 1987. The adolescence of institutional theory. *Administrative Science Quarterly*, 32 (4), 493–511.

Scott, W.R. and Meyer, J.W., 1983. The organization of societal sectors. In: J.W. Meyer and W.R. Scott, eds. *Organizational Environments: Ritual and Rationality*. Beverly Hills: Sage, 129–153.

Siti-Nabiha, A.K. and Scapens, R.W., 2005. Stability and change: an institutionalist study of management accounting change. *Accounting, Auditing and Accountability Journal*, 18 (1), 44–73.

Slager, R., Gond, J.-P., and Moon, J., 2012. Standardization as institutional work: the regulatory power of a responsible investment standard. *Organization Studies*, 33 (5–6), 763–790.

Steinfeld, E.S., 1998. *Forging Reform in China: The Gate of State-Owned Industry*. Cambridge: Cambridge University Press.

Stern, E., 2011. China adopts EVA: an essential step in the Great Leap Forward. *Journal of Applied Corporate Finance*, 23 (1), 57–62.

Stern, J.M., Stewart, III G.B., and Chew, D., 1995. The EVA™ financial management system. *Journal of Applied Corporate Finance*, 8 (2), 32–46.

Stern, J.M., Shiely, J.S., and Ross, I., 2001. *The EVA Challenge: Implementing Value-Added Change in an Organization*. New York: Wiley.

Stewart, III G.B., 1991. *The Quest for Value*. New York: HarperCollins.

Szamosszegi, A. and Kyle, C., 2011. *An Analysis of State-owned Enterprises and State Capitalism in China*. Washington, DC: U.S.-China Economic and Security Review Commission.

Tolbert, P.S. and Zucker, L.G., 1983. Institutional sources of change in the formal structure of organizations: the diffusion of civil service reform, 1880–1935. *Administrative Science Quarterly*, 30 (1), 22–39.

Tucker, B. and Parker, L., 2014. In our ivory towers? The research-practice gap in management accounting. *Accounting and Business Research*, DOI: 10.1080/00014788.2013.798234.

Vollmer, H., Mennicken, A., and Preda, A., 2009. Tracking the numbers: across accounting and finance, organizations and markets. *Accounting, Organizations and Society*, 34 (5), 619–637.

Wong, L., 2005. Corporate governance in China: a lack of critical reflexivity? *Advances in Public Interest Accounting*, 11, 117–143.

Woods, M., Taylor, L., and Fang, G.C.G., 2012. Electronics: a case study of economic value added in target costing. *Management Accounting Research*, 23 (4), 261–277.

Wooten, M. and Hoffman, A.J., 2008. Organizational fields: past, present and future. In: R. Greenwood, C, Oliver, K. Sahlin, and R. Suddaby, eds. *The Sage Handbook of Organizational Institutionalism*. Thousand Oaks: Sage, 130–147.

World Bank, 1994. *Thailand Sector Report: Increasing Private Sector Participation and Improving Efficiency in State Enterprises*. Singapore: the World Bank East Asia and Pacific Regional Office.

World Bank, 1995. *Meeting the Challenge of Chinese Enterprise Reform*. Washington, DC: The World Bank.

World Bank, 1997. *China's Management of Enterprise Assets: The State as a Shareholder*. Washington, DC: The World Bank.

World Bank, 2002. *Exercising Ownership Rights in State Owned Enterprise Groups: What China Can Learn from International Experience?* Washington, DC: The World Bank.

World Bank, 2012. *China 2030: Building a Modern, Harmonious, and Creative High-Income Society*. Washington, DC: The World Bank.

Yang, C. and Modell, S., 2013. Power and performance: institutional embeddedness and performance management in a Chinese local government organization. *Accounting, Auditing and Accountability Journal*, 26 (1), 101–132.

Yindeepit, D., 2010. *State Enterprise Performance Appraisal*. Bangkok: State Enterprise Policy Office.

Young, M.N., Ahlstrom, D., and Bruton, G., 2004. The globalization of corporate governance in East Asia: the transnational solution. *Management International Review*, 44 (1), 31–50.

Zajac, E.J. and Westphal, J.D., 2004. The social construction of market value: institutionalization and learning perspectives on stock-market reactions. *American Sociological Review*, 69 (June), 433–457.

Zawawi, N.II.II. and Hoque, Z., 2010. Research on management accounting innovations: an overview of its recent development. *Qualitative Research on Accounting and Management*, 7 (4), 505–568.

Zietsma, C. and Lawrence, T.B., 2010. Institutional work in the transformation of an organizational field: the interplay of boundary work and practice work. *Administrative Science Quarterly*, 55 (2), 189–221.

Zietsma, C. and McKnight, B., 2009. Building the iron cage: institutional creation work in the context of competing proto-institutions. In: T. Lawrence, R. Suddaby, and B. Leca, eds. *Institutional Work. Actors and Agency in Institutional Studies of Organizations*. Cambridge: Cambridge University Press, 143–177.

Appendix 1. Key regulatory guidelines for EVA^{TM}

The calculation of EVA^{TM} follows the following basic formula:

$$EVA^{TM} = Net\,Operating\,Profit\,after\,Taxes - Capital\,Charge,$$

where Capital Charge is determined as:

$$Capital\,Charge = Capital\,Employed \times Weighted\,Average\,Cost\,of\,Capital\,(WACC).$$

The following table summarises the regulatory guidelines for Chinese and Thai SOEs, respectively, across some key, technical elements of EVA^{TM} as a performance management system.

	SASAC guidelines	SEPO guidelines
Capital charges	Based on uniform WACC of 5.5% for majority of SOEs. Exceptions are made for highly policy relevant (4.1%) and highly leveraged SOEs (6%)	Based on variable WACCs across SOEs depending on industry-specific risk profiles
Financial accounting adjustments	Some compulsory adjustments (e.g. R&D expenses, non-operating income, projects in construction)	SOEs may choose between 12 recommended adjustments (e.g. construction in progress, provisions, extra-ordinary items, non-interest-bearing liabilities)
Weight of EVA^{TM} in corporate performance league tables	40% (from 2010)	Initially 15%. Thereafter around 10% (after 2006)
Requirements to disaggregate EVA^{TM} across hierarchical levels	Compulsory from 2010. Weight of EVA^{TM} in internal league tables increasing from 5% to 30%	No requirement, but SOEs may choose to do so if they deem it suitable
Linking of incentives to EVA^{TM} metrics	Compulsory for 'responsible persons'. Optional though recommended at lower managerial echelons	Compulsory for Chief Executive Officer of SOEs. Optional at lower managerial echelons
Role of EVA^{TM} in target setting	In principle, EVA^{TM} targets should be no less than the average EVA^{TM} result of the preceding three years. In practice, this is often breached as a result of subjective adjustments	Part of annual budgetary negotiations and varying target levels across SOEs. No objective benchmarks

Appendix 2. Overview of interviews

Interviews in the field of Chinese SOEs

		Date			
Interviewee	Duration (min.)	2009	2010	2011	2012
Deputy Minister, Ministry of Finance	120	4/09			
	30		5/08		
	90			23/09	
	20			28/09	
Policy advisor, University of Beijing	Full day			26/9	
Senior fellow, Research centre, Ministry of Finance	60 (phone)				30/7
Deputy Head of Performance Review Division 1 , SASAC	60	11/ 08			
	45	4/09			
	45		6/08		
	60			5/09	
	60			24/09	
Officer, Performance Review Division 1, SASAC	30			24/9	
Head of Performance Review Division 2, SASAC	Full day (interview/ observations)				5/11
					6/11

(Continued)

Appendix 2. Continued.

Interviewee	Duration (min.)	2009	2010	2011	2012
			Date		
Deputy Head of Performance Review Division 2, SASAC	Full day (interview/ observations)				5/11 6/11
Officer, Performance Review Division 2, SASAC	Full day (interview/ observations)				5/11 6/11
Officer, Performance Review Division 2, SASAC	Full day (interview/ observations)				5/11 6/11
Officer, Performance Review Division 2, SASAC	Full day (interview/ observations)				5/11 6/11
Deputy Director, Internal Performance Bureau., SASAC	20 30		6/08	5/09	
Head of, Supervision Bureau, SASAC	90			1/11	
Deputy Chairman, Supervision Bureau, SASAC	30			1/11	
Secretary, General Office, SASAC	20				5/11
Total number of interviews		3	3	7	9

Interviews in the field of Thai SOEs

Interviewee	Duration (min.)	2009	2010	2011	2012
			Date		
Senior Executive and Fiscal Advisor, Ministry of Finance	120		12/10		
Deputy Director, SEPO	60		10/12		
Head of SOE Performance Evaluation Division, SOE Performance Management and Evaluation Bureau, SEPO	85		14/09		
	40 85 35		11/10	02/08	12/05
Fiscal Analyst (Professional Level), SOE Performance Management and Evaluation Bureau, SEPO	60		11/10		
Analyst, SOE Performance Management and Evaluation Bureau, SEPO	30			22/08	
Fiscal Analyst (Professional Level), Policy and Planning Bureau, SEPO	60			16/09	
Account Officer, State Securities Management Bureau, SEPO	30			16/09	
Vice Director, TRIS Co., Ltd.	60			17/01	
Chairman, SST	60		07/10		
Ex-Country Manager, SST	45		29/12		
Ex-Associate Consultant, SST	40			27/12	
Head and Analyst, Business Planning Department, Corporate Business Unit, PTT Ltd	120		29/09		
Vice President, Business Planning Department, Oil Business Unit, PTT Ltd	80		19/11		
Analyst, Business Planning Department, Oil Business Unit, PTT Ltd	60		19/11		
Senior Analyst, Research and Development Department, Corporate Business Unit, PTT Ltd	90		24/12		
Planner, Strategic Planning Department, PTT Ltd	45		01/12		
Total number of interviews		0	12	6	1

The 'performativity thesis' and its critics: Towards a relational ontology of management accounting

ED VOSSELMAN[a,b]

[a]Institute for Management Research, Radboud University Nijmegen, The Netherlands;
[b]Zijlstra Center for Public Control and Governance, Vrije Universiteit Amsterdam, Amsterdam, The Netherlands

This paper explores accounting's mediating role in bringing theoretical statements from economics into life. It addresses the so-called performativity thesis that claims that economic theory does not just observe and explain a reality, but rather shapes, formats and performs reality. Accounting mediates in that process by creating cognitive boundaries that embed societal practices in economic theory. However, the performativity thesis is not without criticisms. Its main criticisms concern a lack of proof of the thesis; an overestimation of the power of economics to extend beyond the virtual; and a lack of a critical stance. In order to bring more nuance in the discussion on the performativity thesis the paper reflects on evidence from the field of accounting. The review of accounting studies reveals how accounting, to different degrees, is implicated in strategic and operational activities in markets and organisations and how it is a performative mechanism of economisation. Moreover, in order to accentuate the 'good' in society and to challenge the 'bad', the paper suggests a further development of (critical) management accounting research into the performativity of both economics and other social theories. A relational ontology of management accounting that is *in politics* and that is sensitive to 'unlocalisable' virtual powers of social-historical formations of management accounting may be developed.

Keywords: calculative agencies; calculability; performativity; virtualism

Introduction

In a functionalist view accounting is passive and has no intrinsic societal consequences. It is a device for decision-making and control and as such it is in the hands of individual human actors. The human decision-maker is active and up front; accounting is passive and comes in later as a neutral tool. This passive role of accounting is consistent with the dominant conceptual metaphor that describes the essence of accounting: accounting is an instrument (Amernic and Craig 2009).

In a passive mode, accounting is a form of re-presentation. It turns absence into presence. It re-presents specific objects or flows as they are spacio-temporally situated in the real world. The act of re-presentation, however, is not without problems. Different objects and flows have different re-presentational performances, and the techniques of re-presentation differ in their capacity to re-present (Kalthoff 2005). Although as a technology accounting came in as a 'visible sign system before writing' (Ezzamel and Hoskin 2002, p. 35) reaching back to ancient Egypt (Ezzamel 2012), the act of accounting may be seen as a practice of economic writing (Krämer 1996, Kalthoff 2005). Economic writing has both a memory and a transformation function (Luhmann 1998). From a functionalist view, the accounting records that result from this practice reflect what is happening in the real world and serve as memory anchors. The objects and flows in the real world are considered to be independent of their re-presentation through the practice of writing (accounting). Thus, reality is external to and prior to its re-presentation by accounting. Once accounting has anchored the objects and flows, the numbers and figures can be traced back to the real situation without problems. The accounting records render the objects and flows visible; they reflect the 'truth'. By representing objects and flows the accounting records not only make it possible to forget, but also enable transportation. The records thus transcend local contexts. They enable a travel through time and space (Robson 1992). Accounting thus mirrors, stores and transports.

The functionalist view of accounting and the centralisation of the human actor are consistent with economics. (Institutional) economics puts human actors up front. For example, in a principal-agency theory (Ross 1973, Stiglitz 1974, Jensen and Meckling 1976, Jensen 1983) the principal and the agent are naturalised ontologies. Out of their self-interests agents intend to behave rationally and sometimes opportunistically. They transact in markets. Seen from a principal-agency theory perspective accounting is part of a solution to the agency problem as it is related to a divergence of interests between a principal and an agent; both the principal and the agent are prior to accounting. An (institutional) economics perspective thus conceptualises accounting as 're-presentation of something' (Rheinberger 1992, 1997) and 're-presentation for someone' (Rheinberger 1992, 1997); accounting is considered to provide a reflection of reality 'out there' that is prior to accounting. Accounting is a monitoring device to the principal that mitigates information asymmetry. Within an economic perspective the dominant metaphor of accounting is indeed that of an instrument (Amernic and Craig 2009).

The functionalist view of the practice of economic writing may be criticised because of its lack of attention for the possibilities of writing (and thus of accounting) to break through spacio-temporal limitations of objects and flows and to create. That is, accounting may not only reflect, store and transport, but may also perform. Accounting may be a practice of *operative* writing. In practices of operative writing (Krämer 1996) accounting represents objects and flows, but at the same time permits operations with these objects and flows. Accounting tools, then, are symbolic machines and the objects and flows are indifferent towards the symbols used in these machines. Accounting numbers do not simply re-present an object or a flow, but present an operation which is performed on them and of which the numbers are the result (see also Kalthoff 2005, p. 83). That is, accounting is performative. Kalthoff (2005) demonstrates this performative function of accounting by exploring calculation in banking practices of risk management. The practices are embedded in calculation categories, algorithms, rules, procedures and formats. Accounting technologies re-present objects, but at the same time permit operations with these objects, thus transforming and modifying them, for instance, into a profit and loss statement or, in case of the granting of loans to corporations, into a report on the basis of which a decision regarding the acceptance or rejection of a loan is taken (Kalthoff 2005).

In a practice of operative writing the accounting 'machine' manufactures a re-presentation of spacio-temporal objects and flows. Reality, then, does not exist independently of the accounting practice. Rather, reality is internal to its re-presentation; it is shaped through the practice of its re-presentation. This practice is not just a 're-presentation of something' or a 're-presentation for something', but it is a 're-presentation as creation' (see Rheinberger 1992, 1997, for an elaboration on this distinction). By manufacturing a re-presentation, accounting is performative. It does not serve to find a 'truth'. Against this background it is in need of internal plausibility; the practice of accounting has to be 'correct'. To that end, the rules of the game have to be respected and followed.

From an actor-network theory (Callon 1986, 1999, Latour 1992, 1999, 2005, Law 1999, Callon *et al.* 2011) perspective accounting is conceptualised as an actant.[1] Not only does the performativity of accounting refer to its re-presentation-as-creation, but it also entails mediation between actants in a network. In interaction with other actants it shapes who and what counts. As an actant, the 'presence' manufactured by accounting is symmetrical to human actors; it has material agency.[2] That is, accounting is active and has an impact in a collective of humans and other-than-humans. It is made to act by others in a relational network; that is, it performs. It helps changing the actions and actants in the network. In terms of Miller and O'Leary (2007), it is a 'mediating instrument'. This actor-network theory perspective thus differs fundamentally from an economics perspective. Rather than to centralise the human subject, the main purpose of actor-network theory approaches is to *de*centralise it. The core of human agency is perceived as a technically framed and performed interaction (Latour 1999).

Although in extant 'alternative accounting research' (Baxter and Chua 2003) the Latourian version of actor-network theory has been dominant (for a recent review, see Justesen and Mouritsen 2011), a focus on the performative impact of accounting on society also calls for a more in depth investigation into 'Callonistics' (Fine 2003). Essentially, 'Callonistics' refer to the so-called performativity thesis (Santos and Rodrigues 2009). The 'performativity thesis' states that rather than explaining and/or predicting a reality that is prior to and independent of economic theory, economics is succeeding in the materialisation of its ideas and of the behavioural assumptions that are at the heart of the theory. Economics may produce Homo Economicus. Accounting is considered to be a mediator in the materialisation of Homo Economicus and its interaction patterns in markets or in market-like spaces.

However, the performativity thesis is not without critics. For instance, Santos and Rodrigues (2009) claim that there is no strong evidence that economics produce Homo Economicus. Fine (2003, 2005) criticises the lack of an underlying theoretical framework that accounts for the mechanisms that are at play in constituting markets and Homo Economicus. Moreover, although agreeing with the idea that economics has a societal impact, Miller (2002, 2005) questions if the theoretical statements in economics have the power to get *materialised* in the real world. Finally, be it from different angles, both Whittle and Spicer (2008) and Roberts (2012) challenge actor-network theory (including Callonistics) for its lack of critical commitment.

This paper addresses the societal impact of accounting and accountability as these are related to the performativity thesis and related criticisms. In order to bring further clarity to the performativity thesis, the paper examines evidence from the field of accounting. The main question is whether and how extant accounting research brings more nuances in the discussion on the performativity of economics. Moreover, in order to accentuate the 'good' in society and to challenge the 'bad', the paper suggests a further development of (critical) management accounting research into the performativity of economics by focusing on the politics in management accounting as it is implicated in concrete-contingent socio-material networks.

The remainder of the paper is organised as follows. First, Callonistics is discussed in more detail, followed by a discussion of its main criticisms. The paper then reviews a number of micro-studies that (explicitly or implicitly) address the performativity of economics and accounting. The mini-review reveals how accounting indeed mediates in bringing notions of instrumental rationality and accountability as incorporated in economics into life, both in (financial) markets and in organisations. The paper thus provides support for the performativity thesis and reveals some of the micro-mechanisms that are at play in performing economics. In order to further improve the societal contribution of management accounting research based on Callonistics and on actor-network theory in general, a development towards a relational ontology that is *in* politics is then advocated. It is claimed that such an ambition has the potential to add a critical flavour to actor-network theory inspired management accounting research.[3]

Callonistics

Socio-technical agencements

To Callon, economic practices are not treated as an ontologically independent sphere of the social world. There are reciprocal relationships between societal practices and economic theory. Economic theory re-presents societal practices and intervenes in them. To a large extent, economic theory frames and formats societal practices. In line with this way of thinking, what is at stake with accounting is *not* a nexus between a reality-out-there and the image that shows through an accounting 'mirror', but a nexus between accounting and theoretical statements, particularly statements from economics. As a form, or as an other-than-human, an actant, accounting mediates in bringing economic theory into life (Callon 1998a). Re-presentation and intervention are entangled, they cannot be separated; accounting represents and intervenes at the same time. In the strongest sense, it helps to create and distribute Homo Economicus.

Rather than being a priori naturalised ontologies, economic agents result from the framing and distribution of calculative agencies. A calculative agency is 'a self-interested agency obsessed by the calculation-optimization of his or her own interest' (Callon 2007a, p. 346). Such a calculative agency is not simply a result of the diffusion of autonomous values, norms and conceptions of the world that serve as intermediaries through which abstract ideas or theories act upon economic agents. Rather, such an agency is the result of the diffusion of socio-technical institutions. Therefore, to account for the framing and distribution of calculative agencies it is necessary to substitute socio-technical institutions for individuals whose brains are embedded in values and norms guiding them. The socio-technical institutions are called 'agencements'[4] because there is an entanglement of human actors and materialities (Callon 2005). An 'agencement' is an assemblage that puts Homo Economicus at the centre. It is a hybrid collective that comprises humans as well as other-than-humans such as material and technical devices and texts, and that is distributed through a 'performation' of economics, which is the impact of economics outside the theory itself (Callon 1998b, p. 23). Such hybrid collectives provide actants with a capacity to act and to give meaning to actions.

Thus, the performativity of economics essentially is a political process through which 'Homo Economicus' is framed and equipped with 'prostheses which help him in his calculations and which are, for the most part, produced by economics' (Callon 1998b, p. 51). Homo Economicus is a calculative agency that can only perform under specific circumstances and that has to be equipped with certain material: economic theories and models, paper, information technology, computers, calculation methods, statistical programmes and more:

> The appearance and spread of this new species (i.e. homo economicus) can be understood only if we agree that agency, and especially what we call human agency, does not depend only on evolving and adaptive processes taking place gradually over long periods (as they are studied, for instance, by paleoanthropology). Human agency is a distributed agency that goes beyond the somatic resources

of the individual; it is the variable outcome of a complex process of engineering. This agency can be described more precisely as a socio-technical agencement consisting of material elements, texts and discourses, competencies and embodied skills, routines and so on. Human STAs are variable, evolving and, above all, increasingly dependent on human activity itself. (Callon 2007a, p. 142)

Callon (2007b) identifies this assemblage, this artefact as Homo Economicus *version 2.0*. Similar to his predecessor, Homo Economicus version 1.0, version 2.0 is linked up with scientific management as developed by Frederick Winslaw Taylor. Having the identity of an agent Homo Economicus remains to be a 'puppet on a string'. Yet, compared to his predecessor, as a consequence of available prostheses he has more strategic space available.

The 'performativity thesis' endorses an understanding of human action that is largely dependent upon the structural configurations of the socio-technical institutions and the networks in which human action takes place (Santos and Rodrigues 2009). The implication of this is that individual action discloses the nature of socio-technical institutions or 'agencements' rather than robust and naturalised behavioural traits of human actors (Callon 1998a, 2005, 2007b). Accounting mediates in the creation and operation of such agencements, thus contributing to the performativity of economics. It thus assists in successfully enacting the patterns of behaviour postulated by economics. In other words, accounting helps to bridge the gulf between theoretical statements regarding behavioural patterns of individuals and real behaviour. It mediates in distributing calculative agencies rather than serving as a tool for a naturalised, rationally acting individual. Accounting mediates in shaping who and what counts. It is part of reality, part of the network. It is an actant rather than an instrument in the hands of human beings that possess 'natural' traits such as individual rationality and opportunism. Thus, rather than being solid characteristics of human beings, rationality and instrumentality are shaped by mediating socio-materialities (Orlikowski 2007). In mediating in the construction of agencies, of spaces in which they meet and of the boundaries between things and people, accounting is symmetrical to human actors. The question is not whether accounting reflects economic reality (a truth) or not, but whether accounting is able to perform and enact a reality corresponding to what it says.

As Callon (2005) states, the anthropology that characterises any individual as an autonomous subject, capable of rational choices, and responsible for his or her behaviour, is becoming pervasive. To a large extent, it is through accounting that economics occupy a key position in giving actors a capacity to act.

The spaces between agencies

The calculative agencies are not completely isolated from each other. Economic theory also produces the spaces within which encounters between the agencies take place. These spaces may be markets (Callon 1998a) or organisations; in case of a 'performation' of principal-agency theory the latter will be a 'nexus-of-contracts' – organisation (Jensen and Meckling 1976, Jensen 1983) or a market-bureaucracy. Similar to a market, a nexus-of-contracts organisation is a space for pursuing private interests. From organisational economics reasoning, under certain circumstances, compared to the space of the market the nexus-of-contracts organisation may economise on transaction costs. As a consequence, individuals can reach their goals more efficiently. In order to reach such efficiency and to prevent opportunistic behaviour from occurring at the level of the organisation a regulatory institution is needed. The institution codifies a number of critical 'rules of the game' (Jensen 1983, p. 326) by allocating decision rights and specifying performance evaluation- and reward systems. The main purpose of these institutions is to safeguard against potential opportunistic behaviour. That is, the institutions facilitate cooperative interactions between organisational participants by preventing an opportunism-prone minority to pursue its self-interest 'with guile' at the expense of the collective (cf. Williamson 1975, 1979).

In order to enable Homini Oeconomici to meet, boundaries between people and things have to be created. In order to enable circulation 'goods' have to be transformed into 'things' that go from hand to hand. Such circulation is both production and qualification. The circulation qualifies the goods so that they enter the world of the users. Callon (2005) calls this 'singularisation'. However, market circulation or circulation in a market-bureaucracy also implies that this attachment induces a transaction after which the agencies involved are quits (Callon 2005). Transactions are necessarily reduced interactions. They are the result of framing activity that produces powerful mechanisms of exclusion. Many elements have to be excluded from the market or nexus-of-contracts (market-bureaucracy) frame, at least for the moment of the transaction. The transaction is enabled through the (at least temporary) exclusion of other factors that cannot be included within the calculation. Calculation and the circulation of goods in markets and in market bureaucracies require accounting tools and practices. Accounting tools and practices provide prostheses for human beings to become calculative.

Although the core of calculative behaviour thus seems to be the result of a process of disentanglement (Miller 2002, 2005), Callon insists that the spaces in which agencies meet are characterised by both disentanglement and entanglement. As Callon states, the market produces 'a stage on which the process of entanglement-disentanglement can be managed by the agents engaged in the transaction' (2005, p. 7). He exemplifies this as follows (Callon 2005): if person A buys a car from person B they have to get rid of issues such as global warming, traffic congestion and problems of road safety (disentanglement). They then can focus on 'the qualification of the car' that A is '(maybe) going to buy and on the process of that car's particular attachment to the world of the buyer (entanglement)' (Callon 2005, p. 7):

> Concrete markets have the singularity of teeming with multifarious actors and entities and at the same time of constantly being framed, shaped, rarefied in a sense, to organize market transactions and ensure their aggregation. (Callon 2005, p. 8)

Moreover, Callon notes that success is bound to be a temporary achievement. Therefore, the agencies and their behavioural patterns eventually have to cope with overflows, i.e. reactive responses to reality as it is the result of 'performation' of economic theory. Future research not only has to account for the mechanisms through which calculative agencies, the spaces in which they operate and the boundaries between things and people are framed, but it will also have to account for the way overflows are coped with. Rather than viewing overflows as 'accidental' as economists do, Callon defines an overflow as a phenomenon that is not unexpected but rather a norm and unavoidable (see also Christensen and Skærbæk 2007, p. 106). While framing produces order, overflow produces disorder and threatens the framing attempts. Framing triggers matters of concern that may evolve into political issues. The answers to these issues may in turn have an impact on the organisation of economic activity (Callon 2007b, p. 139).

The performativity thesis and its critics

Callonistics have met criticisms. Major criticisms come from different angles. They particularly concern a lack of proof of the performativity thesis; an overestimation of the power of economics to extend beyond the virtual and to materialise; and a lack of a critical stance. This section deals with these criticisms in more detail.

A lack of proof

First, critics claim that there is a lack of proof of the performativity thesis. Santos and Rodrigues (2009) claim that there is no strong evidence that economics produce Homo Economicus. 'In particular, and this is the strongest sense in which economics can be said to be performative, economists can produce, through their engineering efforts, the "calculative agencies" postulated by neoclassical economic theory, that is, homo economicus' (Santos and Rodrigues 2009, p. 990). However, Santos and Rodrigues mistakenly substitute economi*sts* for economi*cs*. Callon does not claim that economists are performative, but that economics is. In other words, the performativity thesis is not on deliberate actions of 'centralised' economists that aim to shape society. Rather, it is about theoretical statements being actants that are made to act by many other actants (amongst them accounting) in concrete-contingent socio-material networks. The performativity of economics is a network effect, not the result of deliberate actions of human beings (i.e. economists) that are outside the network. Santos and Rodrigues continue to state that they can support the *weaker* claim that economics, rather than being performative in the shaping of calculative agencies, is performative in market building, thereby contributing to the commodification of social life. In their view, the emergence of calculative agencies might be simply the result of this commodification of social life, associated with the processes of market expansion. 'In this more lenient notion, economics is performative whenever it is used in market building' (Santos and Rodrigues 2009, p. 990). Again, this points to a misconception. In Callonistics, the main point is not 'economic engineering' or 'social engineering' (Santos and Rodrigues 2009); it is 'heterogeneous engineering'. Economics is *not used* by others to help building markets, is *not an instrument*, but *is* an *actant* in socio-material networks, involved in the shaping of markets and its inhabitants.

Similarly, Fine (2003, 2005) points to a lack of proof. Fine (2003, 2005) claims that the performativity thesis lacks a theoretical framework that discerns the mechanisms at play, both at the micro-level of individuals' behaviour and at the macro-level of the logic of the market economy and its main institutions. Without such a framework, Fine argues, 'the idea that economists constitute markets is simply a tautology or an assertion of causation without supporting argument' (2003, p. 480). But again, it is not the economists' intentional activity to constitute markets that is at the heart of the performativity thesis, but the capacity of theoretical statements situated in concrete-contingent socio-material networks to perform markets. Such power can be explained by researchers who enact such networks, as will be demonstrated in the review section.

Virtualism

Second, it is claimed that markets are not materialised on the basis of theoretical statements, but that markets only exist in a virtual world (Miller 2002, 2005), that, at a macro-level, contradicts with a real world. Thus, the performativity thesis gives too many credentials to economics. To Miller, economic theory does not succeed in influencing the phenomena in reality. Economic theory is not part of a network but is separate from it. Miller separates re-presentation from real practising, from intervention. He sees a *macro*-contradiction between a real world and a virtual world. To him, rather than a network effect, the performativity of economic theory is directly related to the power of its discourse:

> ... .that we live in a period of history where we can see the increasing ability of certain powerful discourses, including that of economists, to realize themselves as models in the world through their increasing control over that world. That is their increasing ability to be performative. (Miller 2005, p. 4)

Miller compares economists with priests. He observes, for instance, that both theorists and practitioners such as management consultants and accountants have spread the gospel of shareholder
value as a next phase of successful business:

> And behind the management consultants lay the stern priesthood of the IMF laying out the terms of
> pure capitalism to which the country must conform or be punished for its heresy. (Miller 2005, p. 4)

To Miller, the performativity of economics lies in its success to virtually control the world and not
in its ability to realise the model of the market. The market remains to be an ideological model and
does not become an empirical phenomenon, a real object. Rather than a description of practice the
market is a moral and ideological system whose intention is to create the normative conditions for
exchange. Miller claims that Callon is making the same mistake as economists do: taking a
re-presentation of economic life for its practice. To Miller, science has to account for the
extraordinary power of this act of re-presentation to reconstitute the world (macro) in its
image. It has to account for *virtualism* (Miller 1998, 2003). It has to position the virtual world
against the real world in which transactions always take place in a particular moral framework.
In the real world, everyone wishes to feel that their economic transactions are also expressions
of their larger sense of 'being'. To this end, transactions are ritualised as formal exchanges that
draw attention to this ideal congruence of being and practice.

   Where Callon thinks that the performativity of economics is reflected in the construction of
real agencies, of spaces in which these agencies meet and of the boundaries between things
and people, Miller claims that the ability of performative action to realise the model of the
market is still comparatively rare. He states that Callon's emphasis on calculation and disentanglement results in an attempt to rescue the conventional notions of the market, but for no particularly good reason. Miller's anthropological argument is that the market is an ideological model
rather than an empirical phenomenon. He, moreover, criticises the notion of 'calculativeness'
as it is incorporated in the socio-technical agencements. He claims that in reality decision-
making is not (and cannot be) what economics states. In reality, decision-making is not a
matter of disentanglement, but is a totalising affair. In Miller's view the way to 'profitability'
is not through disentanglement, but through further entanglement. The better an organisation
acknowledges the rich mixture of factors that account for profitability (in whatever sense) the
more it is likely to be successful. The question then becomes whether the business organisation
could ever be entangled enough to reflect the totalising acts of the stakeholders. The power of
economists and accountants to create a virtual world then becomes problematic. It might create
distortions; the simplifications of the disentanglements that are expected of market transactions
might decrease efficiency. Profitability and success is more than specified performance and
contra-performance. An effective assessment of value is the true basis for 'profitability', for
success of the organisation. Exchange is always embedded in values. This does not make the
exchange less calculative, but it does imply that the calculations become more and more
complex. Creating a market is pretending that calculation is relatively simple; the calculation
of value is reduced to a quantitative instrument. But is this simplification of calculation real practice? By giving a positive answer to this question, in the eyes of Miller, Callon becomes a quin-
tessential economist who attempts 'to reduce value to price by seeing value as that which
overflows the frame, instead of seeing it as that which constitutes ordinary transactions'
(Miller 2002, p. 231):

> A possible analogy is to think of Callon as presenting to us the bare bones of transactions. He hacks off
> the flesh to show the relative solidity of the market principles inside. But skeletons are not agents, they
> are the dead, remnants left when that which gives agency is stripped away. We can theorize such bare

bones academically but that is not how economies or economic agents operate. As actors they are always burdened by flesh and life and relationships. Instead, as argued in *Virtualism*, we can find in practice an increasing tendency for market ideology to gain the power to remove all other externalities as distortions. This is an actual and growing phenomenon in the world that we really ought to be paying attention to instead of false grails of inherent market logics. (Miller 2002, p. 232)

To Miller it is the difference between true and false conceptions of reality and human nature, the difference between reality and its re-presentation that needs studying.

Miller's virtualism considerably differs from Callon's views. Callon claims that:

the capitalist form of the economy *assumes* an organization of markets in which there are both calculative agencies (equipped and formatted to calculate profits, maximize shareholder value, reduce production or distribution costs) and the controlled rarefaction of relations and encounters between agencies, obtained primarily by singularizing goods and setting up systems of circulation of agencies and goods. (2005, p. 15)

There is no contradiction between worldviews and values of economists on the one hand and reality on the other hand, there is just a multiplication of differences, gaps, displacements and translations. In other words, there are asymmetries and relations of domination that they sustain. These relations are produced by socio-technical institutions (agencements) that produce 'as many attachments as detachments, as many entanglements as disentanglements' (Callon 2005, p. 16).

To Callon, there is no real truth up front which can then be put against the 'virtual world' of economics. Economics and accounting both are engaged in the dynamics of power struggles. Science (economics and other (social) sciences) are not outside reality, but are part of it. They are all *in* the network. The ultimate aim of the social sciences is to engage in 'different anthropological projects struggling to impose their conceptions and the implementation thereof' (Callon 2005, p. 11). Callon agrees with Miller that the social sciences can help to transform the world. But he disagrees about the strategy with which to achieve that. He does not want to search for the truth while at the same time combatting the illusions that mask the strength of the powerful, but aims to participate, along with certain actants who are in a position to produce small differences. He aims to show that humans act in multiple and uncertain forms (Callon *et al.* 2011) and that other 'worlds' are possible. The main differences between virtualism and 'Callonistics' are summarised in Table 1.

A lack of a critical stance

Third, Callonistics is criticised for its lack of a critical stance. Drawing on Fournier and Grey (2000) as a sensitising framework, Whittle and Spicer (2008) claim that actor-network theory

Table 1. Virtualism against Callonistics.

Virtualism	Callonistics
There is '*ex ante*' reality 'out there' (a reality prior to theory)	Reality is in the process of knowledge creation
Scientific activity aims at representing the 'truth' and at combatting illusions (for instance those created by economics)	Scientific activity intervenes in transforming the world
Theory is outside reality	Theory is inside networks, it participates
Economic theory creates a virtual world that is linked to reality through beliefs, values and norms	Economic theory is brought into life through performative mechanisms and practices

has a commitment to realism (it 'relies on the assumption that social life can be observed objectively by scientists using esoteric concepts' (p. 9)), positivism (social life 'is understood through a process of scientific verification' (p. 9)) and conservatism (the knowledge is 'explained without a reflexive examination of the philosophical and political assumptions that accompany the researcher' (p. 9). Although this makes the actor-network theory valuable for making detailed descriptions of accounting and organising, according to Whittle and Spicer (2008) it is poorly equipped to address the issues that make up critical studies in accounting and management, particularly the issues of instrumental reasoning and asymmetrical relations of power, reinforced by the appearance of 'neutral' research (Alvesson and Willmott 1992, 1996, Adler 2002). Callonistics might be accused of just describing how accounting is engaged in situational power struggles, how it mediates between economic theory and practice without aiming to judge whether this is good or bad, or true or false. It accepts the economic man and does not a priori reject this creature. To some, Callonistics is, therefore, a poor resource to draw upon for 'ANT has tended to walk and talk more and more like the stick figure *Homo Economicus* from neoclassical economics for some time now' (Mirowski and Nik-Khah 2007, p. 190). However, I agree with Roberts and Wilson (2012) that in the notion of the 'performativity' of economics there is perhaps an attempt visible to remedy the paranoia of the ego as it is incorporated in the construct of Homo Economicus.

Moreover, Whittle and Spicer's modernists mode of critique may be questioned in a more fundamental way (Alcadipani and Hassard 2010). In recent Callonistics (and in actor-network theory approaches in general) reality is internal to the process of knowing or internal to its re-presentation; it is re-presentation as creation. This makes the knowledge production a *political* process. To Latour (2005), political relevance is related to the grasping of complexities and multiplicities by registering as many associations as possible in order to find possibilities to change a state of affair. There is always a concern for the possibility that things could be 'otherwise' and that reality is not a 'destiny' (Law 2007). Moreover, in the research practice the researcher does *not* describe but *enacts*; he or she re-presents as creation. Not only does this challenge the positivistic character of Callonistics, but in the notion of 'enactment' it is also expressed that the narratives are 'versions of the better and the worse, the right and the wrong, the appealing and the unappealing' (Law 2007, p. 15). Accounts are produced through politics; 'the good is being done as well as the epistemological and the ontological' (Law 2007, p. 15). In other words, accounts are not just political, but *ontologically political* (Mol 1999, 2002, Law 2004, Law and Urry 2004). The real is implicated in the political and vice versa. Things might always be otherwise (Law 2008). One result of thinking in ontologically political terms is that 'every time we make reality claims in science we are helping to make some social reality more or less real' (Law and Urry 2004, p. 396, see also Alcadipani and Hassard 2010).

The notion of ontological politics challenges both a 'naturalisation' of objects and the way politics is usually understood. Rather than 'naturalisations' both the researcher himself and his enactments are consequences of research practices. As for politics, this is traditionally understood as something that gives voice by and in itself (Latour 2007). However, rather than being a specific domain of life or an essence itself, politics turns around the re-presentation of the assembling of multiple realities within many different practices and arenas. Every account is a political account, and all kinds of 'others' are allowed to object to the accounts (Latour 2005). Rather than focusing on the stabilisation of relations actor-network theory approaches thus focus on *controversies* surrounding things that are in the making.

Whereas Whittle and Spicer (2008) questionably claim that actor-network theory approaches suffer from realism, positivism and conservatism, Roberts (2012) claims that Callonistics pay no attention to underlying virtual powers of the socio-historical formation of capitalism and related neoliberalism. In his critique, Roberts (2012) claims that actor-network theory tends to over-identify with how concrete-contingent actor networks are enrolled at the expense of analysing how such networks are also internally mediated through underlying or virtual *historically emerging and developing* capacities, potentials and powers, particularly that of capitalism. A critique of Callonistics, therefore, is that it explores the translations of actor networks in time—spaces, without relating them to different 'planes of immanence' (Deleuze and Guattari 1994), that is to 'those underlying potentials, powers and capacities of a historical system that fold over and refract into one another in a rich ontological "absolute horizon"' (Roberts 2012, p. 38). To a large extent these systems cannot be localised, they are 'unlocalizable' (Roberts 2012, p. 37). For example, socio-technical arrangements or agencements may be seen as *immanent moments* in the drive to enhance the productivity and efficiency of the workforce that is immanent moments of capitalism. However, actor-network theory-based approaches reject immanence and tend to focus on 'planes of organisation' (Deleuze and Guattari 1994); they enact a specific reality and describe what (non-visible) principles organise it. As a consequence, the claims made by Callonistics may be restricted to thick descriptions of hitherto hidden principles of concrete–contingent relations, to narratives and to stories. Moreover, by rejecting the notion that concrete-contingent networks are *in immanence* the research lacks a basis to make critical evaluations.

Although Roberts (2012) indeed may be pointing to a flaw in actor-network theory-based research, it is also true that a number of researchers who are inspired by Callonistics or actor-network theory in a broad sense stress the importance of socio-historical formations as, for instance, neoliberalism (Miller 2008, Friedman 2010).

Evidence from the field of accounting

Extant accounting research offers anecdotal evidence for the performativity of economics. Without referring to either actor-network theory or to Callonistics, Miller's (1991) study into the mechanisms through which discounted cash flow (DCF) techniques were promoted in the UK in the 1960s offers an early example of accounting's mediating power in bringing neoclassical behavioural assumptions into life.

Some recent studies that address the issue are more directly related to Callonistics or actor-network theory. In the next section, a mini-review of relevant accounting studies is provided. The studies convincingly demonstrate how accounting is a performative mediator between economics and real-life practices. Accounting proves to be more than just a representational practice that creates a (distortive) virtual reality. Rather, the ontologically political accounts reveal how economic statements and accounting may go beyond the virtual, thereby challenging Daniel Millers 'virtualism'. Representation and intervention prove to be entangled. Be it to different degrees, in collective practices the performativity of economics is recognisable.

Accounting as a mediator in markets

Vollmer *et al.* (2009) reflect on the significance of Callon's concept of performativity in the Social Studies of Finance. It was brought there by Callon (1998b), and subsequently specified by MacKenzie (2006), MacKenzie and Millo (2003) and Didier (2007), addressing 'the blurred distinction between re-presentational and interventionist uses of economic models by financial practitioners' (Vollmer *et al.* 2009, p. 622). Financial markets are seen as socio-technical agencements. Calculability and value assignment are intrinsic to the working of such markets. Numbers are assigned to entities (be they financial securities or consumable goods), which endows these entities with relative stability and enables their circulation throughout society.

Against the background of the financial crisis, Roberts and Jones (2009) explore how self-interested behaviour and, thus, the cognitive construct of Homo Economicus is constructed through calculation in financial markets. In particular, they explore the mediating role of accounting in creating and sustaining market relationships, both feeding the illusion of rational individual behaviour and the fear and panic as the market fell. They observe that the work of framing/disentanglement was massive. They conclude that 'accounting in its capacity to recognize or disentangle profits within a stream of transactions has provided the motive, means and realized gains (and now losses) for all concerned' (Roberts and Jones 2009, p. 865). However, it proved that interests and risks were inadequately assigned to entities; interests lie between rather than within individuals or institutions. In Callon's language they conclude that 'accounting is key in reproducing a sense of self as "isolated – too isolated – and autonomous – too autonomous", such that it is largely blind and/or indifferent to the unintended "side effects" of the calculated' (Roberts and Jones 2009, p. 865). Interests in the sense of a complex web of inter-institutional networks and relationships ('interests') were rendered largely invisible by accounting. Here, rather than turning absence into presence accounting turned presence into absence; it obscured all kinds of moral hazard in the network of relationships:

> So the tension that becomes visible here is between inter-dependencies (inter-ests) that were systemic and the calculations of individual and institutional 'self' interest that were seemingly indifferent to these. The real hazard, however, was not just the lack of care exercised in the borrowing, lending, tranching, rating, leveraging, insuring and buying of these 'pass through' products. It was also that, in reality, they turned out to be anything but 'pass through' since the unanticipated consequences of this carelessness then revisited agents at every point in the networks. The error of 'self' interest lies in the way in which it imagines the self as separate and separable from others. Its calculation conceives of others only in instrumental terms, and so it remains blind or simply indifferent to the consequences of its conduct for others. (Roberts and Jones 2009, p. 866)

Accounting as a mediator in organisations

Calculation is a cognitive operation that requires commodification and standardisation. As calculability is increasingly visible in modern (public) organisations that develop into the direction of market bureaucracies (e.g. in health care, universities and housing corporations), questions about the performativity and economics are perpetuated. Apart from attention to the performativity of accounting in markets, this calls for attention in the scientific accounting discipline for framing and overflowing in organisations.

An illustration that accounting may go beyond the construction of a virtual organisation and may transform day-to-day organisational practices (and, thus, may be *in* and *not outside* reality) is provided by Keevers et al. (2012). They provide an account of how so-called Results-Based Accountability (RBA), as a mandated exogenous change imposed by funding agencies, became implicated in transforming the everyday social justice practices in locally based community organisations. Related to dominant managerial discourses (fuelled by economics) in the public sector RBA is an instrument to govern and manage service provision across the purchaser–provider divide. RBA is an 'intentional structure' (Ahrens and Chapman 2007) that seeks to ensure effective and efficient government spending and to strengthen transparency and accountability in the public sector. As such it is closely related to theoretical statements from economics. Keevers et al. (2012) show how the discursive-material practice of RBA interferes with the situated local community practices. Although the advocates (consultants) of RBA (Friedman 2005) take a re-presentationalist position by naturalising RBA as a mirror and by stressing that accountability and performance measurement methods should not interfere with the service (thus revealing the perspective that RBA is outside the network, that reality is prior to its representation), Keevers *et al.* (2012) convincingly show that RBA is not an instrument in the hands of a centre that measures and acts from a distance without interfering in the day-to-day practices. Rather, it interacts with and shapes the phenomena that become (Barad 2007) in the local communities. That is, RBA is performative. It iteratively reconfigures that which is included and excluded from mattering in day-to-day local practice. Incorporated in computerised case-management RBA becomes an actant; in the day-to-day practices the relationship between the professionals and the 'young people' (the target group of the local communities) changed in a relationship between the professional, the 'young person' and the computer as an actant:

> Thus meaning, matter and power relations are produced and constrained through the iterative intra-actions of the government department, its bureaucrats, the young person, their youth workers, managers, the outcomes-based accountability reporting database on the machine and the administrative system of Southern Youth. These structural relations of power are materialized, contested and (re)produced through a range of local practices including the numbers and notes recorded in the computer. (Keevers *et al.* 2012, p. 114)

In this case, the RBA system is far from a system that creates a virtual world by just mapping reality. Rather, it imposes another form of organising. It re-shapes locally based community organisations in the image of the funding agency. At the local, RBA practices establish a shift in focus from situationally embedded practices to practices in which a correspondence between desired results ('reality') on the one hand and its measurement and graphing on the other hand is reached. Thus, the analysis demonstrates that the introduction of RBA:

> anchored in a computerized case-management monitoring technology and entangled with funding tied to individualized outcome targets, is unravelling some of the daily organizing practices of social justice that create a sense of belonging, assist young people to have a sense of control over their lives and build hope for their futures. (Keevers *et al.* 2012, p. 116)

Keevers *et al.* (2012) implicitly illustrate the disentanglement of humans and things and the framing of rarified interaction. They highlight the invisibility of relational aspects of practice. By introducing RBA, the focus is shifted from interaction to transaction; the delivery of services is placed at the foreground, while reciprocity and a sense of belonging are backgrounded. The professional practices change from a totalising affair in which entanglement is the norm to a disembedded and disembodied affair that is controlled from a distance. By introducing RBA, a form of instrumental rationality is introduced that changes real professional practices. Thus, RBA does not simply create a virtual world. It does not only provide an incomplete and distortive re-presentation of the practices, but also at the same time it interferes with the practices. RBA is performative in the sense that it brings a re-presentationalist mode of accounting and accountability into life, thus obscuring the status of RBA 'as itself a form of culturally and historically situated activity, manifested in specific practices and associated artifacts' (Suchman 2007, p. 187, Keevers *et al.* 2012).

While Keevers *et al.* (2012) illustrate how forms of instrumental accountability frame day-to-day practices within a specific organisation, Christensen and Skærbæk's (2007) contribution is to demonstrate that the Callon-lens is apposite in order to better understand widely experienced trends in public sector change. They draw on the notions of framing and overflow to show why public sector accountability innovations are likely to produce an unexpected outcome. More specifically, they show how two changes in accountability techniques in separate jurisdictions (Denmark and New South Wales) were distracted in their implementation. The innovations (or reforms) were meant to provide information to the general public and were promoted by a central agency that explains and directs the implementation. However, the innovations were fragile accomplishments that produced a variety of outcomes that were not compatible with the original aim. It is found that the actor-networks of the accountability innovations developed in such a way that the central agencies became the primary audiences, thus resulting in:

> inordinate attention to issues about resource usage rather than issues of performance. That is, the spending agencies (who were also the accountability reporters) anticipated the needs of the public spending guardians (Wildavsky 1974) and the resultant accountability innovation was diverted from its publicly argued purpose. (Christensen and Skærbæk 2007, p. 104)

This research thus shows why public sector innovations may produce unexpected results. It is shown how in both jurisdictions the 'accountability frame' is constituted by a range of objects and materialities such as White Papers, Statutes, guidances and the accountability reports themselves. These materialisations produce cognitive boundaries 'within which interactions – the significance and content of which are self-evident to the protagonists – take place more or less independently of their surrounding context (Callon 1998a, p. 249).' The accountability frames thus produce the actions and the entities. The paper also shows how the framed interactions produce a number of overflows and how, as a consequence, the accountability frame is transformed in a resource frame as it was also present in the budgeting process. The research supports the argument that framing is a fragile and imperfect effect by pointing to a number of overflows of the innovative accountability frame. One important overflow is that the audience to which the accountability innovation is aimed is not the audience to which the reporting agency performs. A second important overflow is that the reporting agency does not correctly understand and accept the frame of the audience of the accountability reform. Third, reporting agencies produce broad rhetoric promising multitudinous effects to convince various decision-makers; and, fourth, the reporting agencies publish a variety of 'inside secrets' to gain trustworthiness for the report.

Apparently, as the reporting practices continue the overflows do not result in re-framing. This may be due to the fact that the overflows do not produce heated situations; the political debate therefore remains unresolved and the accountability innovations became part of resource allocation politics in which the more powerful institutions influencing decisions about budgets became the primary audience rather than the citizens or other stakeholders. The active network actors effectively manage the overflows and therefore the reporting process remains stable. Although 'the emergence of the accountability innovation can be seen as a means of stabilizing democracy', 'the operation of the reform provides a sense of reinforced managerial control' (Christensen and Skærbæk 2007, p. 126). As a consequence of the framing activity the central agencies became more indispensable.

The accountability innovations are illustrations of an advancement of New Public Management (Hood 1995), a movement that advanced the ideas of (institutional) economics through investments in accounting and performance management. As the study shows how institutions influencing economic decision-making manage to stay in control, keeping the frames of existing calculative agencies and their interaction patterns stable and preventing them from the inclusion of overflows resulting from democratic powers, the study may be seen as supportive of the performativity thesis. It shows how the interaction for the main part excludes 'citizenry'. It is an illustration of the performativity of New Public Management, a managerial discourse which is closely related to (institutional) economics thinking. Whether the innovations will be persistent across time and whether the framing effects are first an endeavour and later an achievement (as Callon claims) remains an open question. As long as the overflows remain 'cold' and do not provoke concerned groups to resist against the innovation practices the situation will not change.

While Christensen and Skærbæk (2007) address a situation in which the overflows hardly produce matters of concern with other stakeholders and thus do not significantly result in reframing, Skærbæk and Tryggestad (2010) investigate a situation in which overflows do produce such matters of concern. They address framing, overflowing and re-framing within a company that faced major changes in its environment and market: the Ferry Division (since 1995 known as Scandlines) of the Danish government-owned railway company DSB (Danish State Railways). Their work provides answers to questions regarding active roles of accounting in formulating an adaptive strategy. It is illustrated how accounting is not an instrument in the hands of humans to improve an efficient implementation of strategy, but is an actant that creates strategy and strategic actors. Skærbæk and Tryggestad (2010) show how a strategy not to liquidate the Ferry Division but to further develop it is mutually constituted by accounting devices. Strategy and strategic actors are constituted in a double movement of framing and overflowing. On the one hand, the accounting devices in the form of budgets and balance sheets create frames: taken for granted boundaries within which actors interact. They are thus formative in (re)creating strategy and strategic actors. On the other hand, as it is impossible for the accounting frames to internalise every interest in the strategic decision-making process, the accounting frames create overflows. For example, the responsibility accounting system created overflows because the interests of the captains of the ships were improperly included. The captains did not accept the responsibility that was inscribed in the responsibility accounting system because 'the role of captain called for the professional skills in commanding and navigating ships and the captains defined their role in those terms' (Skærbæk and Tryggestad 2010, p. 116) instead of in terms of an economic agent. Their (professional) interests and views were thus excluded from the responsibility accounting frame. This produced overflows in terms of emerging concerns and resistance. The captains were an 'emerging concerned group' (Callon 2007b) that mobilised maritime law to defend its professional position. Unexpectedly, the captains emerged as strategic actors that were outside the original strategic centre (the CEO). The overflows that they produced were 'hot' and the accounting experts had to deal with them, and had to reframe the accounting devices. In doing so, the accounting devices did not stay faithful to the CEO but also shaped identities of new strategic actors (i.e. captains). The new strategic actors learned about alternative accounting metrics and overtime learned about their possibilities and constraints.

Skærbæk and Tryggestad's study analyses the framing, overflowing and reframing of strategising within a public organisation. It illustrates how the framing through accounting devices triggers matters of concern. Through framing, overflowing and reframing accounting is performative in creating calculability and in bringing behavioural assumptions from economic theory into life. The paper convincingly shows how strategising is characterised by both disentanglement (through framing) and entanglement (through overflows), by both detachment and attachment. In doing so, it is supportive of Callon's argument that disentanglement and entanglement have to be taken together. However, the paper also illustrates a failure of shaping the captains into purely calculable men; they effectively resisted to become responsible and calculable 'agents' in the sense of a principal-agency theory. They succeeded, however, in becoming strategic actors by successfully acquiring calculative equipment and by learning about its affordances and constraints.

Whereas Callon positions the concept of performativity[5] in the process of economisation, Cushen studies performativity in the context of financialisation. As Caliskan and Callon (2010, p. 2) state, 'to speak of economization is to consider that economies, in all of their diversity, depend heavily upon divergent and often controversial analyses – both scholarly and lay – that define, explain and enact economic forms of life'. In the context of economisation the study of 'performativity' includes all the theoretical and practical, expert and lay knowledge, know-how and skills developed and mobilised in the process of designing and managing calculative agencies or socio-technical agencements (Callon 2007a, Caliskan and Callon 2009, 2010). An important characteristic of this concept of performativity is that it is a collective engagement extending beyond the academic world. Performativity relates to 'economics at large'; it is not simply the result of the work of confined economists who increasingly perform *in vitro* experiments, but also of 'economists in the wild' performing *in vivo* experiments, thus entailing a proliferation of issues and matters of concern resulting from framing operations (Callon 2007a). The role of economics at large is thus thoroughly political (Caliskan and Callon 2010, p. 20).

Cushen (2013) draws on a Callonistic notion of performativity in the context of *financialisation* rather than economisation. Similar to economisation, financialisation is seen as a performative phenomenon which elevates the role of accounting in organisations. Financialisation refers to the increasingly significant role of financial markets, financial actors and financial motives in daily life (Epstein 2005). Cushen (2013) documents how financialisation pervades everyday life within an Irish subsidiary of a publicly listed, high-technology, knowledge-intensive and multinational corporation.

Cushen (2013) explores how financialisation within this subsidiary is defined precisely by the stream of performative interventions the organisation at large takes to live the narrative of financialisation, to deliver returns and ultimately to be a model of shareholder value creation. In order to become performative the narratives are in need of socio-technical agencements comprising calculative equipment in the form of accounting. The paper particularly explores the relation between financialisation and accounting, thus taking a path also followed by Ezzamel *et al.* (2008). Cushen (2013) documents how accounting is an important performative mechanism in the process of financialisation. Budgets, ROI-calculations and benchmarking help constructing socio-technical agencements (calculative agents) that perform the optimistic narratives of financialisation. Thus, accounting helps in creating performative hegemony of the financialisation programme. The case study particularly identifies how budgets enable the structures and narratives which prioritise capital interests at the corporate governance level to be replicated inside the organisation. In the subsidiary:

> directors were required to continuously justify and reduce subsidiary expenditure, craft optimistic narratives and achieve a myriad of performative interventions to secure capital investment from Group. Line managers and employees were required to deliver ever changing performative interventions, cut costs and also craft optimistic narratives to secure capital investment and work on projects. (Cushen 2013, p. 328)

However, as Callon states 'the world conveyed by the statement is only realized after a long collective effort' (2007a, p. 313). The performative hegemony of financialisation is only realised through performative interventions, including 'continuous Group mandated changes to products and services, locally developed revenue generating initiatives, redundancies, outsourcing, centralization, re-organizations and on-going reduction of operational expenditure' (Cushen 2013, p. 328). Particularly, the paper documents how budgeting practices served as the mechanisms through which these performative interventions were transmitted and delivered by lower hierarchical levels. The paper also documents how accounting mechanisms such as budgeting created behavioural scripts; operational targets were deemed wholly achievable and lower managers had to be compliant and silent. There was a 'suppression of voice and a reluctance to highlight concerns' (Cushen 2013, p. 329). However, the performative hegemony of financialisation also had counterperformative consequences. In terms of Callon, the process of financialisation apparently produced overflows; potential problems were just ignored, thus causing a risk of failure in the product markets. This counter-performativity proved to simultaneously weaken and perpetuate the hegemony of financialisation.

Conclusions and discussion

The reviewed studies in accounting and accountability reveal that accounting not simply represents (for) something, is not simply a mirror, but is created as a re-presentation. Moreover, it re-presents and intervenes at the same time; representation and intervention are entangled. Accounting proves to be performative. All of the reviewed studies support this claim. The studies reveal how accounting creates calculability in strategic and operational practices in markets and organisations and how it may change who and what counts. How accounting creates and sustains market relationships and feeds the illusion of rational individual behaviour (Roberts and Jones 2009); how the creation (or framing) of performance indicators and measures may change professional practices through materialisations in the form of inscriptions and computers in the name of efficiency and accountability (Keevers et al. 2012); how the framing of accountability practices meant for a broader audience may make the present network actors, the funders, more indispensable (Christensen and Skærbæk 2007); how accounting produces calculability frames that shape strategies and that trigger matters of concern, thus giving shape to new strategic actors (Skærbæk and Tryggestad 2010); how accounting is a performative mechanism in a process of financialisation that impacted operational and managerial practices (Cushen 2013). In all cases, accounting is performative, not only in the sense that it creates re-presentations, but also in the sense that it mediates between actors and actants. It is not performative in the sense that it is in the hands of 'priests' that, through discursive strategies, try to convince others that the accounting-representations reflect a (desired) reality, but through discursive-material practices and materialisations it intervenes in the construction of actions and actors. As such, the reviewed studies are supportive of Callon's claim that the performativity of economics is not the simple result of discourses that reflect certain ideologies, values and beliefs, but of power struggles in concrete-contingent networks in which economics and accounting are engaged. Such struggles may indeed lead to a multiplication of translations. Insofar as ideologies, values and beliefs mattered it was through materialisations in the form of texts and inscriptions rather than to 'priesthood'.

As an actant in the network, accounting not only turns absence into presence, helps turning theoretical statements into existence, but it is also engaged in the transformation of already existing 'presence', as is shown by the studies of Keevers et al. (2012) and Skærbæk and Tryggestad (2010). Moreover, as shown by Roberts and Jones (2009) it may be active in turning presence into absence. Through a strong emphasis on reproducing a sense of Self that resembles Homo Economicus inter-institutional networks and relationships ('inter-ests') were rendered largely invisible by accounting. Moreover, forms of moral hazard were obscured. Here, accounting seems to produce exclusion rather than inclusion; rarified interaction rather than a proliferation of the social. Therefore, Roberts and Jones (2009) offer a very strong demonstration of the claims in the performativity thesis.

Accounting's mediating role is related to the intensity with which overflows entail a re-framing activity. Depending on whether there are 'strategists in the wild' (Skærbæk and Tryggestad 2010) accounting may enhance (Roberts and Jones 2009, Keevers et al. 2012) or hinder (Skærbæk and Tryggestad 2010) instrumental rationality and rarefaction of interaction patterns. In the case of the Ferry Division (Skærbæk and Tryggestad 2010) strategic decision-making takes the direction of a 'totalising affair' as described by Miller (2002), yet such 'totalising' occurs through dialectic processes of disentanglement and entanglement. Here, the issues at stake are 'hot' and induce political reactions to the accounting frames by different actors. This implies a proliferation of the social, and an inclusion of interests of others. Here, as exemplified by the captains defending their professional status, the behavioural assumptions of economics are not fully brought into life; the captains refuse to take the full shape of Homo Economicus. On the other hand, in the case of the financial markets (Roberts and Jones 2009) calculative agencies are distributed, and rarified transactions are framed *inter alia* on the basis of statements from finance theory. Overflows are not addressed; this is portrayed as one of the reasons for the ultimate emergence of the financial crisis.

Towards a relational ontology of management accounting

In Callon's performativity thesis the focus is on the 'performation' of (institutional) economics. Miller and Power (2013) further analyse the relationship between organising, accounting and economics. From their views, Callonistics would point to a particular way through which accounting, organising and economising could be claimed to be mutually constitutive. They identify four roles of accounting: territorialising, mediating, adjudicating and subjectivising. Accounting helps 'territorialising' in the sense that it recursively produces the calculative spaces in which there is rarified interaction between calculative agencies. Moreover, accounting *mediates* between economics and goal directed efficient behaviour by calculative agents. It links up different actors and spaces with statements from economic theory. Accounting *adjudicates* by evaluating, rewarding and punishing calculative agencies, and by determining failings and failures. In its strongest sense, accounting *subjectivises* in the sense that it helps producing Homo Economicus version 2.0.

However, in specific networks accounting may also be performative (i.e. it may also territorialise, mediate, adjudicate and subjectivise) in many different ways. As there is a multiplicity of practices there may be concrete-contingent networks where economics is less performative while competing theories are more performative. For example, there may be societal practices that do not construct an 'agent' as it is represented in institutional economics (in Callon's terms Homo Economicus version 2.0), but a 'steward' (Davis *et al.* 1997).[6] To actor-network theory researchers it might be a challenge to enact such networks, and thus, to help accentuating and developing socio-technical arrangements of stewardship rather than calculative agencies. Similar to 'agents', stewards take shape as a consequence of their relations with others, both humans and other-than-humans, and it might be a challenge to accounting academics to enact the actor-network of a steward, and, thus, to narrate (Czarniawska 2009) stewardship. For instance, Segal and Lehrer (2012), through a case study of the Edmonton Public Schools, explore the extent to which stewardship can be institutionalised. It would be interesting to explore the performativity of stewardship theory in the shaping of stewards and their interaction patterns.

The choice for such a research project would be a political one. Politics then is connected to the topic and is not an essence in itself. It is *in* the process of producing knowledge. It is connected to choices of and in the enactment of concrete multiple contingent networks through which, for instance, education and related issues of accounting and accountability are practiced. Accounts based on Callonistics are not only ontologically relational, but also ontologically political; the real is implicated in the political and vice versa. Things might always be otherwise (Law 2008). In actor-network theory, there is a 'burning desire to have new entities detected, welcomed and given a shelter' (Latour 2005, p. 224).

My claim would be that actor-network theory (and, thus Callonistics) may become critically engaged with accounting and management by enacting multiple practices and by defending that some practices are more favourable than others. This has already been done outside the field of accounting, for instance, in studies of health care (Mol 2008) and animal feeding (Law and Mol 2008). Although not explicitly taking an actor-network theory approach and not explicitly drawing upon the concept of performativity as developed by Callon, Vaivio (1999) has demonstrated how systematic performance management (the 'quantified customer') was involved in power struggles that revealed the importance of tacit knowledge of sales people. More studies might be conducted that enact both instrumental accountability (or accountability as transparency; Roberts 2009), thereby demonstrating the performativity of (institutional) economics, and more intelligent (Roberts 2009) and relational accountability, thereby demonstrating the performativity of other theories. Next, a comparison between these studies could then particularly focus on the different ways through which accounting territorialises, mediates, adjudicates and subjectivises (Miller and Power 2013) in these different settings. Moreover, by particularly helping to enact intelligent and relational practices of accountability, research might serve to redress an all too extreme performativity of institutional economics that results in a self-fulfilling prophecy of opportunistic behaviour (Ghoshal and Moran 1996, Ferraro *et al.* 2005) and other pernicious societal consequences (Chua 2011). In doing so, accounting researchers help to make some reality (i.e. a reality of relational accountability and stewardship) more real, while simultaneously making the reality of instrumental accountability and Homo Economicus less real.

In short, future research might underscore the politics in management accounting. Such politics is not located in a separate sphere and is not prior to practices, but comes through in concrete practices in dispersed social-material networks. Rather than being the transcendent 'explanans' for management accounting the politics has to be explained, it is the 'explanandum'. Research into the politics of management accounting underscores how the (calculative) agencies or 'agencements' are not 'natural' or 'destiny', but how they become assembled in complex networks in which humans and other-than-humans interact. The research re-presents how accounting as it interacts with other actants territorialises, mediates, adjudicates and subjectivises (Miller and Power 2013) in concrete-contingent networks. Such networks contain elements that may reside both inside or outside a focal organisation or an organisational relationship; they cross boundaries. The research accounts for the performativity of economics as well as for the performativity of other theories. It highlights that both the 'good' and the 'bad' are made up in multiple practices and it can serve to undermine the 'bad' and to underscore the 'good' by enacting and comparing specific local practices, thus helping to change states of affaires. In doing so, a relational ontology of management accounting would be developed that acknowledges that accounting is not an essence in itself, but can only exist in processes of knowing in networks, and is in politics. Such a development should also be sensitive to the notion that concrete-contingent networks are 'in immanence', thus also illuminating that virtual and 'unlocalisable' historically developing systems of ideology and power are underlying the working of networks.

The development of such a relational ontology of management accounting might help in changing states of affairs in society.

Acknowledgement

The paper benefited from discussions at a seminar of the Research Center on Accounting and Control Change, January 2013, Nijmegen. The clear guidance by the Associate Editor, Sven Modell and the helpful reviews were highly appreciated. The usual disclaimer applies.

Notes

1. Although the term 'actor' is part of the name of the theoretical approach ('actor-network theory'), Latour (1992) prefers the term 'actant' above the term 'actor' because the term 'actor' has a human connotation. The term 'actant' refers to all acting entities, both human and non-human. In this paper, both terms ('actant' and 'actor') will be used interchangeably.
2. Scholars differ as to how they theorise the status of non-human agency relative to human agency. For instance, Callon (1986) and Latour (2005) posit these agencies to be symmetrical; both humans and other-than-humans are symmetrical in the sense that they are both made to act by many others. The other-than-humans are not simply in the hands of humans. Others see humans and other-than-

humans as interwined (Pickering 1995) or entangled (Suchman, 2007). The basic point is that other-than-humans (for instance, accounting) have an impact in concrete socio-material networks.
3. See Modell (2013) for the development of a parallel discussion to make *institutional* accounting research more critical.
4. Callon borrows the term from Deleuze and Guattari (1998).
5. Callon uses the term 'performativity' in a developed sense that goes beyond a social constructivist sense of the term. From a social constructivist perspective human actors may be engaged in politically laden struggles, fighting with each other on their different views. Accounting, then, is performative when it assists the most powerful human actors in reaching their aims. In a more developed sense, accounting is performative when it produces possibilities and constraints related to economic models or frameworks. It has unexpected effects.
6. This is consistent with a suggestion by Callon (2007a) to include the issue of how 'the anthropology of economics is constantly confronted with other, equally performative, anthropological programs' (p. 347) in the research agenda.

References

Adler, P., 2002. Critical in the name of whom and what? *Organization*, 9 (1), 387–395.

Ahrens, T. and Chapman, C.S., 2007. Management accounting as practice. *Accounting, Organizations and Society*, 32 (1), 1–27.

Alcadipani, R. and Hassard, J., 2010. Actor-network theory, organizations and critique: towards a politics of organizing. *Organization*, 17 (4), 419–435.

Alvesson, M. and Willmott, H., 1992. *Critical Management Studies*. London: Sage.

Alvesson, M. and Willmott, H., 1996. *Making Sense of Management*. London: Sage.

Amernic, J. and Craig, R., 2009. Understanding accounting through conceptual metaphor: accounting is an instrument? *Critical Perspectives on Accounting*, 20 (8), 875–883.

Barad, K., 2007. *Meeting the Universe Halfway: Quantum Physics and the Entanglement of Matter and Meaning*. London: Duke University Press.

Baxter, M. and Chua, W.F., 2003. Alternative accounting research. *Accounting, Organizations and Society*, 28 (2–3), 97–126.

Caliskan, K. and Callon, M., 2009. Economization, part 1: shifting attention from the economy towards processes of economization. *Economy and Society*, 38 (3), 369–398.

Caliskan, K. and Callon, M., 2010. Economization, part 2: a research programme for the study of markets. *Economy and Society*, 39 (1), 1–32.

Callon, M., 1986. Some elements in a sociology of translation. In: J. Law, ed. *Power, Action and Belief*. London: Routledge & Kegan Paul, 196–233.

Callon, M. ed., 1998. *The Laws of the Markets*. New York: Blackwell Publishers.

Callon, M., 1999. Actor-network theory – the market test. In: J. Law and J. Hassard, eds. *Actor Network Theory and After*. Oxford: Blackwell Publishers, 181–195.

Callon, M., 2005. Why virtualism paves the way to political impotence. A reply to Daniel Miller's critique of *The Laws of the Markets*. *Economic Sociology*, 6 (2), 3–20.

Callon, M., 2007a. What does it mean to say that economics is performative? In: D. MacKenzie, F. Muniesa, and L. Siu, eds. *Do Economists Make Markets? On the Performativity of Economics*. Princeton, NJ: Princeton University Press, 311–357.

Callon, M., 2007b. An essay on the growing contribution of economic markets to the proliferation of the social. *Theory, Culture & Society*, 24 (7–8), 139–163.

Callon, M., Lascoumes, P., and Barthe, Y., 2011. *Acting in an Uncertain World*. Cambridge, MA: MIT Press.

Christensen, M. and Skærbæk, P., 2007. Framing and overflow of public sector accountability innovations – a comparative study of reporting practices. *Accounting, Auditing and Accountability Journal*, 20 (1), 101–132.

Chua, W.F., 2011. In search of successful research. *The European Accounting Review*, 20 (1), 27–39.

Cushen, J., 2013. Financialization in the workplace: hegemonic narratives, performative interventions and the angry knowledge worker. *Accounting, Organizations and Society*, 38 (4), 314–331.

Czarniawska, B., 2009. Commentary: STS meets MOS. *Organization*, 16 (1), 155–160.

Davis, J., Schoorman, D. and Donaldson, L., 1997. Towards a stewardship theory of management. *Academy of Management Review*, 22 (1), 20–47.

Deleuze, G. and Guattari, F., 1994. *What is Philosophy?* Trans. G. Burchill and H. Tomlinson. London: Verso.

Deleuze, G. and Guattari, F. 1998. *A Thousand Plateaus: Capitalism and Schizophrenia*. London: Athlone.

Didier, E., 2007. Do statistics 'perform' the economy? In: D. MacKenzie, F. Muniesa, and L. Siu, eds. *Do Economists Make Markets? On the Performativity of Economics*. Oxford: Princeton University Press, 276–310.

Epstein, G.A., 2005. Introduction: financialization and the world economy. In: *Financialization and the World Economy*. Cheltenham: Edward Elgar.

Ezzamel, M., 2012. *Accounting and Order*. London: Routledge.

Ezzamel, M. and Hoskin, K., 2002. Retheorizing accounting, writing, and money with evidence from Mesopotamia and Ancient Egypt. *Critical Perspectives on Accounting*, 13 (3), 333–367.

Ezzamel, M., Wilmott, H., and Worthington, F., 2008. Manufacturing shareholder value: the role of accounting in organizational transformation. *Accounting, Organizations and Society*, 33 (2–3), 107–140.

Ferraro, F., Pfeffer, J., and Sutton, R.I., 2005. Economics language and assumptions: how theories can become self-fulfilling. *Academy of Management Review*, 30 (1), 8–24.

Fine, B., 2003. Callonistics: a disentanglement. *Economy and Society*, 32 (3), 478–484.

Fine, B., 2005. From actor network theory to political economy. *Capitalism Nature Socialism*, 16 (1), 91–108.

Fournier, V. and Grey, C., 2000. At the critical moment: conditions and prospects for critical management studies. *Human Relations*, 53 (1), 7–32.

Friedman, M., 2005. *Trying Hard is not Good Enough: How to Produce Measurable Improvements for Customers and Communities*. Victoria: Trafford Publishing.

Friedman, D., 2010. A new mentality for a new economy: performing the Homo Economicus in Argentina. *Economy and Society*, 39 (2), 271–302.

Ghoshal, S. and Moran, P., 1996. Bad for practice: a critique of the transaction cost theory. *Academy of Management Review*, 21, 3–47.

Hood, C., 1995. The 'New Public Management' in the 1980s: variations on a theme. *Accounting, Organizations and Society*, 20 (2–3), 93–109.

Jensen, M.C., 1983. Organization theory and methodology. *The Accounting Review*, LVIII, 319–339.

Jensen, M.C. and Meckling, W.H., 1976. Theory of the firm: managerial behaviour, agency costs and ownership structure. *Journal of Financial Economics*, 3 (4), 305–360.

Justesen, L. and Mouritsen, J., 2011. Effects of actor-network theory in accounting research. *Accounting, Auditing and Accountability Journal*, 24 (2), 161–193.

Kalthoff, H., 2005. Practices of calculation: economic representations and risk management. *Theory, Culture & Society*, 22 (2), 69–97.

Keevers, L., Treleaven, L., Sykes, C., and Darcy, M., 2012. Made to measure: taming practices with results-based accountability. *Organization Studies*, 33 (1), 97–120.

Krämer, S., 1996. Sprache und Schrift oder: Ist Schrift verschriftete Sprache? *Zeitschrift für Sprachwissenschaft*, 15 (1), 92–112.

Latour, B., 1992. Where are the missing masses? The sociology of a few mundane artefacts. In: W.E. Bijker and J. Law, eds. *Shaping Technology/Building Society*. Cambridge, MA: MIT Press, 225–258.

Latour, B., 1999. On recalling ANT. In: J. Law and J. Hassard, eds. *Actor Network Theory and After*. Oxford: Blackwell Publishers, 15–25.

Latour, B., 2005. *Reassembling the Social: An Introduction to Actor-Network Theory*. Oxford: Oxford University Press.

Latour, B., 2007. Turning around politics. A note on Gerard de Vries' paper. *Social Studies of Science*, 37 (5), 811–820.

Law, J., 1999. After ANT: complexity, naming and topology. In: J. Law and J. Hassard, eds. *Actor Network Theory and After*. Oxford: Blackwell Publishers, 1–14.

Law, J., 2004. *After Method: Mess in Social Science Research*. London: Routledge.

Law, J., 2007. Actor Network Theory and Material Semiotics. Available from: http://www.heterogeneities.net/publications/LawANTandMaterialSemiotics.pdf [Accessed 5 September 2007].

Law, J., 2008. On sociology and STS. *Sociological Review*, 56 (4), 623–49.

Law, J. and Mol, A., 2008. Globalisation in practice: on the politics of boiling pigswill. *Geoforum*, 39 (2), 133–43.

Law, J. and Urry, J., 2004. Enacting the social. *Economy and Society*, 33 (3), 390–410.

Luhmann, N., 1998. *Die Gesellschaft der Gesellschaft*. Frankfurt/Main: Suhrkamp.

MacKenzie, D., 2006. *An Engine, not a Camera: How Financial Models Shape Markets*. Cambridge, MA: MIT Press.

MacKenzie, D. and Millo, Y., 2003. Constructing a market, performing theory: the historical sociology of a financial derivatives exchange. *American Journal of Sociology*, 109 (1), 107–145.

Miller, D., 1998. A theory of virtualism. In: J. Carrier and D. Miller, eds. *Virtualism: A New Political Economy*. Oxford: Berg, 187–215.

Miller, D., 2002. Turning Callon the right way up. *Economy and Society*, 31 (2), 218–233.

Miller, D., 2003. The virtual moment. *Journal of the Royal Anthropological Institute*, 14 (1), 57–75.

Miller, D., 2005. Reply to Michel Callon. *Economic Sociology*, 6 (3), 2–13.

Miller, P., 1991. Accounting innovation beyond the enterprise: problematizing investment decisions and programming economic growth in the UK in the 1960s. *Accounting, Organizations and Society*, 16 (8), 733–762.

Miller, P., 2008. Calculating economic life. *Journal of Cultural Economy*, 1 (1), 51–64.

Miller, P. and O'Leary, T., 2007. Mediating instruments and making markets: capital budgeting, science and the economy. *Accounting, Organizations and Society*, 32 (7–8), 701–734.

Miller, P. and Power, M., 2013. Accounting, organizing and economizing: connecting accounting research and organizational theory. *Academy of Management Annals*, 7 (1), 555–603.

Modell, S., 2013. Making institutional accounting research critical: dead end or new beginning? Working Paper, Manchester Business School.

Mol, A., 1999. Ontological politics. A word and some questions. In: J. Law and J. Hassard, eds. *Actor Network Theory and After*. Oxford: Blackwell Publishers, 123–162.

Mol, A., 2002. *The Body Multiple: Atherosclerosis in Practice*. Durham, NC: Duke University Press.

Mol, A., 2008. *The Logic of Care: Health and the Problem of Patient Choice*. London: Routledge.

Mirowski, P. and Nik-Khah, E., 2007. Markets made flesh: performativity, and a problem in science studies, augmented with consideration of the FCC auctions. In: D. MacKenzie, F. Muniesa, and L. Siu, eds. *Do Economists Make Markets?* Princeton, NJ: Princeton University Press, 190–224.

Orlikowski, W., 2007. Sociomaterial practices: exploring technology at work. *Organization Studies*, 28 (9), 1435–1448.

Pickering, A., 1995. *The Mangle of Practice: Time, Agency and Science*. Chicago, IL: University of Chicago Press.

Rheinberger, H.J., 1992. Experiment, difference, and writing, 1. Tracing protein synthesis. *Studies in History and Philosophy of Science*, 23, 305–331.

Rheinberger, H.J., 1997. *Toward a History of Epistemic Things: Synthesizing Proteins in the Test Tube*. Stanford, CA: Stanford University Press.

Roberts, J., 2009. No one is perfect: the limits of transparency and an ethic for 'intelligent' accountability. *Accounting, Organizations and Society*, 34 (8), 957–970.

Roberts, J.M., 2012. Poststructuralism against poststructuralism: actor-network theory, organizations and economic markets. *European Journal of Social Theory*, 15 (1), 35–53.

Roberts, J. and Jones, M., 2009. Accounting for self interest in the credit crisis. *Accounting, Organizations and Society*, 34 (6–7), 856–867.

Roberts, J. and Wilson, N., 2012. Against economic (mis)conceptions of the individual: constructing financial agency in the credit crisis. *Culture and Organization*, 18 (2), 91–105.

Robson, K., 1992. Accounting numbers as inscription: action at a distance and the development of accounting. *Accounting, Organizations and Society*, 17 (7), 685–708.

Ross, S., 1973. The economic theory of agency: the principal's problem. *American Economic Review*, 63 (1), 134–139.

Santos, A.C. and Rodrigues, J., 2009. Economics as social engineering? Questioning the performativity thesis. *Cambridge Journal of Economics*, 33 (5), 985–1000.

Segal, L. and Lehrer, M., 2012. The institutionalization of stewardship: theory, propositions, and insights from change in the Edmonton Public Schools. *Organization Studies*, 33 (2), 169–201.

Skærbæk, P. and Tryggestad, K., 2010. The role of accounting devices in performing corporate strategy. *Accounting, Organizations and Society*, 35 (1), 108–124.

Stiglitz, J.E., 1974. Incentives and risk sharing in sharecropping. *Review of Economic Studies*, 41 (2), 219–255.

Suchman, L., 2007. *Human-Machine Reconfigurations: Plans and Situated Actions*. 2nd ed. New York: Cambridge University Press.

Vaivio, J., 1999. Examining 'the quantified customer'. *Accounting, Organizations and Society*, 24 (8), 689–715.

Vollmer, H., Mennicken, A. and Preda, A., 2009. Tracking the numbers: across accounting and finance, organizations and markets. *Accounting, Organizations and Society*, 34 (5), 619–637.

Whittle, A. and Spicer, A., 2008. Is actor network theory critique? *Organization Studies*, 29 (4), 611–629.

Wildavsky, A., 1974. *The Politics of the Budgetary Process*. 2nd ed. Boston, MA: Little, Brown & Co.

Williamson, O.E., 1975. *Markets and Hierarchies: Analysis and Anti-Trust Implications: A Study in the Economics of Internal Organization*. New York: Free Press.

Williamson, O.E., 1979. Transaction cost economics: the governance of contractual relations. *Journal of Law and Economics*, 22 (1), 3–61.

Relevant interventionist research: balancing three intellectual virtues

KARI LUKKA[a] and PETRI SUOMALA[b]

[a]Turku School of Economics, Accounting & Finance, University of Turku, Turku, Finland;
[b]Department of Industrial Management, Tampere University of Technology, Tampere,
Finland

This paper argues for a balanced approach to considering the three intellectual virtues of
Aristotle, brought forth by Flyvbjerg [2001. *Making Social Science Matter: Why Social
Inquiry Fails and How It Can Succeed Again*. Cambridge: Cambridge University Press] –
techne, episteme and phronesis – and links them to recent debates on the relevance of
management accounting research. The intellectual virtue of phronesis is viewed as opening
an avenue for conducting management accounting research that is societally relevant and the
interventionist research (IVR) approach is suggested to form one natural platform for such
research. The paper underlines that the intellectual virtue of episteme, being related to
theoretical relevance, is a necessary element in all scholarly endeavours and that IVR has so
far tended to suffer from being too much focused on the intellectual virtue of techne and
thereby practical relevance only. The method of 'engaged scholarship' is offered as one
fruitful option for balancing the three intellectual virtues and conducting research that is
relevant to several dimensions.

Keywords: management accounting; discursive logical argument; relevance; intellectual
virtues; phronesis; interventionist research

1. Introduction

The starting point of this paper is the observation and claim of Flyvbjerg (2001) – based on Aristotle (1955) – that there are several, rather than just one, intellectual virtues that researchers can
pay attention to: episteme, techne and phronesis. The major aim of this paper is to cross-examine
this three-item typology of intellectual virtues and especially the idea of phronetic social science
(PSS) – the one forcefully promoted by Flyvbjerg regarding social sciences – against the key
ideas of interventionist research (IVR). For Flyvbjerg, PSS represents science which has a practical, yet simultaneously value-sensitive agenda, leading to 'social science that matters'. Flyvbjerg
regards PSS as applying the virtue of techne 'with head on it' (making it thereby phronetic),
whereas for him, techne alone represents 'headless social engineering'. PSS stresses the

importance of dialogue with the targets of research and that values and power issues are taken into consideration.

The purpose of PSS research can vary from conceptual clarification to developing frameworks to critique, and as PSS can be interventionist; its linkages to IVR are a natural target for closer examination. IVR revolves around making an impact in the world through research and can be defined as a longitudinal case study approach (with variations), in which active participant observation and sometimes also the implementation of development ideas brought forward by the field researcher are deliberately used as a research asset in order to produce theory contribution (Jönsson and Lukka 2007, Suomala and Lyly-Yrjänäinen 2012). IVR is often blamed to represent only 'social engineering', which in Aristotle's terms lean on techne. Our paper challenges this limited, but widespread tendency of IVR, and explores the inherent linkages of high-quality IVR with phronesis, indicating the potential of IVR in this direction.

However, while we agree with Flyvbjerg regarding his major claim of the need for more PSS kind of research, we also challenge his view that underplays the potential of social sciences regarding episteme. We argue that IVR – similarly to all scholarly endeavours – should always have, and would benefit from, episteme-related purposes, too. In our view, Flyvbjerg's position regarding episteme is not only radically outdated and limited when it comes to social sciences, but also hard to defend in the long run as a viable position for the academe. We stress that lacking epistemic virtue, the academe would over time lose its voice in society. After all, also social scientists get their central *raison d'etre* from their epistemic strengths, even if they of course need not be their only asset.

We advance an argument for the need of a balanced employment of the three intellectual virtues in IVR and social sciences overall. Regarding how such balanced research could be conducted, the issue of the interface between theory and practice is in focus. We will draw from recent advances in the management literature, especially from the notion of 'engaged scholarship' of Van de Ven and Johnson (2006) and Van de Ven (2007) and that of the 'practice epistemology' of Jarzabkowski *et al.* (2010). These two notions are in line with our thoughts as to how a balanced cooperation between techne, episteme and phronesis can work. Accordingly, knowledge can well be developed in a collaborative effort between academics and practitioners, a view that has for a long time been largely neglected in business studies research. In the research designs of engaged scholarship, the role of the researcher can vary from non-interventionist to a more or less strongly interventionist one. IVR approaches would have certain notable strengths when engaged scholarship is nurtured in the spirit of practice epistemology.

Finally, we will open up the notion of relevance in management accounting research, arguing that this concept is typically understood too narrowly as referring to practical relevance only (linking it thereby tightly but narrowly to only techne). Defining the notion of relevance broadly as something that is of significance for something else,[1] we suggest that relevance should be linked to all three intellectual virtues raised by Flyvbjerg (2001), yet with differing angles to interpret it. Hence, techne relates to the practical relevance of a study, episteme to its theoretical relevance and phronesis to its societal relevance. While theoretical relevance should be viewed as a necessity for all scholarly projects, we generally argue for a balanced consideration of the three intellectual virtues as well as the three dimensions of relevance, both in IVR and in management accounting research overall.

The paper is structured as follows. In the next section, we will introduce the three intellectual virtues of episteme, techne and phronesis, focusing on the main ideas of PSS, and cast them against the core of IVR. Subsequently, we will develop our argument for the need of episteme both in IVR and social sciences overall. In the section that follows, engaged scholarship will be brought forth as a method to bridge the attempts of researchers and practitioners to advance knowledge, well suitable for IVR, too. This will lead us to reconceptualise the notion of relevance and argue for the need and usefulness for a balanced consideration of the three intellectual virtues in IVR and management accounting research overall. The paper ends with conclusions.

2. PSS and IVR

Flyvbjerg (2001) draws directly from Aristotle when he mobilises his key notions referring to three different kinds of intellectual virtues: episteme, techne and phronesis.[2] For Flyvbjerg, episteme is viewed to concern universals and the production of knowledge which is invariable in time and space with the help or analytic rationality, corresponding to the modern scientific ideal in natural sciences and responding to 'know why' types of questions. Techne again is craft and art, and as an activity it is concrete, variable and context-dependent, being based on practical instrumental rationality and responding to 'know how' type of questions. While also phronesis is closely connected to action and is context-dependent, it deals with ethically practical wisdom and knowledge of how to behave appropriately in each particular circumstance. Phronesis is linked to value rationality as opposed to technical rationality and is often translated as 'prudence' or 'practical common sense' (Flyvbjerg 2001, pp. 55–7). Flyvbjerg extends the original notion of phronesis by Aristotle by stressing the importance of connecting power issues to it based on the works of Habermas and particularly Foucault.

Flyvbjerg (2001) argues that social scientists are typically not sufficiently aware of these three different intellectual virtues, with unfortunate consequences, and especially that the long-lasting tendency to imitate natural sciences in strongly focusing on episteme will unlikely never be a way out from the Science Wars type of critique of low quality or pre-paradigmatic social science. While natural sciences are at their strongest regarding episteme, in that regard, social sciences are at their weakest, Flyvbjerg argues. He insists this is essentially due to the facts that knowledge about human activities cannot exclude context which the notion of 'ideal theory' seems to require and that social sciences are bound to their inherent double reflexivity – that there are subjects at both ends of the inquiry. He argues that instead of episteme (or techne) social sciences would find a fruitful direction, and solid ground for development, from adopting phronesis as its corner-stone, leading to a largely new kind of social science, a phronetic one – a social science that would matter in society.

For Flyvbjerg (2001), the primary objective for social science is not to provide a theoretical mirror for a society but to provide society with knowledge that can be used as input to the dialogue on topical social challenges and solutions – 'carry out analyses and interpretations of the status of values and interests in society aimed at social commentary and social action, i.e. practice' (p. 60). When seeking to fulfil this objective, according to Flyvbjerg, research has to address four wide questions, which are inherently value-rational: 'Where are we going?', 'Is this desirable?', 'What should be done?' and finally 'Who gains and who loses and by which mechanisms of power?' (2001, p. 60).

Given that the full answers to the questions phrased by Flyvbjerg are impossible to produce and that even partial answers might be hard to formulate by research, what can then be done? To begin with, Flyvbjerg advises that the researcher must not settle with practising 'science' in general but she has to make it explicit, whether she is practicing episteme, techne or phronesis. Concerning the selection from, or emphasis between, these three virtues, Flyvbjerg advocates the potential of social sciences in terms of techne and especially phronesis, whereas he is extremely doubtful regarding the qualities of social research as to episteme. Regarding research setting and approach, this stance would lead the researcher towards context-specific inquiry and appreciating case-based research, which can draw from the power of examples and thus create depth that complements the breadth produced by large sample surveys or archival-based studies, for instance.

For methodological guidance of conducting PSS, Flyvbjerg offers nine principles that make it up as 'pragmatically governed interpretation of studied practices' which is 'an analytic project, but not a theoretical or methodological one' (2001, pp. 129–40):

(1) Focusing on values, the researcher must reject both the view that central values are universal and the view of relativism (that any set of values is as good as another); instead the researcher seeks to draw from the studied context and situation and tries to capture the common view among the group or setting under study.

(2) Placing power at the core of analysis. In addition to values, power serves as another key element of context being analysed. For a phronetic researcher, power is quite elusive and versatile; not negative or positive per se, but something that is exercised and produced within and between institutions and structures.

(3) Getting close to reality.[3] Researchers try to anchor their studies in the context that are being studied (without necessarily going native in the ethnographic sense) and establish close relations to stakeholders in order to stimulate reactions and interest to the research, which is to test and evaluate the findings and their value

(4) Emphasising little things. The researcher seeks to build as general findings as possible, but through a procedure that takes off by putting effort towards understanding details and 'little things'.

(5) Looking at practice before discourse. Phronetic research sees actual daily practices and actual deeds as more fundamental targets of analysis than discourse or theory. At the outset, each individual practice is documented in itself without taking positions regarding 'the truth-value and significance ascribed by participants to the practice studied'. At the second stage, the researcher seeks to establish the relations from the local practices to the wider context.

(6) Studying cases and contexts. Judgment is regarded as central to phronesis, and since judgment lies in specific contexts, phronetic researchers draw from case-exemplars in order to understand judgment – be the cases experienced or narrated.

(7) Asking 'how?' and doing narrative. Building an understanding and explanation of any given phenomenon is believed to start by asking 'how' questions. Narrative, for one, is regarded as a fundamental vehicle for not only 'making sense of experience', but also as a means to recognise future alternatives or scenarios before actually encountering them.

(8) Joining agency and structure. Practices, actors and structures ought to be studied together while understanding that they are profoundly intertwined. Micro- and macro-level analyses should be combined, not between separate studies, but within individual studies in order to understand how structures shape individual choices and which structural consequences of individual actions are.

(9) Dialoguing with a polyphonic voice: research is not regarded as the one voice of claiming authority. Instead, the interpretations provided by the phronetic research are understood as inputs for societal dialogue and practice, which serve as the actual test for the interpretations produced. In this test, the strength of interpretation depends upon the acceptance of validity claims underpinning the interpretation.

Flyvbjerg's (2001) view on PSS has much in common with the typical characteristics of IVR. IVR can be defined as a longitudinal case study approach (with variations), in which the researcher's active involvement and participant observation is used as a research asset for building access and creating the possibility of gathering in-depth empirical data, and eventually, for producing a theory contribution. A characteristic feature of IVR is that the researcher is an active participant in the real-time flow of life in the field, and therefore she has to be able adopt an insider's viewpoint (the emic perspective) to the issues at hand in order to produce theory contribution (the etic perspective). IVR frequently relates to attempts to develop and implement innovations in practice, most explicitly when the constructive research approach – one variant of IVR – is applied (Kasanen *et al.* 1993, Jönsson and Lukka 2007, Suomala and Lyly-Yrjänäinen 2012).

Of Flyvbjerg's list of methodological guidelines for PSS, getting close to reality, looking at practice before discourse, and studying cases in their contexts are typical features of IVR, too (Suomala and Lyly-Yrjänäinen 2012). In IVR, the researcher is an active actor in the real-time flow of life in the field. For coping with and for balancing between various interests present in cases, she has to adopt, or at least consider, the emic (insider's) perspective to the issues at hand. IVR is often a problem-solving oriented venture with explicit connections to challenges present in practice. In IVR, the researcher typically participates in an organisational change project and faces the practical challenges together with the representatives of the case organisation, and it has an element of field experimentation, during which a novel or typically something not yet fully diffused is put into an empirical test (Jönsson and Lukka 2007).

We fully support the main claim of Flyvbjerg (2001): phronetic intellectual virtue is potentially important and is something, which is largely omitted and should be more in the picture in the social sciences. Phronesis adds a powerful aspect to the repertoire of social sciences and its central idea is well in line with the potential of IVR. That said, we do not argue that *all* interventionist studies should be deeply phronetic, but rather that it should be kept in mind as one important aspect to be considered and in some cases developed in a full-blown manner. All interventionist researchers should pay attention to the value issues at stake in their studies and ponder whether they are happy with them or not.[4] The list of phronetic questions Flyvbjerg presents is highly relevant in this regard. If the researcher feels there are issues around these questions, she has the hard choice to make, whether she wishes to go towards phronetic analysis and interventions in a deeper manner, potentially including critique of the current state of affairs and attempts to, for instance, emancipate people from their iron cages. Such research is not without risks and can jeopardise the researcher's ability to continue conducting her study. Even if the researcher would be able to avoid any signs of arrogance and indications of 'I just know it better' attitude, conflicts can easily arise and the outcome can, at worst, be denial of further access to the field. Indeed, the researcher needs a lot of human skills and prudence to be able to conduct a full-blown phronetic study to completion. But despite these obvious risks, phronetically oriented research should be viewed as an important alternative within IVR – and for all social scientists, for that matter – adding to its potential regarding societal relevance.

3. The need for episteme in social sciences

Faithful to the original characterisations of episteme by Aristotle, Flyvbjerg (2001) suggests that social scientists should just abandon the virtue of episteme, since they will always lose the Science Wars, if episteme is the battleground. We counter-argue this particular claim of his. On the one hand, winning the Science Wars can hardly be viewed as an end per se. On the other hand, rather than just leaving the battleground of episteme, social scientists could alternatively argue that the Science Wars are simply a misguided battle, driven by the false idea that all sciences should be evaluated with the same criteria. The monolithic thinking of one methodology fitting for all sciences had its hay-day at the peak of logical positivism in the 1920s (the so-called 'Given View'), but has long been rejected in the philosophy of science and has become widely criticised in the context of accounting research, too (Lukka and Mouritsen 2002). Flyvbjerg falls into a trap as he seems to accept and adopt precisely those epistemic criteria that natural scientists put forth in the Science Wars – leading him to strikingly dismiss the virtue of episteme in social sciences. In our view, there is no reason whatsoever to accept precisely those epistemological criteria that natural sciences insist on as the only ones – but actually vice versa.

Consequently, while we are generally very much in accordance with the views of Flyvbjerg (2001) regarding PSS, we are far from convinced of his strong dismissal of episteme in social sciences. To us Flyvbjerg seems even too faithful to Aristotle when he defines episteme in a very narrow, and from the viewpoint of social sciences and humanities, clearly limited and outdated manner. While Aristotle no doubt was one of the greatest thinkers of all times, there has been some development in scholarly thinking regarding episteme in the last 2300 years, which needs appreciation, too. And even Flyvbjerg himself is not able to be consistent regarding his dismissal of episteme as he talks about generalisation from case studies and applies several theoretical models and frameworks as building blocks of his arguments – these are certainly epistemic resources.

For us Flyvbjerg (2001) defines theory in such an extreme manner (with attributes such as being explicit, universal, abstract, discrete, systematic, complete and predictive) – indeed as may be typical of natural sciences – that he happens to build a straw man, which is then easy for him to dismiss from the social science viewpoint: such social science theories are very obviously impossible due to the reasons Flyvbjerg correctly captures. Adopting instead a more liberal notion of theory, particularly by not linking it to complete and abstract universals only, leaves room for meaningful theories (episteme) also in the social sciences. Even though things can never be assumed to be stable (or complete or universal for that matter) when human action is in question, this does not imply that everything would be changeful all the time. There are at least semi-stable patterns of human behaviour and causal linkages on which we can base our own projections and action choices – yet being all the time conscious that institutional settings, rules and routines can change (Kakkuri-Knuuttila et al. 2008).

Accordingly, we argue that social sciences cannot, and should not, do without episteme. Instead of abandoning episteme in social sciences and focusing on phronesis only, we should find ways of nurturing a balanced approach, which would leave room for the potential of all three intellectual virtues. At least in management accounting, there can be theories that help us to understand how and why things are as they are (reflecting episteme), but also theories helping us to understand how to make things work (techne) as well as theories helping us to cope appropriately with particular situations involved with power and value-related deliberations (phronesis).

Abandoning episteme would certainly be disastrous for the social scientists, especially in the longer run. Would social scientists one-sidedly only conduct phronesis targeted studies, forgetting epistemic purposes, they would sooner or later lose their capacity of having anything to offer. Hence, we do not support the idea of abandoning the intellectual virtue of episteme in social sciences, but vice versa: We think in this era of increasing instrumentalism and cynical publish or perish mentality in the academe, stressing episteme in the name of true scholarship is perhaps more important than ever before (cf. Humphrey and Lukka 2011).

4. Episteme in IVR

The need for carefully considering episteme is burning in the case of IVR, which has so far predominantly stuck to the virtue of techne. Having followed what is going on in and around IVR in management accounting for a longer time (and in several different scholarly roles), the authors of this paper have observed, how many IVR studies that are floating around in conferences and seminars as working papers get tough treatment in scholarly journals and seldom get published there.

Their destiny is often to get published in less prestigious research journals or in professionally tuned outlets – or even remain eventually unpublished. Why is the situation like this?

One likely reason for this is the background and interests of the IVR authors. They tend to be practice-oriented researchers, who often also run consulting practices alongside their academic work. Their typical interests lie in solving problems that emerge from their contacts with practitioners and they are perhaps not used to profound thinking in theoretical terms and problematising things theoretically. Hence serious questions raised by reviewers and editors in high-quality scholarly journals regarding the theoretically motivated research question and theory contribution tend to sound distant and artificial to them as their efforts are targeted to solving practical problems with their client organisations. All this is typical of techne and can largely be grounded from the viewpoint of that particular intellectual virtue.

Often the authors of IVR papers likely feel puzzled about the expectations they face in research journals' review processes. A typical defensive counterargument from their side is that journals just wish to function in their academic ivory towers and do not understand the 'real world out there', which IVR is able to capture and say something about. Another defence is to argue that this is a paradigmatic issue: research journals just do not wish to offer IVR a chance, since the empirical linkage is obtrusive and thereby out of the box when evaluated by the scientific criteria of the mainstream. There may be some truth in both of these counterarguments: surely there is an issue of gap between academic and practical knowledge in accounting (Jarzabkowski *et al.* 2010) and surely there are genres and politics in the academe, understandable through the notion of paradigm (cf. Lukka 2010). However, and even more importantly, the other side of the coin is that IVR papers just tend to be weak regarding episteme, even if that notion would be understood way more liberally than what Flyvbjerg proposes based on Aristotle.

We argue that IVR – like any mode of scholarly research, for that matter – can, and should, be always interested in the virtue of episteme and that there is no reason whatsoever why IVR could not do that. There are always possibilities to problematise theoretical issues around matters that may at first glance look only practical. The bottleneck of IVR in this regard is normally that it does not occur to the researchers early enough that also their studies are expected to make theoretical points. All research projects, including IVR ones, are arguably wisest to start with the heavy thought work of developing a research question that is theoretically strongly motivated. That said, especially in IVR projects the researcher needs to be flexible in this regard during the course of the project and be ready to revise the research question while she goes. This does not yet mean that she would be allowed to throw away this key aspect of any scholarly study.

Although there currently seems to be something of a movement for IVR within management accounting academe accompanied with several calls for such research (Labro and Tuomela 2003, Jönsson and Lukka 2007, Malmi and Granlund 2009, Quattrone 2009, Suomala and Lyly-Yrjänäinen 2012), it is noteworthy that the justification of IVR is articulated quite differently between these specific calls. Particularly regarding the role of theory and theory contribution, we can recognise nearly opposite schools of thought amongst the proponents of IVR in management accounting.[5] For Malmi and Granlund (2009), IVR is about solving practical (and accounting related) problems with practitioners, where the process also includes a phase during which the presented local solutions for identified problems are brought to a more global level by 'synthesizing' them 'to a more general form' (p. 613). Furthermore, it becomes clear that Malmi and Granlund (2009) recognise the role of theory in IVR, but rather than underscoring it as an outcome, they highlight it as an input or a resource one should draw from during the course of research: 'Our position is favourable to interventionist approaches, as in our view the potential of generating directly applicable yet *theoretically informed* solutions to practitioners is important to pursue.' (p. 613, emphasis added). In his commentary, Quattrone (2009) – although criticizing some of the assumptions and definitions made by Malmi and Granlund (2009) – fundamentally shares the generally positive stance towards IVR. It is particularly interesting that while engaging in a debate on management accounting theories and theorising, Quattrone (2009) demonstrates explicit support for IVR not due to its potential related to theoretical development, but for its capability to affect the non-academic world:

> The paper also makes an important point when it calls for interventionist research given that across the two sides of Atlantic and elsewhere, there is a widespread feeling that some accounting publications lack relevance for, and produce very limited effect on the non-academic world. (Quattrone 2009, p. 622)

In contrast to these examples, some authors have put higher emphasis on the role of theory development when building a justification to IVR as an approach. Jönsson and Lukka (2007) underscore that theoretical contributions are a 'must' in all types of research – and no less so in IVR. However, they point out that the evidence from the existing examples of IVR studies shows that theory development is in many cases underplayed at the expense of presenting somewhat anecdotal empirical findings and focusing on solving practical problems of target organisations. In other words, while theoretical relevance should be an elemental virtue in IVR, making a theoretical contribution when simultaneously working meaningfully within a flow of real-life events is a true challenge for a researcher and the success in this venture cannot be assumed – not least because the logics of practice and theory can significantly and fundamentally differ from each other (Van de Ven and Johnson 2006, Jönsson and Lukka 2007). Similarly, Suomala and Lyly-Yrjänäinen (2012) share the view that IVR should not be seen merely as a pragmatic exercise, but that theoretical relevance is something to be pursued in parallel to providing value for the participating organisations. However, based on an extensive account of conducted IVR studies, Suomala and Lyly-Yrjänäinen (2012) also identify a number of challenges related to pursuing theoretical contributions through IVR, including the substantial length of research processes, incentive structures favouring practical results (possibly without a need for theoretical elaboration), the lack of visibility of the theoretical potential prior to committing oneself to working in the field and finding a balance between individual capabilities needed for the different facets (practical/theoretical) of the IVR process.

As it seems evident that although there is no full consensus on the need for, and potential of, IVR to produce theoretically relevant results, it nevertheless becomes clear from the debate that most authors interested in IVR distinguish between the types of relevance – typically by referring to a dichotomy between theoretical relevance and practical relevance. Concerning the core of our paper, it is interesting that authors seem to either explicitly or implicitly hint that placing increasing emphasis on either one of the domains would somehow lead to sacrificing another. This juxtaposing view is analogously present also in the retrospective accounts on critical accounting research as articulated by Neu *et al.* (2001, p. 736): 'Indeed the cynical might argue that we have emphasized third-party theorizing instead of direct practice, focusing on academic scholarship in "learned" journals where the only contact with the "real world" is mediated through the screen of the reviewers'. This observation leads us to ponder whether, and if so how, it would be possible to respect both of these goals simultaneously and to find a balance within the IVR process that leads not only to practically, but also theoretically relevant results, which would facilitate IVR in management accounting contributing to wider societal debates as well. Applying the taxonomy of intellectual virtues of Flyvbjerg (2001), this leads us to explore whether and how episteme could be combined with techne or phronesis or both of them. Indeed as reminded by Jarzabkowski *et al.* (2010), there are reasons to understand the relationship between, and the very idea of, theory and practice more dynamically than just representing two opposite elements present in a dichotomy. For Jarzabkowski *et al.* (2010, p. 1194) theories ' … are living, breathing guesses, frameworks and general principles that are brought into being as practitioners use and adapt them in their everyday practice'. This view sets the ground for our analysis of the next section, which focuses on the notion of engaged scholarship.

5. Engaged scholarship and IVR

Van de Ven and Johnson (2006) acknowledge the potential tension between theory and practice, but seek to establish a resolution between them without sacrificing either one.[6] They establish three different frames for understanding the gap between theory and practice and propose a collaborative knowledge production method called 'engaged scholarship' for improving both the relevance of research for practice and the level of scientific knowledge. In other words, they simultaneously share the interest in serving practice and acknowledge the fundamental idea of scientific research as having the obligation to produce new theoretical knowledge. Their analysis proceeds through the explication of three kinds of framings of this relationship.

First, the difference between practice and theory can be framed as a *knowledge transfer problem*. It is understood that the problem has many underpinnings, including the form and content of knowledge produced within research so that the knowledge cannot be expediently applied in practice (Van de Ven and Johnson 2006), the lack of effort, in that researchers pay too little attention to interpreting the results together with practitioners (Mohrman *et al.* 2001) and the ineffective structure of the supply chain for knowledge without necessary intermediaries between academics and practitioners (Starkey and Madan 2001). However, as Van de Ven and Johnson (2006) point out, it is problematic to parse the issue between theory and practice as a knowledge transfer problem as any 'supply chain' we can imagine between the two is not likely to be unidirectional and the worlds that the supply chain might connect and represent distinct virtues of science (cf. Flyvbjerg 2001).

This relates to the second framing, according to which theory and practice can be understood to represent *two separate domains of knowledge*. Following the reasoning of Flyvbjerg (2001), researchers ought to select between being primarily involved in either producing theoretical or practical knowledge – both of the forms having the potential to be regarded as valid and relevant, but representing different contexts and purposes of knowing (Van de Ven and Johnson 2006). However different the content of knowledge may be, Van de Ven and Johnson (2006) suggest that there is a set of criteria that applies flexibly but universally for determining the relevance of knowledge. These include the power of knowledge to describe the events present in a situation, capability to explain and produce answers to 'why' questions, ability to predict and thus set expectations for future events, and the value of knowledge in gaining control over situations and engaging in effective actions. Knowledge is understood to be relevant within a context and related to a situation if all of these criteria (or at least some of them to a certain degree) are met.

Despite this common set of four criteria, regarding the production of relevant knowledge, it is important to identify the difference in how epistemic and practical knowledge is advanced. As explained by Van de Ven and Johnson (2006, pp. 806–7), epistemic knowledge develops ' ... through a comparison of the relative contributions and perspectives provided by different models' whereas 'practical knowledge advances through a more subjective involvement of one who knows and acts.' So when accepting this view of two separate worlds there is no actual 'problem' between theory and practice – perhaps other than that both would be appreciated in their own right. Reed and March (2000, p. 55) put this somewhat bluntly:

> Both the pressure toward relevance and the acquiescence to it are misguided. The main advantage of
> an academic institution can be found in academic research and its contribution to knowledge. It is not

in trying to identify factors affecting organizational performance, or in trying to develop managerial technology.

While we can appreciate this as a healthy reminder of the importance of having and separating between different institutional roles in society, in the long run, the academe hardly can suffice by disregarding the interconnectedness it may or may not have with other parts of society.

The third framing of Van de Ven and Johnson (2006) – and the one they promote – suggests that theory-building and practice can work together even though there are issues to be addressed in order to accomplish this. In other words, the lack of interconnectedness between theory and practice can be regarded as a *knowledge production* problem – and precisely here the idea of engaged scholarship enters the scene (Van de Ven and Johnson 2006). This involves that research-ers should not only ask the right questions and produce practice-based scientific knowledge together with managers, but also put more effort into disseminating the results together (Pettigrew 2001).

The central idea of engaged scholarship is a serious collaboration of researchers and prac-titioners in generating new knowledge together, thereby producing 'knowledge that meets the dual hurdles of relevance and rigor for theory as well as practice in a given domain' (Van de Ven and Johnson 2006, p. 809, cf. Hodgkinson *et al.* 2001 and Jarzabkowski *et al.* 2010). Intel-lectual arbitrage between the collaborating parties (Harrison 1997) and even emerging conflicts can be viewed as contributing to this process of mutual knowledge production. Engaged scholar-ship essentially represents an idea of integration: theory and practice are not depicted as distinct worlds, but as complementary aspects of a holistic knowledge production process – the process having a dual aim. One of the aims lies within practice and another within theory (Pettigrew 2001). As Van de Ven and Johnson (2006, p. 809) phrase it:

> Instead of viewing organizations as data collection sites and funding sources, an engaged scholar views them as a learning workplace (idea factory) where practitioners and scholars coproduce knowl-edge on important questions and issues by testing alternative ideas and different views of a common problem.

Thus, the principles of engaged scholarship include those that are capable of bridging interests of practitioners and researcher from the outset to the last phases of a project.

When introducing engaged scholarship in more detail, Van de Ven and Johnson (2006) advise us to identify 'big questions', which by definition would motivate all the stakeholders of the research process. How to come up with these kinds of big questions might be a challenge, but it is nevertheless advised that it is better to obtain diverse perspectives of several stakeholders than rely on the cognitive capabilities of a single one – that is the researcher alone. The second principle relates to the way in which an engaged research project is organised. Van de Ven and Johnson (2006) advocate divergent compositions of research teams, however with clearly negotiated roles and responsibilities (cf. Amabile *et al.* 2001). It is highlighted that 'a lone fieldworker' model can only seldom work, but that a team of individuals ('a collaborative learning community') with versatile backgrounds and experiences is needed for analysing, reflect-ing on and interpreting the questions and observations related to the on-going study. In addition to collaboration, engaged scholarship favours a relatively long duration of field work, which contrib-utes to building trust between individuals and thus facilitates deeper access into the field. Third, an engaged scholar seeks to maintain a critical attitude when reflecting theoretically on the findings by comparing competing models or theories. While this kind of triangulation is recognised widely regarding various types of data (Yin 1994), Van de Ven and Johnson (2006) extend the call for triangulation to concern also theories. The fourth and final principle of engaged scholarship claims that while scholarly and clinical roles can be identified as separate entities, they are and should be intertwined in order to promote the production of knowledge that meets the criteria of relevance in terms of practice and theory.

The natural starting point of an IVR process seems to be well in line with the first principle of engaged scholarship as in the outset of an IVR project it is necessary to identify and explicate 'big questions' in a sense that they resonate with the interests of several stakeholders: researchers and case organisations – and often also the organisations that provide the researchers with financial resources. Otherwise, it would be extremely difficult to negotiate access to the field and set up the research project in the first place. Furthermore, a continuous evaluation and balancing of interests is valuable throughout the project for keeping the project running smoothly and eventually securing its outcomes. Based on our experience, we support the view presented by Flyvbjerg (2001) that details matter: interventionist researchers might consider it necessary to dig really deep into organisational practices in order to be able to eventually draw a big picture with relevant theoretical underpinnings.

The suggestions made by Van de Ven and Johnson (2006) related to the organisation of engaged scholarship are also in line with good IVR practices. Long duration of field work to secure valid data, and collaborative learning communities within IVR projects are inherent features of good interventionist projects. Most of the IVR projects that the authors are familiar with span from two to five years in duration, and during the life cycle of the project, it is fairly typical that the field researcher(s) will reach a status resembling a full organisational membership (Suomala and Lyly-Yrjänäinen 2012).

In terms of the critical stance towards competing theoretical bases, the interventionist researcher ought to be extremely alert to taking the best out of the project at hand. During a field study, a researcher is likely to face many versatile phenomena that call for rich theoretical understanding and sometimes also willingness to flexibly reposition the research theoretically when something unexpected is emerging. In addition, researcher's flexibility within the theoretical frame might not be enough. To be able to succeed in IVR, researchers would benefit from a balanced set of efforts to develop not only their theoretical awareness and expertise, but also their social skills and knowledge on the topical challenges present in companies. This seems to be in line with the position by Van de Ven and Johnson (2006) in respecting both the clinical and scholarly roles of researchers.

6. Reconceptualising relevance and balancing the three virtues

We argue that the notion of relevance, which frequently enters the scene when IVR and the theory–practice interface are explored and has been understood in a too narrow fashion in management accounting research: it has served too much to merely juxtaposing theory and practice rather than engendering constructive debate. Practice-oriented researchers have used the notion of relevance as a weapon for challenging more theoretically oriented researchers essentially claiming that they sacrifice relevance while nurturing episteme and the role of theory. On the other hand, researchers emphasising the importance of theory development have sometimes downplayed the aspect of pragmatic relevance with respect to research findings and deliverables. This has resulted not only in a limited understanding concerning the notion of 'relevant research' but also – and perhaps more fundamentally – in a lack of convergence regarding how to conduct research so that its relevance could be ensured.

We suggest that key to resolving this puzzle is to acknowledge that relevance as a concept should be conceived much more widely than what has been done so far. We suggest that the notion of relevance should not only refer to the practical usefulness of the findings of an individual piece of research, but that it can equally well be used to describe the epistemic potential of an entire research stream or understood as its impact on long-term policy development relating to its societal implications. In a nutshell, we argue that 'relevance' is a general sign and an attribute of good research, and as a concept it primarily captures whether the research matters or not.[7] Hence, it does not need to be limited to referring to the extent of direct and immediate pragmatic implications, but research can be relevant in many ways and through many kinds of processes – that sometimes only materialise in the long run. Hence, we suggest an explicit reconceptualisation of the notion of relevance implying that it covers all three intellectual virtues: episteme, techne and phronesis. In this section, we particularly focus on the potential of IVR in this respect by offering guidelines for conducting relevant IVR, as understood in this many-sided fashion.

For reaching a balance between the three virtues, and building more holistically relevant research, the phronetic dimension of IVR projects would deserve increasing attention. In this respect, the state-of-the-art of management accounting research is somewhat diverse. It seems that critical accounting researchers do conduct phronetic inquiry and analysis within research projects drawing from either direct or indirect interventions in practice. As discussed by Neu *et al.* (2001), these studies have potential towards societal relevance, given that they are able to actually facilitate desired outcomes by challenging common sense and by preventing the isolation of academics from other important interest groups in society. In this sense, a phronetic and thereby societally relevant inquiry calls for equilibrium of several issues; it is to a great extent built on the epistemic core of science (since it is the substance that particularly the academics can bring into different social contexts), but it should also be able to operate at a level that makes it possible to resonate with common perceptions – either agreeing or disagreeing with them.

Outside the critical school, IVR in management accounting has predominantly emphasised the impact on local practices and managerial challenges (Suomala and Lyly-Yrjänäinen 2012), thus underscoring especially the virtue of techne and thereby practical relevance. At the same time, epistemic resources and potential – and thereby theoretical relevance – have remained without full utilisation, and a good balance between the three virtues has not been typically achieved within individual studies. A likely major consequence of this is that only a very limited number of published IVR studies have appeared in high-quality accounting journals (notable exceptions including Malmi *et al.* 2004, Wouters and Roijmans 2011 and Wouters and Wilderom 2008). For improving the legitimacy and impact of IVR within academia and elsewhere in society, more effort towards epistemic and phronetic quality of IVR is required.

So how to improve the balance of contributions of IVR for achieving higher societal relevance? By following the guidelines provided by Flyvbjerg (2001), IVR in management accounting could be much more informed by and concerned with emerging needs and practices related to production and use of accounting information in organisations. Especially bearing in mind, the first guideline for PSS offered by Flyvbjerg (2001), i.e. focus on values, interventionist researchers could consider the role and significance of management accounting practices and management accounting information less as a given, and thus seek to establish valid interpretations of them in different circumstances and contexts. In these ventures, it becomes necessary to also address power issues around management accounting techniques and put effort into explicating the role of values within the processes of control. When conducted in dense collaboration between researchers and managers where researchers are primarily responsible for importing theories into the process and practitioners are responsible for bringing topical challenges on the table, IVR can serve as an approach promoting engagement and dialogue on research findings and their practical implications. It can thus represent a forum for 'polyphonic' voices to surface (Flyvbjerg 2001).

To illustrate our argument for a balanced approach, we draw from the study by Lyly-Yrjänäinen (2008) on the cost effects of component commonality. It represents interventionist management accounting research that primarily addresses the virtues of techne and episteme.

Hence, it is a rather typical – yet rare – example of published IVR in management accounting. It was conducted in the context of solving a number of practical engineering and accounting-related problems of specific organisations, the field evidence being reflected on the theories of commonality and cost accounting literature. As the study provided several feasible technical approaches for advancing component commonality in an engineering-to-order context and it empirically verified the cost implications of such approaches, the dimension of techne was strongly present in the study. However, and what has been generally underdeveloped in IVR so far, the study also set high standards for its epistemic quality. The epistemic potential materialised by explicating how the contextual variables that had been fairly implicitly addressed in earlier commonality literature, have a great impact on the cost effects resulting from increased commonality.

Thus by recognising the quality of the work with respect to two virtues, we do not intend to use the study by Lyly-Yrjänäinen (2008) as an example of unsuccessful IVR in management accounting. Instead, we use the study as a reference point for elaborating on the possibility of balanced approach and the further potential related to increasing emphasis on phronesis. In other words, we ask what Lyly-Yrjänäinen's work would have looked like had it been designed more explicitly towards phronetic ideas, thereby being better linked to its potential regarding societal relevance, and what could have been achieved by building on a more balanced approach to the three virtues.

We conduct this brief exercise by drawing from and reflecting upon the nine methodological principles offered by Flyvbjerg (2001) for PSS, outlined above in this paper. To begin with, there were a number of strategies in the study by Lyly-Yrjänäinen (2008) that are clearly in parallel with Flyvbjerg's guidance: getting close to reality, emphasising little things, looking at practice before discourse, studying cases and contexts, and asking 'how' as recommended principles convey aptly what was done by Lyly-Yrjänäinen. However, there are four out of nine principles by Flyvbjerg that were not fully present in this study.

First, for Lyly-Yrjänäinen (2008) component commonality as an engineering approach clearly represents a broader agenda of productivity improvement. It is fair to say that improving productivity – and indeed profitability of the focal company – was accepted in the study as a given value. There were no explicit considerations of alternative underpinning values, or possible changes in the systems of values that the commonality developments may have induced. More focus on alternatives – and perhaps somewhat competing – values such as craftsmanship, personal motivation or learning could have produced important insights on the ways component commonality shapes organisations and thus also on managerial implications of commonality. As a result, the analysis could have produced a more comprehensive account on the management of commonality drawing from the positive consequences, but also from the tensions and conflicting interest related to commonality from the perspectives of different individual roles and companies in the supply chain.

Second, increasing commonality was considered in the study in a quite power-neutral way. It was accepted as an element of management's agenda without considering its possible linkages to the ways power is being exercised in the studied environment. This was mainly the case because the management's perspective was dominant in the study. When the employees' or suppliers' perspectives were brought forward, it was done in a relatively power-neutral way, for instance, by addressing how the employees deal with technical expertise required in the process of physical assembly. However, by explicating the relationships between commonality and power the view of commonality as a phenomenon could have been broadened. For example, increased component commonality could have been addressed as a vehicle for exercising power with respect to supplier companies (in fact, increased commonality was a factor diminishing the role of specific suppliers by lowering the mutual dependence) and customers (considering for instance that increased

Table 1. Intellectual virtues and corresponding dimensions of relevance.

Intellectual virtue	Dimension of relevance
Techne	Practical relevance
Episteme	Theoretical relevance
Phronesis	Societal relevance

commonality is likely to decrease the relative bargaining power of customers when negotiating on new deliveries).

Third, Flyvbjerg (2001) advocates joining agency and structure in inquiries. He suggests that practices, actors and structures ought to be studied together in understanding that they are profoundly intertwined. Even though practices and actors were under a very close scrutiny, the process of 'joining' was not really happening in the study by Lyly-Yrjänäinen (2008); particularly as the structures where actors and practices were situated were left without comprehensive elaboration. Whereas according to Flyvbjerg micro- and macro-level analyses should be combined not between separate studies but within individual studies in order to understand how structures shape individual choices and which are the structural consequences of individual actions, the analysis by Lyly-Yrjänäinen focused predominantly on the micro (that is firm) level. While this strategy resulted in high relevance in a managerial sense in the local context (by providing managers' with validated managerial tools), it probably led to some unused potential with respect to broader societal impact and legitimation of social commentary.

Finally, regarding PSS as a dialogue with a polyphonic voice, the study by Lyly-Yrjänäinen (2008) does not differ much from most of the studies in management accounting – perhaps apart from the fact that the developed solutions have been actually implemented in practice and discussed intensively, not only with managers of the case company, but also with executives of other companies facing similar challenges. Indeed, in IVR several voices are inherently present already during the field study phase of the research, and the idea of market tests typical in a constructive research approach (Kasanen *et al.* 1993, Labro and Tuomela 2003) can be understood as one element in IVR that quite naturally serves as a reminder of the phronetic virtue. But realising the phronetic potential of IVR in a broader sense calls for more than polyphonic field research processes. The findings and implications of research could be communicated to broader society using a variety of engagement strategies relying on personal involvement of researchers (Scapens 2012). Also in the case of Lyly-Yrjänäinen (2008), at the time the study was reported, only little was known regarding how the interpretations produced by the research actually can serve as inputs for societal dialogue and practice, but it remained dependable upon the researcher's future efforts and activities. Making a phronetic impact is thus not only a matter of a single study but a matter of long-term engagement.

7. Conclusions

Our analysis around the three intellectual virtues of Aristotle, which Flyvbjerg mobilises, allows us to conclude that all three virtues – techne, episteme and phronesis – are relevant to IVR (and probably for all social scientists) and that their balanced consideration and use is to be recommended. As for the notion of relevance, we suggest its reconceptualisation, implying a broader understanding than viewing it as relating to the practical dimension only – the two other important dimensions being theoretical relevance and societal relevance. Our analysis essentially leads us to seeing the three intellectual virtues of Flyvbjerg (2001) and the three dimensions of relevance as closely linked and complementing each other (Table 1).

We posit that relevance, when understood in this broader sense, would helpfully add to our understanding as to how the goodness of pieces of research can be seen in a more pluralistic and open-minded light. This three-folded notion of relevance relates to the aspect of contribution, while the other major aspect of the goodness of research is its credibility, encompassing issues like validity and reliability.

We agree with Flyvbjerg (2001) that there is much uncharted room for development in the phronetic dimension of social studies and argue that phronesis fits particularly well to the repertoire of IVR. The phronetic approach is apt to opening new avenues for research that is societally relevant. However, in contrast to Flyvbjerg, we maintain that progress in the dimension of episteme – but understood in a more updated and broader manner than what Flyvbjerg (2001) does – has to be a necessary part of all research endeavours, including IVR. After all, developing theoretical understanding is the eventual *raison d'etre* for the academe. For IVR, this leaves several possible viable combinations: techne and episteme, phronesis and episteme as well as techne, phronesis and episteme.

Despite recent signs of increasing attention to IVR in the academe, its current state-of-the-art in management accounting is still somewhat unfortunate in the sense that the intellectual virtue of techne is overly and too one-sidedly emphasised, phronesis is too rarely in the picture and episteme, the corner stone of any scholarly research project, is too seldom sufficiently developed. 'Social engineering' types of studies dominate the IVR in management accounting, inherently limiting their theoretical and societal value and relevance. We feel that the starting point for resolving these issues of IVR is to first become conscious of the nature of the problem and then looking for fruitful ways out of it, some of which are outlined in this paper. In particular, we suggest that the agenda of engaged scholarship, completed with employing the idea of phronesis, offers one fruitful avenue for such progress in IVR.

Acknowledgement

We thank Sven Modell and the anonymous reviewer for their insightful and helpful comments on prior drafts of this paper.

Notes

1. According to the Oxford Advanced Learner's Dictionary, the word 'relevant' refers to (a) something 'closely connected with the subject you are discussing or the situation you are thinking about' or (b) 'having ideas that are valuable and useful to people in their lives and work'. http://oald8. oxfordlearnersdictionaries.com/dictionary/relevance#relevant, retrieved 18 October 2012.
2. Actually Aristotle's *Nicomachean Ethics* (1955) includes a broader conceptual system regarding the intellectual virtues than just this three-item classification. In addition to the mentioned three categories, he also distinguished 'wisdom' and 'intellect' and the relationships between his complete set of five categories are highly complex. In this paper we follow Flyvbjerg (2001) and focus on just the three first categories of Aristotle.
3. The notion of 'reality' is philosophically many-sided and challenging and plunging deep into discussions on it does not fit into the scope of this paper. We content ourselves here to suggest reading Flyvbjerg as referring to 'practice' or 'everyday life', when he talks about 'reality'.
4. It is questionable whether an IVR study focusing on, for instance, techne would be quite ethical, if the researcher is not convenient with the values that are at stake. In that case the critical label of 'headless social engineering' would indeed go to the point.
5. A recent example of the discussion around the question of relevance is the special issue of *QRAM* published in 2012 (9:3) with a title 'Qualitative approaches to practice-relevant management accounting research'.
6. Van de Ven (2007) is a broader analysis of the same theme.

7. We argue that this broader notion of relevance falls under the concept of 'contribution', one of the two major factors when evaluating the goodness of any piece of research. The other major factor contributing to such goodness is 'credibility', covering sub-issues like validity and reliability. Cf. e.g. Whetten (1989), Lukka and Modell (2010) and Alvesson and Sandberg (2011).

References

Alvesson, M. and Sandberg, J., 2011. Generating research questions through problematization. *Academy of Management Review*, 36 (2), 247–271.

Amabile, T., Patterson, C., Mueller, J., Wojcik, T. Odomirok, W., Marsh, M., and Kramer, S.J., 2001. Academic-practitioner collaboration in management research: a case of cross-profession collaboration. *Academy of Management Journal*, 44 (2), 418–435.

Aristotle, 1955. *The Ethics of Aristotle: The Nicomachean Ethics*. Baltimore: Penguin.

Flyvbjerg, B., 2001. *Making Social Science Matter: Why Social Inquiry Fails and How It Can Succeed Again*. Cambridge: Cambridge University Press.

Harrison, P., 1997. A history of an intellectual arbitrage: the evolution of financial economics. *History of Political Economy*, 29 (4), 172–187.

Hodgkinson, G.P., Herriot, P., and Anderson, N., 2001. Realigning the stakeholders in management research: lessons from industrial, work and organizational psychology. *British Journal of Management*, 12 (Special issue), 41–48.

Humphrey, C. and Lukka, K., 2011. (AC) Counting research: the value of qualitative outlook. In: B. Lee and C. Cassell, eds. *Challenges and Controversies in Management Research*. New York, NY: Routledge, 174–195.

Jarzabkowski, S.M. and Scherer, A.G., 2010. Organization studies as an applied science: the generation and use of academic knowledge about organizations. *Organization Studies*, 31 (9/10), 1189–1207.

Jönsson, S. and Lukka, K., 2007. There and back again. Doing interventionist research in management accounting. In: C. Chapman, A. Hopwood and M. Shields, eds. *Handbook of Management Accounting Research*. Vol. 1. Amsterdam: Elsevier, 373–397.

Kakkuri-Knuuttila, M.-L., Lukka, K., and Kuorikoski, J., 2008. Straddling between paradigms: a naturalistic philosophical case study on interpretive research in management accounting. *Accounting, Organizations and Society*, 33 (2/3), 267–291.

Kasanen, E., Lukka, K., and Siitonen, A., 1993. The constructive approach in management accounting research. *Journal of Management Accounting Research*, 5, 241–264.

Labro, E. and Tuomela, T.-S., 2003. On bringing more action into management accounting research: process considerations based on two constructive case studies. *European Accounting Review*, 12 (3), 409–442.

Lukka, K., 2010. The roles and effects of paradigms in accounting research. *Management Accounting Research*, 21 (2), 110–115.

Lukka, K. and Modell, S., 2010. Validation in interpretive management accounting research. *Accounting, Organizations and Society*, 35 (4), 462–477.

Lukka, K. and Mouritsen, J., 2002. Homogeneity or heterogeneity of research in management accounting? *European Accounting Review*, 11 (4), 805–811.

Lyly-Yrjänäinen, J., 2008. Component commonality in engineering-to-order contexts: contextual factors explaining cost management and management control implications. Doctoral dissertation, Tampere University of Technology, Tampere.

Malmi, T. and Granlund, M., 2009. In search of management accounting theory. *European Accounting Review*, 18 (3), 597–620.

Malmi, T., Järvinen, J., and Lillrank, P., 2004. A collaborative approach for managing project cost of poor quality. *European Accounting Review*, 13 (2), 293–317.

Mohrman, S.A., Gibson, C.B., and Mohrman, A.M., 2001. Doing research that is useful to practice: a model and empirical exploration. *Academy of Management Journal*, 44 (2), 357–375.

Neu, D., Cooper, D.J., and Everett, J., 2001. Critical accounting interventions. *Critical Perspectives on Accounting*, 12 (6), 735–762.

Pettigrew, A.M., 2001. Management research after modernism. *British Journal of Management*, 12 (Special issue), 61–70.

Quattrone, P., 2009. 'We have never been post-modern': on the search of management accounting theory. *European Accounting Review*, 18 (3), 621–630.

Reed, J.S. and March, J.G., 2000. Citigroup's John Reed and Stanford's James March on management research and practice. *Academy of Management Executive*, 14 (1), 52–64.

Scapens, R.S., 2012. Commentary. How important is practice-relevant management accounting research? *Qualitative Research in Accounting & Management*, 9 (3), 293–295.

Starkey, K. and Madan, P., 2001. Bridging the relevance gap: aligning stakeholders in the future of management research. *British Journal of Management*, 12 (Special issue), 3–26.

Suomala, P. and Lyly-Yrjänäinen, J., 2012. *Management Accounting Research in Practice. Lessons Learned from an Interventionist Approach*. New York, NY: Routledge.

Van de Ven, A.H., 2007. *Engaged Scholarship: A Guide for Organizational and Social Research*. New York, NY: Oxford University Press.

Van de Ven, A.H. and Johnson, E., 2006. Knowledge for theory and practice. *Academy of Management Review*, 31 (4), 802–821.

Whetten, D.A., 1989. What constitutes a theoretical contribution? *Academy of Management Review*, 14 (4), 490–495.

Wouters, M. and Roijmans, D., 2011. Using prototypes to induce experimentation and knowledge integration in the development of enabling accounting information. *Contemporary Accounting Research*, 28 (2), 708–736.

Wouters, M. and Wilderom, C., 2008. Developing performance measurement systems as enabling formalization: a longitudinal field study of a logistics department. *Accounting, Organizations and Society*, 33 (4/5), 488–515.

Yin, R.K., 1994. *Case Study Research: Design and Methods*. 2nd ed. Thousand Oaks, CA: Sage.

Index

Note: Page numbers in *italics* represent *tables;* Page numbers in **bold** represent **figures;** Page numbers followed by 'n' refer to notes